Best wishes to Gary and Gudrun Larsen
I have fond memories of working
with Gary, a fine aviator and
a great investigator
all the best to you both

Paul R. Misencik
17 March 2018

Sally Townsend, George Washington's Teenage Spy

Paul R. Misencik

McFarland & Company, Inc., Publishers
Jefferson, North Carolina

LIBRARY OF CONGRESS CATALOGUING-IN-PUBLICATION DATA [new form]

Names: Misencik, Paul R., 1940– author.
Title: Sally Townsend, George Washington's teenage spy / Paul R. Misencik.
Description: Jefferson, North Carolina : McFarland & Company, Inc., Publishers, 2016. | Includes bibliographical references and index.
Identifiers: LCCN 2015040401| ISBN 9780786499878 (softcover : acid free paper) | ISBN 9781476622552 (ebook)
Subjects: LCSH: Townsend, Sally, -1842. | New York (State)—History—Revolution, 1775–1783—Secret service. | United States—History—Revolution, 1775–1783—Secret service. | United States—History—Revolution, 1775–1783—Participation, Female. | Women spies—United States—Biography. | Spies—United States—Biography.
Classification: LCC E280.T73 M57 2016 | DDC 327.12092—dc23
LC record available at http://lccn.loc.gov/2015040401

BRITISH LIBRARY CATALOGUING DATA ARE AVAILABLE

ISBN (print) 978-0-7864-9987-8
ISBN (ebook) 978-1-4766-2255-2

Front cover image of Colonial lady © 2016 Joseph C. Justice Jr./iStock/Thinkstock

Printed in the United States of America

McFarland & Company, Inc., Publishers
  Box 611, Jefferson, North Carolina 28640
    www.mcfarlandpub.com

To my wife and best friend Sally,
my daughter Karen, my son-in-law Tom,
my son Paul Jr., my daughter-in-law Altamira, and
especially my grandsons, Diego and Mateo;
two young men who will one day
make history on their own.

Table of Contents

Preface

Much has been written about the Culper Ring spy network, which operated on Long Island and in New York City. Recently there has been a 2014 television miniseries about the Culper Ring that, while being somewhat historically and factually inaccurate, has piqued public interest in the secret war of the American Revolution. While a lot has been written and romanticized about the men who spied for the American cause against the British in New York and on Long Island, there has been scant substantive information presented about the women who also risked their lives assisting the Culper Ring. Some few examples come to light, like Anna Smith Strong, whose laundry line signaled the Culpers' rendezvous location in Conscience Bay near Setauket, and Mary Underhill, who with her husband ran the boardinghouse where members of the Culper Ring stayed in New York. But despite tantalizing clues about the existence of a woman agent or agents assisting the Culpers, there is no account based on factual, documentary information about women agents who may have assisted the Culper Ring in ferreting out military intelligence from under the noses of the occupying British army.

Frank Knox Morton Pennypacker, in his book *General Washington's Spies on Long Island and in New York*, Vol. II,[1] was the first to allude to a mysterious female spy who was simply known as "355." Corey Ford in his work *A Peculiar Service*[2] expanded on the legend of 355, and since then, the story of 355 continued to grow until it has gained acceptance in many circles as being factual. However, the entire story of 355 was based on one obscure coded message from Abraham Woodhull that read, "By the assistance of a 355 of my acquaintance [we] shall be able to outwit them all."[3] In actuality, the number "355" did not refer to a specific person, but was the Culpers' generic code designation for "lady." Early on, this vague reference to a 355 also piqued my interest, and like many other interested historians, I searched British and American records and followed other available leads in an attempt to uncover the identity of the elusive 355. It took me a while to accept the idea that 355 was indeed only a coded number designating "lady" and did not pertain to a specific female operative, as would more likely be the case if the "a" were omitted before the number 355. However, while I became convinced that the mysterious and romantic 355 written about by Corey Ford and subsequent novelists did not exist in the sense that they portrayed her, it certainly did not mean that there was no woman who actively gathered intelligence for the Culper Ring. It was then that I began to take a very close look at all of the women who were associated in one way or another with the principal members of the spy network. In a way, this book came about as a result of my research into the possible identity of the woman that Abraham Woodhull referenced as "a 355" of his acquaintance.

I began studying the espionage aspects of the Revolutionary War over thirty years ago as a young airline pilot based in New York City. I studied everything I could get my hands on that had relevance to the Culpers. Over the years, in an attempt to get a better sense of their world, I visited most of the places where the Culper spies lived, worked, and visited. Admittedly, some of those sites posed a challenge, but through persistence and the goodwill of the local residents, I was able to gain access to most places. I crept among the reeds of the secret coves of Conscience Bay where Caleb Brewster and his whaleboat commandos hid out, and I walked the little sand spit over which they dragged their whaleboat to avoid the British outpost on Mount Misery Point. In my search for other written works or documents that pertained to the Culpers, I sneezed my way through dusty used-book bookstores in New York City and across the breadth of Long Island, and not so surprising, found that others over the years shared my interest in Washington's Long Island spy network. In this way I uncovered several treasures pertaining to the Long Island spies, including signed first editions of Morton Pennypacker's works, Corey Ford's *A Peculiar Service*, Carl Van Doren's *The Secret History of the American Revolution*, and many, many others. Three small booklets by Kathleen Fullam titled "The Adventures of the Setauket Spy" and Dorothy Horton McGee's *Sally Townsend Patriot* provided an added awareness of woman caught up in the maelstrom of war and how they coped under martial law of an enemy occupation. It was only logical that many of them, like their male counterparts, would fight back, but they had to learn to fight back in their own unique way. Women like Mary Underhill, Anna Smith Strong, and the lovely teenager Sally Townsend indeed took part in the war, and their efforts certainly contributed to the American victory in the Revolution, but unlike the men who shouldered muskets during the war, the women had to learn to be stealthy warriors. The prevailing attitude at the time was that women as the weaker sex were incapable of posing a danger to something as formidable as the mighty British army. Ironically, the fact that they were considered the delicate, vulnerable, and weaker sex happened to be their greatest strength. In their ubiquity, they were for the most part invisible to the occupying army as they carried on with their everyday, mundane chores. Looking deeper into their efforts, I realized that any one of those "355s" who worked in support of the American war effort was possibly the lady that Woodhull referred to at the time. However, as I continued my research, it became apparent to me that it really didn't matter which particular woman was the subject of Woodhull's cryptic coded message. They all contributed in one way or another, but what is more important is how the clandestine accomplishments of these brave patriot women furthered the American cause.

The accounts in this book are centered in Oyster Bay, which lay approximately midpoint between New York City and Setauket. It details the activities in New York City and on Long Island during the long British occupation from 1776 through 1783 and how one young teenage girl became involved in the war for American independence.

I would like to express my appreciation to those historians who preceded me in uncovering and detailing a good bit of the documentary and anecdotal evidence pertaining to the events in this book. I am also indebted to the following groups for their assistance with my research: Robert Delap of the New-York Historical Society; Dr. Debra Antoncic of the RiverBrink Art Museum, Queenston, Ontario; Harriet Gerard Clark of the Raynham Hall Museum; the Oyster Bay Historical Society; Three Village Historical Society of East Setauket, Long Island, New York; the Huntington Library, Huntington, Long Island, New York; the William F. Clements Library at the University of Michigan, in Ann Arbor, Michigan; the New York Genealogical and Biographical Society; the Fred W. Smith National Library at George Washington's Mount Vernon Estate; the Historical Society of Pennsylvania; Karen Carter of the Smithsonian Institution; the Library of Congress; the National Archives; and other sources of records and documentation too numerous to mention. I would especially like to thank my beautiful wife Sally, who is not only an incredible researcher, an outstanding copy editor, but also a great traveling companion who never seems to tire or lose her enthusiasm for visiting obscure places and ferreting out abstruse data. I also would like to acknowledge my daughter Karen Misencik Carter, her husband Tom, and my son, Paul Jr., without whose love, support and technical assistance, this book would never have been written.

Prologue

By all accounts, Sally Townsend was a very attractive young lady. She was described as petite, vivacious, intelligent and remarkably beautiful, but her large, captivating eyes were her most striking characteristic. In fact, Sally's beguiling eyes were mentioned in the diaries of several British and German officers and were also referenced twice in a 1779 Valentine poem given to her by an admiring British officer: "Thou know'st what powerful magick lies, Within the round of Sarah's eyes." And, "'Fond Youth,' the God of Love replies, 'Your answer take from Sarah's eyes.'"[1]

Sally Townsend of Oyster Bay 1760–1842.

During the long British occupation of Long Island from the autumn of 1776 through the summer of 1783, Sally coyly flirted with young British and German officers. Though they were beguiled by Sally's beautiful, hazel, innocent-looking eyes, her admirers never guessed that those beautiful eyes masked the secret that Sally was a spy for General Washington.

Because there is little documentary evidence of Sally's espionage activities, most of what we can deduce of Sally Townsend's activities is based on circumstantial and anecdotal evidence. However, in studying the world of espionage, the lack of hard evidence is not altogether unusual. For self-preservation, successful spies leave little or no tangible evidence, and it's generally only through failure or in later published memoirs that a spy's activities become public knowledge. Like her brother Robert, Sally was never accused of espionage, nor did she ever publicly admit to spying for the American cause. In fact, even after the war ended and when they were no longer vulnerable, both Robert and Sally remained silent about any of their activities during the British occupation. Because there is very little documentary evidence concerning Sally Townsend's activities as a spy, this book is in reality more a historical synthesis in which I try to combine all available formal documentation and data with informal circumstantial and anecdotal evidence to form a hypothesis of what reasonably may have occurred.

Sally's brother Robert Townsend, using the nom de guerre "Samuel Culper Jr.," along with Abraham Woodhull (Samuel Culper, Sr.) was one of the leaders of the "Culper Ring," which was undoubtedly Washington's most successful spy network. The Culper Ring operated mainly between New York City, Oyster Bay, Setauket, and Fairfield, Connecticut. Because of his penchant for secrecy, Robert insisted that his association with Washington's spy service never be made public, and even during the war, only a few people knew of Robert Townsend's involvement with the spy ring. To illustrate the extent to which Townsend went to maintain the secrecy of his activities in the Culper Ring, even George Washington did not know the true identity of Samuel Culper Jr. Robert further demanded that his association with the Culper Ring should never be revealed even after the war ended. In fact, it wasn't until 1930 that Long Island historian Frank Knox Morton Pennypacker (1872–1956) accidentally discovered Townsend's role as a Culper Ring spy. Morton Pennypacker, as he was popularly known, was a collector of New York and Long Island historical documents. His collection, now housed in the East Hampton Library, amounted to some 20,000 books, papers, and other documents pertaining to the history of Long Island. Among the documents he had collected were several Culper Ring messages as well as an assortment of business papers written by the merchant Robert Townsend. Noticing a similarity in the penmanship, Pennypacker was able to confirm Townsend's identity as Samuel Culper, Jr., through handwriting analysis.

As Robert Townsend was determined to preserve the secret of his espionage endeavors during the Revolutionary War, his sister Sally would certainly share a similar wish not to disclose her activities as a spy even after the war ended. This begs the question why? Why would she and her brother not wish to have their patriotic service during the war made public? There are several likely answers, including the fact that the Townsends were Quakers,[2] a sect that was committed to unwavering pacifism. Its founder, George

Fox, proclaimed in 1661, "We utterly deny all outward wars and strife and fighting with outward weapons, for any end or under any pretense whatsoever, and this is our testimony to the whole world. The Spirit of Christ by which we are guided, is not changeable, so as once to command us from a thing as evil, and again to move us unto it; and we certainly know, and testify to the world, that the Spirit of Christ, which leads us unto all truth, will never move us to fight and war against any man with outward weapons, neither for the Kingdom of Christ, nor for the kingdoms of this world.... Therefore we cannot learn war any more."[3] As Quakers, both Sally and Robert would wish to keep private from their congregation any activities that could be construed as taking part in the war. Another likely reason for Sally and Robert's wish to keep their activities secret was that during the 18th century, spying was looked upon as rather dishonorable in that it required false allegiance and pretended friendship. The famous English playwright Ben Johnson (1552–1637) wrote a bit of doggerel that illustrates the contempt in which spies were held,

> SPIES, you are lights in state, but of base stuff,
> Who, when you've burnt yourselves down to the snuff,
> Stink, and are thrown away. End fair enough.[4]

In another example, Lieutenant James Sprague, an officer in Knowlton's Rangers who was asked to volunteer for a spy mission, responded, "I'm willing to fight the British and, if need be, die a soldier's death in battle, but for going among them in disguise and being taken and hung like a dog, I'll not do it."[5] Certainly the Townsends, who considered themselves honorable people, would not wish to have their family name associated with any disreputable activity, particularly one as odious as spying. Quite possibly, it's for that very reason that the majority of the spies of the Revolutionary War chose not to publicize their espionage activities. In Sally's case, there may also have been more deeply personal reasons that prompted her to keep her wartime espionage a secret. Those reasons include her involvement in the death of a good and noble friend, and the loss of the man she loved.

Regardless of a lack of significant documentary evidence, the accounts of Sally's spy efforts during the Revolutionary War have survived for over two and a quarter centuries. This brings to mind the old adage, "Where there's smoke, there's fire." In addition, it is difficult to imagine that Robert Townsend as a leader of the Culper Ring spy network did not take advantage of the intelligence-gathering opportunities offered by the circumstance that important officers of the British military were living and meeting in the Townsend family home. Even more significant was the fact that at least one of those officers was enamored with his sister Sally, and often included her in his activities. It is also a matter of record that Major John André, a major player in the Benedict Arnold treason plot, visited Oyster Bay and stayed in the Townsend home.[6] Therefore, it is altogether reasonable to assume that, as Long Island historian Frances Irwin stated, "Sally Townsend, keenly on the alert, often sent valuable information to her brother Robert."[7] Keeping all of this in mind, we'll examine the life of Sally Townsend in as much detail as possible and try to piece together the story of General Washington's teenage spy.

I

The Townsends of
Oyster Bay

Sarah, or Sally as she was often called, was the seventh of the eight Townsend children born to Samuel (1717–1790) and Sarah (Stoddard) Townsend (1724–1800).[1] The Townsend children were: Solomon (1746–1811), Samuel (1749–1775), William (1752–1805), Robert (1753–1838), Audrey (1755–1829), David (1759–1785), Sarah "Sally" (1760–1842), and Phebe (1763–1841). The Townsends were a prosperous Oyster Bay, Long Island, family who were socially and politically active and were popular pillars of Long Island society. They were Quakers, or "Friends" as the sect referred to themselves, and in 1660, Samuel's great-great-grandfather John Townsend moved his family to Oyster Bay, because Quakerism was more readily accepted there.[2] Even so, while their religious beliefs were tolerated, Quakers were forced to pay for the privilege of practicing their religion. Queen's County records show that in December of 1756, John Willet, the county treasurer, submitted a list of Quakers in Oyster Bay from whom two pounds each had been collected.[3] There evidently was a

A silhouette in the bedroom of Sally Townsend of an unidentified female purported by some sources to be either of Sally Townsend or one of her sisters, Phebe or Audrey (author's photograph, courtesy Collection of the Friends of Rynham Hall, Inc.).

9

large Quaker population in the area. In 1672, George Fox, the founder of Quakerism, visited Oyster Bay and preached to a large gathering from what is known as "Council Rock," a large rock located on an old Matinecock Indian council ground. Fox wrote in his diary that there was a sizable congregation of Quakers in Oyster Bay. Although Samuel Townsend's wife, Sarah, was raised an Anglican, she was more inclined toward the Quaker beliefs. The Townsend family history describes it thusly: "He [Samuel] was a member of meeting by birthright, his parents being strict Friends, and his wife [Sarah], though baptized in the Episcopal Church, preferred the Friends."[4] The Quaker meetinghouse was located at the northeast corner of Main and South Roads, a very short distance from the Townsend home.

Samuel was a merchant who imported and sold goods from as far away as Europe, South America and the West Indies. His merchandise was varied and included luxuries as well as necessities for all levels of colonial society. He dealt in foodstuffs, spices, sugar, wine, rum, ink, lumber, shingles, delft pottery, fabric, dye, nails, furniture, and other commodities for the growing colonial market. Townsend was popular with New Yorkers, because his merchandise was of good quality, and he sold it at reasonable and affordable prices. More importantly, he was an astute businessman, and as a result of his acumen, his business grew rapidly and the family prospered.

Townsend's trade depended on shipping, so he decided to own his own ship rather than pay others to haul his cargoes. In 1747, he had the 25-ton coasting sloop *Prosperity* built[5] and launched into Oyster Bay. The vessel immediately proved itself very lucrative, and as a result, Townsend decided to have more ships built. During the next several years he increased the size of his fleet to five merchant vessels that included the *Prosperity*, the *Solomon*, the *Audrey*, the *Sarah*, and the *Sally*.[6] Townsend's business was well sited. His home was in the center of town, and his wharf and warehouse were conveniently located at the end of Ship Point Lane on Oyster Bay, less than a half-mile from his home.

Samuel Townsend had originally started his general merchandise business in Jericho, Long Island, about six miles south of Oyster Bay, and he lived in Jericho until 1738 when he transferred his mercantile operation to Oyster Bay. In May of 1738, Samuel Townsend purchased a six-acre property on Main Road[7] in the center of town. He paid Thomas Weedon £70[8] for the property, and the lot likely contained a dwelling that Samuel enlarged. The Raynham Hall Museum, which now administers the home, indicates that the original dwelling was built in 1738 as a smaller "two by two" style dwelling with two rooms on the first floor and two rooms upstairs. The home had a central chimney for the fireplaces. Between 1738 and 1743, Townsend enlarged the house considerably, and the completed home was a distinctive "saltbox" style dwelling, fairly large for its time, with eight rooms for Samuel's growing family. The dwelling also had sufficient space to accommodate the office of Townsend's mercantile business. The property was described in the 18th century as "a commodious two-storey house, with four rooms on a floor, situate near the centre of the village on the main road to the Mill, and about 50 rods [275 yards] from the harbour, with a good barn and other outhouses, a well of good water at the door, an excellent spring 20 rods [110 yards] from the house, a good garden, a good bearing orchard."[9]

The Townsend home in Oyster Bay is now called Raynham Hall after the ancestral home in Norfolk, England, that was originally called "Manors of Raynham" or "river" or "water home." It had been granted to a Norman nobleman, Sir Ludovic of Townshende by William the Conqueror. Samuel Townsend of Oyster Bay was descended from that line and was also related to Charles Townshend (1725–1767), the unpopular British politician who in 1767 as Chancellor of the Exchequer initiated the Townshend Acts, which included duties and taxes on goods purchased by American colonists.

The Townshend Acts came about because it was thought that the British victory in the recent French and Indian War had greatly benefitted the Amer-

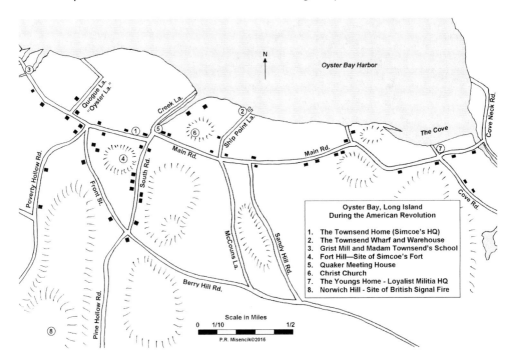

Oyster Bay during the American Revolution, 1775–1783.

ican colonies, and the acts were designed to force the colonies to pay their fair share of the tremendous government debt incurred as a result of the war. The acts imposed duties on basic items like glass, lead, paint, tea and paper imported into the American colonies, and the measure was expected to generate annual revenues of approximately £40,000. However, the Townshend Acts were deeply resented by Americans, who felt the British Parliament unilaterally imposed taxes on the colonists, who had no opportunity to comment or dissent. Quite simply, the measures were viewed as oppressive "taxation without representation," and subsequently provided a great deal of the tinder that ignited the spark of the American Revolution.

The Townsend home in Oyster Bay was not called Raynham Hall during the time Sally and her parents lived there. Sally's father Samuel and his family originally referred to their dwelling as "The Homestead." While some sources erroneously indicate that the house was called Raynham Hall during the American Revolution, it was not given that name until after 1851, when the grandson of Samuel and Sarah Townsend further enlarged the house.

Though the Townsends were practicing Quakers,[10] they did not always

The Townsend home in Oyster Bay (author's photograph).

adhere to the strict religious dictates of that sect. For example, Samuel dressed fashionably, had his clothes cut from expensive fabrics and had them tailored in the latest styles. He did however tend to favor the somewhat muted "Quaker" colors. When he walked through town, he was always stylishly dressed and was accented with trendy and rakish accessories. A family document described Samuel and his attire as "a fine old gentleman, of regular features, straight nose, a large blue eye, high forehead. A snuff-

Historical marker in front of the Townsend home, now the Raynham Hall Museum (author's photograph).

colored or gray suit, with silver knee and shoe buckles, a white stock of cambric lawn gathered in five plaits, fastened behind with a paste buckle, showing no collar, narrow ruffles at the shirt-bosom, gold-headed cane and cocked hat."[11] The Townsend children also wore clothes of the latest fashions, which were not exactly in keeping with Quaker customs. Stricter Quakers may have been inclined to raise their eyebrows at the stylish Townsend appearances. "A certain Solomon Seaman, uncle to Samuel, used to say he hated to see Sam and Sarah Townsend come into meeting, they looked so tall and proud."[12] In spite of their avant-garde dress, the Townsends were definitely Quaker in culture, and they solidly adopted the Quaker philosophy regarding education, industriousness, language, and pacifism.

Samuel and Sarah Townsend were both well educated and believed that education for children should not be neglected. All the Townsend children began their education at early ages. Sally's older brother Robert was the first to be enrolled in classes at "Madam Townsend's" school. Madam Townsend was Sarah Wright Townsend (1719–1780), the wife of John Townsend (1703–1786), who operated the local gristmill. John Townsend's father was also named John (1649–1705) and during his lifetime was known as "Mill John." Around 1661–1662, "Mill John's" father, Henry Townsend (1626–c. 1695), dammed Mill Creek and erected a gristmill there. Henry's grandson John and his wife Sarah operated the mill, while Sarah conducted Madam Townsend's school. The mill was located less than a half mile from Samuel

Townsend's home, and Robert began school there in 1756 at the age of three. The millpond was home to several duck families, which intrigued young Robert Townsend, and although a strict curriculum was generally adhered to in Madam Townsend's school, the toddler Robert occasionally "was allowed diversion with the ducks in the pond."[13]

Sally began her formal education at age six. A page in Samuel Townsend's journal proudly records that "Sarah Townsend went to school to Rebecca Coles ye 27th of October, 1766."[14] However, shortly after Sally became a student of Rebecca Coles, the thirty-eight-year-old Rebecca began to be courted by John Weeks, a sixty-seven-year-old widower. John Weeks was successful in his courtship, as evidenced in the registry of marriages at St. George's Church in Hempstead, which indicates that John and Rebecca were married there on Sunday, July 10, 1768. Apparently the betrothed Rebecca gave up teaching in preparation for her wedding, because another entry in Samuel Townsend's journal states, "Rebecca Coles School ceased ye last of February, 1767. Sarah and Phebe Townsend began school with John Townsend's wife[15] ye 16th March, 1767."[16] Just as their brother Robert had been, Sally and her sister Phebe were now enrolled in Sarah Wright Townsend's school near the gristmill.

Sally's oldest brother, Solomon, had embarked on yet another course of education. In 1760, around the time Sally was born, Solomon was placed as a cabin boy on one of his father's ships in order to learn the intricacies of the family shipping business. At the time, the lad was fourteen years of age, and by the time he turned twenty, he had acquired sufficient maritime skills to be placed in command of his father's newest ship, the brig *Sally*. Solomon captained the *Sally* for more than seven years, plying the usual Caribbean trade routes and even crossing the Atlantic several times to Europe and the Azores. In addition to successfully captaining his father's ship, Solomon acted as his father's business agent, which required a comprehensive knowledge of maritime law, diplomacy, and insurance, and the ability to deal in many different types of currencies. After seven years as captain of the *Sally*, Solomon left his father's employment to become captain of the 300-ton *Glasgow*, a much larger ship owned by the shipping company Walter & Thomas Buchanan & Co. Thomas Buchanan (1744–1815), the principal owner of the company, was married to Almy Townsend (c. 1744–unk.), who was Solomon's first cousin. Almy's father was Samuel Townsend's brother. Thomas Buchanan and the Townsend family were not only related through marriage but were also very close friends. In addition, Samuel and Thomas were close business associates, so there was no question of disloyalty when Solomon left his father's employ to become captain of a ship owned by the husband of his first cousin.

2

The Coming War

After the French and Indian War ended in 1763, tensions began to escalate between the English colonies in North America and the British government in London. A great deal of the friction stemmed from the British Parliament's desire to recoup the tremendous deficits incurred during the French and Indian War, and the Townshend Acts were only one of several initiatives that were designed to extract revenues from the Americans. Among the first of these measures was the Sugar Act, also known as the American Revenue Act or American Duties Act of 1764. It expanded on the Molasses Act of 1733, which had imposed a tax of 6p (six pence) per gallon of molasses. The Molasses Act taxes had never been effectively collected, because the colonists simply avoided the tax by smuggling molasses from the Indies. The newer 1764 measure cut the molasses tax in half to 3p, but also increased procedures to enforce tax collection and to interdict colonial smuggling operations. Interestingly, many Americans built fortunes by circumventing parliamentary taxes through smuggling. Of course, they and their customers who were able to purchase less expensive, untaxed products resented the new parliamentary anti-smuggling measures. That same year, Parliament also passed the Currency Act of 1764, which regulated the paper money issued by the colonies. The various American colonies generally issued their own paper money, which was considered legal tender for public debts, i.e., taxes. However, the colonies often issued more currency than could be redeemed, which resulted in their currency being overvalued and inflationary. This was detrimental to the British government, which was required by law to accept the depreciated colonial currency. The new Currency Act did not prevent the colonies from printing their own money, but it eliminated the designation that it was legal tender for public debts, and therefore did not have to be accepted as payment for taxes and other public obligations. Since hard currency, including gold and silver, was in short supply in the colonies, the Currency Act created financial difficulties for the colonists, who were required to pay taxes and other government fees. Understandably, the two acts of 1764 angered the American colonists. Since they had no elected representatives in the British Parliament, they were not able to argue on their own behalf, and consequently resented this legislation as further examples of taxation without representation.

The following year, to add insult to injury, Parliament passed two significant measures that further angered the American colonists. The first was the Stamp Act of 1765, which stipulated that legal documents, magazines, newspapers, and many other types of records were required to use stamped paper that was made in England, which was embossed with an official revenue stamp. It also specified that these stamp taxes had to be paid in valid British currency, and not with colonial paper money. The American reaction was very strident, because to them it was yet another imperious example of taxation without representation. Public outcries and protests ranged from New England to Georgia, and patriotic organizations like the Sons of Liberty sprang up in the wake of these measures.

The second onerous program was the Quartering Act of 1765. The Quartering Act ordered that local colonial governments were required to provide accommodations and food, basically room and board, to any British soldiers in the area, and that the colonists themselves would have to bear the expense of housing and feeding those troops. What concerned the colonists as much as being forced to house and feed British soldiers was the question of why the British army remained in the colonies now that the French and Indian War was over. It was one thing to have troops in the area during the war, but what was the purpose of a standing British army in the colonies now that the French had been defeated? The colonists, perhaps correctly, assumed that the troops were there to intimidate and coerce the Americans into compliance with Parliament's tax measures.

The parliamentary measures affected the colonial economy, and the colonists responded with increased smuggling activities and with boycotts, which were a general refusal to import British goods. It wasn't long before British merchants began to complain about the significant decrease in American trade. In response, Parliament passed what was known as the Declaratory Act or the American Colonies Act of 1766. This measure attempted to appease the colonists by repealing the hated Stamp Act, but negated any mollifying effect by stating in a face-saving declaration that Parliament's authority extended to the American colonies and that they had the right to pass laws that were binding on the Americans. The Townshend Acts, passed beginning in 1767, included provisions for the crown to pay the salaries of colonial judges and governors directly, instead of allowing the local colonial legislatures to control their salaries. This was intended to limit financial coercion on crown appointees by providing them with increased independence from colonial pressures. The acts also strengthened the means of enforcing trade restrictions through the collection of duties, and by aggressively targeting American smuggling. Not surprisingly, American resistance to the measures increased.

Vocal patriot leaders like Samuel Adams and organizations like the Sons of Liberty portrayed the English government as tyrannical and the British troops in the colonies as an occupying army. The majority of the British and American Loyalists considered those Americans who supported the philosophies of Sam Adams and the Sons of Liberty to be nothing more than a collection of idlers, smugglers and ungrateful, freeloading wastrels who were content to live off the largess of the mother country. Although they were better organized and more vocal, the patriotic factions like the Sons of Liberty were not in the majority. It's estimated that the American colonists were divided into three factions. These included the zealous patriotic movement, which included the Sons of Liberty, and also were often referred to as the "Whigs." The second faction was the Loyalist or "Tory" section of the population that ardently supported the King and Parliament. The third group was the "fence sitters" or those who refused to take sides and wanted no involvement in the confrontation. For the most part, they wanted only to be left alone. It has long been thought that the three factions were roughly equal in number. This was based on an observation made by John Adams in 1815, but historians now believe Adams may have been referring to the French Revolution. It is now thought that prior to and during the early stages of the American Revolution, the patriotic or Whig faction was about 40–45 percent of the population, while the Loyalist or Tory faction was about 15–20 percent of the American colonists. This would indicate that while there were probably twice as many Patriot Whigs as there were Loyalists, there were almost as many neutrals or "fence-sitters" as there were Whigs. Of course, different areas of the colonies had differing concentrations of either Whigs or Tories. Regions like New York and Long Island had a larger than average concentration of Loyalists,[1] but even in those areas where they were in the majority, the Loyalists rarely attempted to form active organizations comparable to the Sons of Liberty. In fact, in most cases, the Loyalists remained fairly passive and only became somewhat active when British army units provided them with a measure of protection. On the other hand, Boston was a hotbed of Sons of Liberty activities, and the great majority of citizens there supported the so-called patriot cause. The Boston Whigs were very strident and prone to action, and therefore, it's not surprising that the first blood was shed in Boston.

The growing animosity between the American colonists and Britain was escalating to the boiling point. British soldiers were frequently subjected to abuse, and predictably it was in Boston where tensions exploded in a volley of gunfire. On the evening of Monday, March 5, 1770, a small group of Boston ruffians began to taunt a lone British sentry who was stationed in front of the Custom House. Hearing the commotion, a squad of British troops was dispatched to rescue their comrade, and as the soldiers formed a cordon around the hapless sentry, the rowdy crowd began to pelt them with snowballs, chunks of ice and any other thing that came to hand. The noise drew more Boston men to the scene, and soon the soldiers found themselves confronted by an angry mob. Captain Thomas Preston (1722–1798), who was in charge of the troops, ordered the civilians to disperse, but it only seemed to further agitate the crowd. Preston again ordered the civilians to disperse, warning them that if they continued their riotous activities, he would be forced to open fire. In the noise and confusion, a nervous soldier mistook the word "fire" as a command, and pulled the trigger of his musket. Startled by the shot, the rest of the squad immediately loosed a volley, and the heavy musket balls tore through the mob, killing five and wounding six others.

After the so-called "Boston Massacre," Patriotic or Whig activities against the British government increased and intensified. Committees of Correspondence were organized by Patriot leaders to coordinate actions between the various colonies, and in effect to circumvent the Loyalist colonial legislatures and royal governors. The Committees of Correspondence were essentially shadow governments, and their main purpose was to rally opposition to the British authorities, plan collective actions, enforce boycotts of British merchandise, and promote American manufacturing of necessary goods. Among their more clandestine activities, they established networks to identify anyone disloyal to the patriotic movement and also to disrupt the imperial structure in each of the colonies. One of their more notorious actions was the celebrated "Boston Tea Party" that was planned and undertaken by the Sons of Liberty.

In December 1773, three East India Company ships arrived in Boston laden with tea. They were the *Dartmouth*, *Eleanor*, and *Beaver*. Provisions of the law required that once the tea was unloaded, the duty or tea tax would have to be paid within twenty days. Even though the shipment was taxed, the tea was heavily discounted and sold at a considerably lower price in order to generate cash flow for the financially troubled East India Company. The East India Company's woes began in 1772, when the old 1767 Indemnity Act expired. The Indemnity Act allowed the East India Company tax relief on tea that was sent to the colonies, however, Parliament's new act in 1772 eliminated most of that tax relief. As a result, there was a 10 percent duty on tea imported into England, but an additional three-pence Townshend tax was added to tea imported into the colonies. To make matters worse, Parliament sought to eliminate foreign competition by enacting a law that specified that the colonists could only import tea from Great Britain. While it was a blatant attempt to benefit the East India Company, the new tax drove up the price of British tea brought into the colonies. The higher price of tea, and the fact that the American colonists refused on principal to pay any tax imposed by a Parliament in which they had no elected representatives, caused tea sales to plummet. The East India Company, however, continued to import tea into Great Britain, and within a short time they had amassed a huge surplus. While the American colonists refused to buy taxed tea from Britain, they did not stop drinking their beloved beverage. Colonial smugglers carried on a brisk trade in Dutch tea, and many families, like the Hancocks of Boston, built their fortunes on contraband tea. Prime Minister Frederick Lord North (1732–1792) looked for a way to make the East India tea competitive with smuggled Dutch tea. North's solution was the Tea Act of 1773. The act restored the full tax refund on tea duty, eliminating the 10 percent tax on imported tea, and it allowed the East India Company to eliminate middlemen by channeling their tea through company agents in the colonies who would place tea on consignment with colonial merchants. The merchants would then sell the tea on commission. Unfortunately for North's plan, the Tea Act of 1773 still retained the three-pence Townshend duty on imported tea. While there was considerable argument in Parliament on whether or not to retain the controversial Townshend duty, Lord North decided to keep it on principle.

Lord North was confident the colonists would buy the tea, because even with the Townshend tax, the East India tea was less expensive than the smugglers could sell their tea. Bohea, the most common variety of tea sold in the colonies, provides a good example. Prior to Lord North's Tea Act of 1773, legally imported Bohea tea, including the three-pence (3d) duty, sold for about three shillings (3s) a pound, while smuggled Dutch Bohea tea sold for about two shillings and one pence (2s 1d) per pound. However, after the Tea Act of 1773, legally imported tea could be sold at 2s per pound, or one pence less than the cost of smuggled tea. The management of the East India Company realized that even though their tea could be sold cheaper than smuggled tea, the colonists would still resent the 3d Townshend duty. As a result, they attempted to hide the tax by paying it in advance in London, or paying it as soon as the tea was off-loaded in the colonies. Unfortunately, their efforts to hide the tax from the colonists failed.

The British government was naively confident that the Americans would buy their cheaper tea. They considered it a "win-win" situation, in that it would break the American embargo on British tea and at the same time provide the East India Company with needed revenue. However, the Boston patriots looked upon this as just another arrogantly devious action on the part of the British government, and they refused to accept any taxed tea on principle. The Committees of Correspondence had been aware of the ships and their cargoes since they departed England, and when they arrived in Boston, a plan of action was put into effect. The Sons of Liberty demanded that the taxed tea be returned to Britain rather than having it unloaded in Boston where the duty would have to be paid, but Royal Governor Thomas Hutchinson and the East India Company refused. On Thursday, December 16, 1773, a band of Sons of Liberty, crudely disguised as Indians, boarded the ships at Griffin's Wharf and destroyed the three shiploads of taxed tea by throwing it overboard into Boston Harbor. The Crown reacted to what became popularly known as "the Boston Tea Party" with a series of punitive measures known as the Coercive Acts, or "the Intolerable Acts," as the American colonists referred to them. One of the acts stripped Massachusetts of self-government by doing away with elections. Instead of elections, the king or the royal governor would henceforth appoint almost all of the positions in the colonial government. In addition, the Port of Boston was closed to all commerce until the East India Company was reimbursed for the loss of their tea. That was a devastating blow to not only the Boston merchants, but also to the ordinary citizens who relied on the trade that came through their port. The act also allowed the Royal Governor to move all trials to another colony or even to Great Britain if he believed it were necessary to ensure a fair trial. This was an equally onerous measure, because plaintiffs could be required to travel at their own expense as far as England to press a suit, and defendants could be transported far from home and family to face trial among strangers.

News of the Crown's punitive actions against the Massachusetts patriots caused many of the Whigs in the other colonies to react in support of their Boston comrades. However, in New York and on Long Island, it was less overt, primarily because of the larger percentage of Loyalists in the population. While there was an active Sons of Liberty presence in New York City, the Whigs were fairly evenly matched in numbers by staunch Loyalists. Long Island appeared to favor the Loyalist cause to an even greater extent, with a large portion of the population supporting the Crown's position. In Oyster Bay, Samuel Townsend's family for the most part avoided being identified with one faction over the other. As Quakers they preferred to be seen as neutral and not be involved in political confrontations. However, it was not easy for anyone, especially the more prominent citizens, to distance themselves from the conflict, and the Townsends were no exception.

As a leading citizen of Oyster Bay and indeed the Province of New York,[2] Samuel Townsend took his status as a civic leader seriously. Samuel served as justice of the peace and town clerk in Oyster Bay. On Monday, March 27,

1775, in his capacity as town clerk, he published a notice that included the suggestion that at the next town meeting, Oyster Bay elect a representative to the New York Provincial Convention. The purpose of the Provincial Convention was to elect delegates to the Continental Congress in Philadelphia, which was considered by most to be Whig-leaning and viewed by the more ardent Loyalists as a dangerous nest of seditious rebels. Townsend's notice read: "March 27, 1775 I have received a letter from the chairman of the committee of New-York, recommending it to the freeholders[3] of Oyster Bay to choose their Deputies so soon as that they may be at New-York by April 20th, the day proposed for the meeting of the Convention; and as our annual Town Meeting is so near at hand, I thought it best previous to said meeting to acquaint the freeholders that I should lay said letter before the meeting, that in the interim they might have an opportunity of thinking whether it will be proper or not to choose a Deputy on that day."[4]

The town meeting was held on Tuesday, April 4, 1775, and of the 247 freeholders who gathered for the meeting the majority were apparently Loyalists or landowners who were not certain of the motives of Congress or were suspicious of anything that smacked of anarchy. Only 42 voted in favor and 205 voted against electing deputies. In fact most of the freeholders objected to having anything to do with "Deputies of Congresses." The record of the meeting described the event: "At the annual Town Meeting, Thomas Smith was chosen Moderator, and after going through the business of the town, Samuel Townsend read the above cited letter and offered it to the consideration of the freeholders and inhabitants; and it was objected by many against having anything to do with Deputies of Congresses, and insisted by some to choose a Deputy. The Moderator proposed to go out and separate, but it was objected to and a poll demanded. The Town Clerk wrote down the votes and at the close of the poll there appeared on the list for Deputy, 42; against, 205."[5] If the vote tally was a true indicator, it was very apparent that the majority of landowners in Oyster Bay were overwhelmingly Loyalists at a ratio of five-to-one.

The Whig faction reacted obliquely. A second meeting was held eight days later on Wednesday, April 12, 1775, for the express purpose of electing a deputy from Oyster Bay, and this time the dissenting majority of freeholders were not invited. To no one's surprise, the vote was 43 to 0 in favor of electing Zebulon Williams as Oyster Bay's deputy to the Provincial Convention. Williams immediately traveled to New York, where he joined his fellow delegates at the Exchange Coffee House. When they met, on Thursday, April 20, 1775,[6] they were not yet aware that the previous morning the war had begun on Lexington Green in Massachusetts.

3

The War Begins

In April 1775, the military royal governor of Massachusetts, General Thomas Gage (1719–1787), received significant intelligence from his highly placed spy in the Boston Sons of Liberty network. The spy was the renowned surgeon Dr. Benjamin Church (1734–c. 1778), who as a member of the Sons of Liberty was a close associate of the likes of Sam Adams (1722–1803), Dr. Joseph Warren (1741–1775), John Hancock (1737–1793), and Paul Revere (1735–1818). Church had risen high in the hierarchy of the Sons of Liberty and was a member of its most secret and exclusive branch, "The Mechanics." Unfortunately for the patriots, Church had been selling some of their most sensitive information to the British authorities for the past several years. His most recent message to Gage contained details of a cache of arms, munitions, and other military supplies that the Sons of Liberty were stockpiling in Concord, Massachusetts. In addition, he included a map of the Concord area that specified in which particular buildings the arms and equipment were stored. When General Gage received this information, he decided to take action, and on the night of Tuesday, April 18, 1775, he dispatched about 700 troops under the command of Lieutenant Colonel Francis Smith (1723–1791) to confiscate or destroy all of the rebels' weapons, munitions, and supplies at Concord. The Sons of Liberty had been constantly monitoring British operations in Boston, and they became aware of Gage's plan almost from the beginning. As soon as the British regulars formed up for their march to Concord, riders like Paul Revere, William Dawes (1745–1799), and Dr. Samuel Prescott (1751–c. 1777) raced through the countryside, where they spread the word of the British regulars' advance, and roused a response by armed patriot "minutemen." The minutemen were American partisan militia units organized in the various towns and hamlets and were expected to respond to an alarm at a "minute's notice." They lived up to their name on the night of April 18 and during the early morning hours of April 19, 1775. As the British moved toward Concord, Lieutenant Colonel Smith's force of regulars began to hear alarm guns and church bells sounding throughout the countryside. Concerned about an ambush, Smith detached Major John Pitcairn (1722–1775) with six companies of light infantry to race ahead of the main body of troops to secure the route to Concord.

Near dawn on Wednesday, April 19, 1775, Pitcairn's advance party of red-coats reached the town of Lexington on the way to Concord. Marching through the fog, they spied a substantial number of armed men[1] formed up on Lexington Green. The Americans were under the command of militia leader Captain John Parker (1729–1775), a local Lexington farmer. Seeing the armed minutemen, Pitcairn stopped his column and ordered his light infantry to form up in line of battle. British troops were trained to change battle formation at the double quick, during which time they shouted and "huzzahed." Apparently they did just so that April morning, as evidenced by most of the surviving accounts. As the British noisily deployed, some of the Americans began to edge away from their formation. Captain John Parker steadied his small force and told the men to stand fast; he said that they had every right as free Englishmen to assemble on their own village green.

Somewhat calmed by Parker's words, the minutemen held their positions. Pitcairn gave orders to fix bayonets, and again the regulars did so loudly with a flamboyant display that was meant to intimidate. They brandished

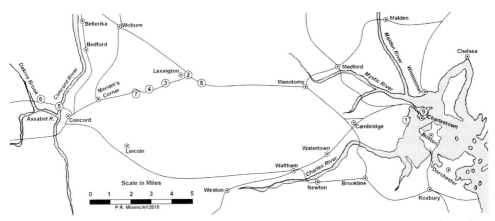

1. Phipps Farm—Midnight—British regulars crossed the Charles River from Boston by boat, then began their march to Lexington and Concord.
2. Lexington Green—Revere arrived here about 12:30 a.m.; Dawes arrived about 1:00 a.m.; Pitcairn's light infantry arrived about 5:00 a.m.
3. Revere and Dawes met Dr. Samuel Prescott, who accompanied them toward Concord.
4. British patrol intercepted Revere, Dawes, and Prescott. Revere was captured; Dawes escaped but did not continue; only Prescott escaped and reached Concord.
5. Concord North bridge—Regulars reached Concord about 9:00 a.m. on the way to Barrett's Farm. Engagement at Concord North Bridge was fought about 10:00 a.m.
6. Barrett's Farm—Because of Prescott's warning, most of the American arms and equipment were moved and hidden. The regulars destroyed what remained.
7. "Bloody Curve"—During the regulars' withdrawal, some of the fiercest action was fought at "Bloody Curve."
8. Gen. Percy's relief column met retreating regulars about 2:00 p.m. and escorted them to Boston via Cambridge and Charlestown.
9. Charlestown Peninsula—Retreating regulars arrived at Charlestown between sunset and 8:00 p.m. The wounded were ferried over to Boston during the night, and the rest of the troops reached Boston the following day.

Lexington and Concord, April 18–19, 1775.

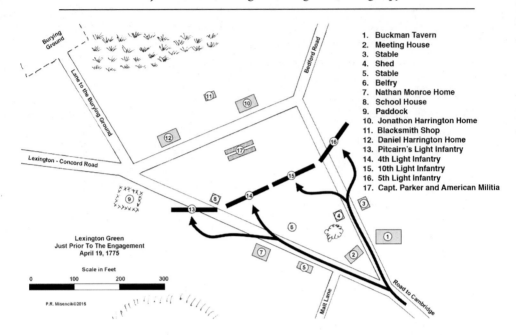

1. Buckman Tavern
2. Meeting House
3. Stable
4. Shed
5. Stable
6. Belfry
7. Nathan Monroe Home
8. School House
9. Paddock
10. Jonathon Harrington Home
11. Blacksmith Shop
12. Daniel Harrington Home
13. Pitcairn's Light Infantry
14. 4th Light Infantry
15. 10th Light Infantry
16. 5th Light Infantry
17. Capt. Parker and American Militia

Lexington Green
Just Prior To The Engagement
April 19, 1775

Scale in Feet
0 100 200 300

P.R. Misencik©2015

Lexington Green, April 19, 1775.

their 18-inch bayonets and noisily attached them to the ends of their muskets. Their movements were accompanied by more loud shouts and huzzahs. Once again Parker tried to steady his men and is supposed to have said, "Stand your ground, men. Don't fire unless fired upon. But, if they mean to have a war, let it begin here!"[2]

Pitcairn casually studied the small force of Americans arrayed on the green and then ordered his long lines of regulars forward on a broad front. It was apparent that Pitcairn meant to advance his line forward and swing the flanks around to envelop and encircle the American militia group. Parker, the American leader, looked at the overwhelming force arrayed against him and was acutely aware that every man in his tiny command was in imminent danger, with the situation getting more explosive by the moment. As the redcoats advanced with fixed bayonets, Parker finally gave the order for his men to disperse. With an audible sigh of relief, the militia broke ranks and began to walk away. Suddenly, a single gunshot split the air. The shot caught everyone by surprise and the dispersing Americans stopped and turned at the sound. At the same time the shot caused a British officer to shout, "Fire," and his platoon fired a point-blank volley at the dispersing Americans. The first volley caused other platoons to fire until within seconds almost all the regulars had fired at the standing Americans from a distance of less than 40 yards. Immediately upon firing, many regulars rushed forward with fixed bayonets and drove the long blades into a number of Americans. Several of the militia were bowled over in the first volleys by the fusillade of heavy musket balls, but a few Americans got off shots in reply. One redcoat suffered a slight leg wound, and Pitcairn's horse was hit and wounded twice. The whole engagement lasted only a minute or so, and it resulted in eight Americans killed outright and 10 more wounded. There were no serious British injuries. Captain Parker's cousin Jonas Parker was one of the dead. The first British volley wounded Jonas, but he stood his ground and fired at the charging regulars, who drove their bayonets into him as he calmly reloaded his musket. The surviving Americans turned and ran, leaving their dead and wounded strewn across the Green. The regulars briefly chased them until the British officers were able to restore order and form up their men. The celebrated Battle of Lexington, where the "shot heard round the world" was fired, was over in a trice.

The British regulars then marched on to Concord, where they destroyed some arms and supplies, but they soon realized that they had stirred up a hornet's nest of resistance. Scores of minuteman units had converged on Concord, and upon learning of the blood spilled on Lexington Green, they were spoiling for revenge. The British troops marched on to Concord's North Bridge, but there they encountered very stiff opposition and suffered their first losses. Even worse for the regulars, hordes of arriving American militia units continued to join the fight. The regulars fought their way through to Barrett's Farm, where according to Benjamin Church's message, most of the American arms and materiel were stashed. However, as soon as the Americans had been warned of the regulars' march from Boston, they had hurriedly moved most of their military goods out of the area, leaving little for the redcoats to find. The regulars destroyed what they could, but besieged by increasing swarms of minutemen, they were forced to withdraw to Boston. So many minutemen and militia units converged on the withdrawing regulars that the redcoats had to fight for their lives the entire way back to the relative safety of the Charlestown Peninsula. The shooting war was on in earnest, and what started out as a fairly routine mission to confiscate some rebel supplies ended in a bloody retreat. If Lord Hugh Percy's (1742–1817) relief force had not met the beleaguered, retreating British regulars and escorted them back to Boston, it is likely that the rapidly gathering numbers of increasingly hostile American minutemen would have wiped the redcoats out to a man. The Americans chased the British all the way back into Boston, where the growing numbers of rebel forces were able to surround and contain the British within the city. The Americans controlled all the surrounding areas, and they maintained a siege of the regulars in Boston, where they sniped and otherwise harassed the beleaguered redcoats whenever an opportunity presented itself. The war had now begun in earnest. It was no longer a political disagreement with the Whigs and Tories as mere political adversaries; now they considered themselves sworn enemies.

On Tuesday, May 23, 1775, the month after the fighting at Lexington and Concord, the 1st New York Provincial Congress convened in New York City. Samuel Townsend was one of the delegates selected to represent Queen's County. This would indicate that he had some affinity with the Whig or patriotic movement. Royal Governor William Tryon (1729–1788) bluntly referred to the Provincial Congress as a rebel organization, since its first adopted resolution was to pledge obedience to recommendations made by the Continental Congress. Notwithstanding Tryon's assessment of the body of delegates as rebellious anarchists, the New York Provincial Congress seemed to reflect a more moderate temperament. In spite of the bloody carnage that had occurred a month earlier in Massachusetts, the Provincial Congress adopted a "plan of accommodation between Great Britain and America,"[3] which urged the New York representatives at the Continental Congress in Philadelphia to exercise extreme caution regarding the quarrel with the mother country, but they also urged the British authorities to repeal the unconstitutional laws affecting the colonies and to acknowledge the right of the colonies to self-taxation. In return, the New York Provincial Congress promised to contribute to the cost of defense and maintenance of the civil government while recognizing England's right to regulate trade. Though they took some militarily defensive measures, like raising troops, stockpiling arms and fortifying New York City, the New York Provincial Congress condemned American plans to invade Canada, because they believed it would impede reconciliation with the mother country. The Provincial Congress hoped for a peaceful solution to the dispute, and even went so far as to welcome Royal Governor Tryon on his return from England in the summer of 1775. In actuality, Governor Tryon was faced with a conundrum. He was aware of and encouraged the moderation of the New York Provincial Congress, but as royal governor, he represented the power and imperial authority of the king. As such, he had no official choice other than to publically regard the Provincial Congress as rebels against the lawful government and indeed against the king of England.

Hopes for an amicable reconciliation between America and Great Britain were dashed on Saturday, June 17, 1775, when American patriots fortified Breed's Hill just across the Charles River from Boston. Predictably, British regulars responded with an attack on the American positions there. The result was an incredibly violent and bloody battle in which the sharp-shooting colonists slaughtered wave after wave of attacking British grenadiers and light infantry. Eventually the Americans' ammunition gave out and their positions were overrun in savage hand-to-hand fighting. The engagement was mistakenly called the Battle of Bunker Hill, but there was no mistaking the fact that England and America were now involved in a bloody, total war which would not end in accommodation or conciliation, but only with victory for one side and surrender for the other.

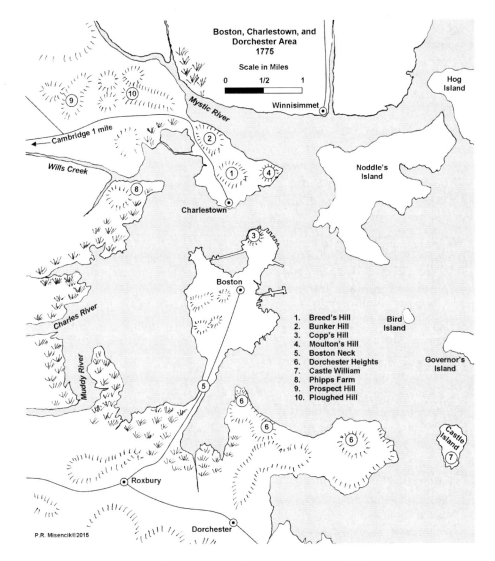

Boston, Charlestown, and Dorchester area in 1775.

After Breed's Hill, the fairly amicable relationship New Yorkers had with Governor Tryon quickly deteriorated, as patriotic New York Whigs became more strident in their opposition to British authority in general and against Loyalists in particular. This patriotic enthusiasm spread among the populace and even to the Provincial Congress where Samuel Townsend was serving. On Wednesday, June 28, 1775, the New York Provincial Congress voted to raise four regiments of troops for the New York Line. Then the following month on Thursday, July 20, 1775, New York Sons of Liberty surprised the British guard and captured a British supply house at Turtle Bay[4] on the East River shore of Manhattan, or York Island, as it was commonly called. In August the Provincial Congress ordered the capture and removal of British cannons from the Battery at the southern tip of Manhattan, and on the night of Wednesday, August 23, 1775, a contingent of Americans went after those guns. Loyalists however, had warned the redcoats of the raid, and they posted a barge load of Royal Marines just offshore. When the American raiders began to haul off some of the cannons, the barge load of redcoats opened fire on them. A brisk firefight ensued during which the Americans successfully fought off the Marines, killing one of the redcoats in the process. However, when the Americans continued to haul away some of the cannons, the 64-gun *Asia* that was stationed just offshore opened fire on them with a violent bombardment of grape and round shot. The savage broadsides from the *Asia* drove the Americans off, and they abandoned their attempt to seize the Battery's cannons. The cannonballs continued to rain down on the fleeing Americans as they made their way uptown, and one shot from the *Asia* penetrated the roof of Fraunces Tavern on Pearl and Broad Streets, several blocks from the Battery. The mood of the Americans was deteriorating so rapidly that by October of 1775, Governor Tryon felt it was no longer safe to live ashore, so he took refuge aboard the *Asia* in New York Harbor.[5]

At the same time, Sally's oldest brother, Captain Solomon Townsend, was having a series of adventures that would keep him away from his family for several years. On Tuesday, October 3, 1775, Solomon, in command of the brig *Glasgow*, arrived in New York where almost immediately, a press gang from the *Asia* forced a large portion of the *Glasgow's* crew into the Royal Navy. In addition, Solomon's plans to visit his family in Oyster Bay were dashed when he was told that his ship would depart as soon as it could be reprovisioned. The *Glasgow* was hurriedly provisioned for twenty-eight days, loaded with Loyalist refugees who wanted to escape New York, and Townsend was ordered to set sail for Boston, where the main British army was located and where Loyalists felt they would be better protected. Before he sailed, Solomon complained to Captain George Vandeput (c. 1717–1800) of the *Asia* that most of his crew had been taken from him, so Vandeput replaced some of the sailors. However, the replacements were not nearly as experienced or capable as the men that were taken from the *Glasgow*. Now, with a ship full of refugees and a mediocre crew, the *Glasgow* left New York. When they arrived in Boston, the Loyalist refugees learned that the city was under siege and completely encircled by the American Army. Food and supplies were scarce, expensive and prioritized for the army and navy. In addition, rumors were rife that the British would not be able to remain in Boston and would likely be forced to evacuate the city. Faced with those realities, most of the refugees on the *Glasgow* did not want to disembark at Boston, and to make matters worse hundreds of Boston Loyalists clamored for passage out of the city. Solomon took on as many of Boston's Loyalists as he could and set sail for Halifax, where the displaced Loyalists were finally put ashore.

In Halifax, the *Glasgow* was quickly loaded with military supplies and materiel and was dispatched back to Boston. Solomon hoped that after stopping in Boston he would be able to continue to New York and then have the opportunity to travel to Oyster Bay to visit with his family. However, when Solomon arrived at Boston, he found that the supply and personnel situation had become so critical that every transport available was being requisitioned for the war effort. Solomon was informed that the *Glasgow*, which had once been a Royal Navy fighting ship, was now recommissioned into the Royal Navy as a transport and that while he could remain captain of the *Glasgow*, he would sail under Royal Navy command. Rather than continue to New York, the *Glasgow* was given revised orders to sail to England, where the ship would become part of the enormous British military supply line. When Solomon reached England, the *Glasgow* was fitted with cannons for protection against American privateers.

During the year 1777, Solomon Townsend sailed the *Glasgow* on several trips between England and North America, transporting British military equipment, supplies and troops. However, by the end of that year, Solomon began to reevaluate his allegiance, and he decided to return to America. In 1778, Solomon received approval from Thomas Buchanan to leave the *Glasgow* in England, so he gave up his command to another captain, settled his accounts and left England for France. In Paris, he met Benjamin Franklin (1706–1790), who in 1776, along with Silas Deane (1737–1789) and Arthur Lee (1740–1792), had been commissioned by the Continental Congress to negotiate a treaty between the United States and France. Franklin and Solomon became good friends and exchanged several personal notes and other tokens of friendship. Franklin introduced Solomon at the French court and showed him many of the sights in the French capital. However, by the summer of 1778, Solomon was eager to return home, and his friend Benjamin Franklin gave him a letter confirming Solomon's loyalty to the United States.

Passey, near Paris, June 27, 1778

I certify to whom it may concern, that Captain Solomon Townsend of New York, mariner, hath this day appeared voluntarily before me, and taken the oath of allegiance to the United States of America, according to the resolution of congress, thereby acknowledging himself a subject of the United States.

B. Franklin[6]

In addition, Franklin commissioned Solomon as a volunteer midshipman in the Continental Navy and secured him a berth on the frigate *Providence* under command of the famous Captain Abraham Whipple[7] (1733–1819) of Rhode Island. Whipple was Rhode Island's first commodore in the fledgling United States Navy, and was one of the navy's most celebrated officers. Whipple gained fame and notoriety when shortly before midnight on Tuesday, June 9, 1772, he led a group of fifty Rhode Islanders in the capture and burning of the British revenue cutter HMS *Gaspée*, which had run aground while chasing an American smuggler. After the event, British Captain James Wallace (1731–1803) of the frigate HMS *Rose* wrote to Whipple declaring, "You Abraham Whipple on June 10, 1772, burned his majesty's vessel *Gaspée*, and I will hang you at the yard arm!" Whipple responded with a note of his own that said, "Sir, always catch a man before you hang him." Among Whipple's more singular accomplishments was his capture, without firing a single shot, of a fleet of ten British merchant vessels sailing from Jamaica and bound for London.

When Solomon Townsend joined the crew of the *Providence*, Whipple placed him in charge of a division of guns, but during the return voyage, no engagements took place. Townsend reached Portsmouth, New Hampshire, in November 1778, where he left the life of the sea. He had been gone for three years, but because he had served in the rebel navy, and the British Army occupied Oyster Bay, Solomon did not want to risk returning home to his family. Instead Solomon traveled to Chester, Orange County, New York, and stayed at the home of his cousin, Peter Townsend (1729–1783), who was owner of Noble, Townsend & Company, proprietors of the Sterling Iron Works. Earlier in 1778, Peter Townsend's Sterling Iron Works had forged "the Great Chain" that was stretched across the Hudson River at West Point to prevent passage of British warships. The 600-yard chain consisted of forged iron links two feet in length, each weighing 114 pounds. In April 1778, the links were carted to New Windsor, where they were joined and floated on log rafts down river to West Point. The chain was massive. Including swivels, clevises, and anchors, the chain weighed 65 tons, and it took several 16-foot waterproofed log rafts to provide buoyancy and support for the chain.

Solomon stayed and worked with Peter and later became successful in his own right as the proprietor of the Augusta Forge near Sterling. He fell in love and courted his cousin Anne (1752–1823), and after he married her in 1783, he purchased an estate adjacent to his father-in-law's property. After the war, Solomon's business began to deteriorate, and when he died in 1811, there was little left of his fortune. Solomon's widow Anne and their children were forced to liquidate the majority of their assets to settle his estate.

Meanwhile, back in New York and Oyster Bay in 1775, Samuel Townsend continued to serve with the 1st New York Provincial Congress until it adjourned on Saturday, November 4, 1775. The 2nd New York Provincial Congress met on Tuesday, November 14, 1775, and continued to meet sporadically during the winter until its session ended on Monday, May 13, 1776. Samuel Townsend was not listed as a member of the 2nd Provincial Congress, most likely because of the death of his son Samuel, who contracted a fever

The author's wife Sally Misencik with links from the "Great Chain" at the United States Military Academy, West Point, New York (author's photograph).

and died while on board one of the family's ships during a trading voyage to the Carolinas.[8] Not much more is known of young Samuel's life other than a listing in one source that indicates he had previously married and had left the Townsend's Oyster Bay home.

When the 3rd Provincial Congress convened on Tuesday, May 14, 1776, Samuel Townsend once again took his seat as a deputy from Queen's County. The fact that his colleagues in Congress held him in high esteem was indicated by his appointment to the thirteen-member committee[9] to draft a constitution for the State of New York. The work of the committee spanned the 3rd and last (4th) Provincial Congress, and on Wednesday, March 12, 1777, their draft was presented to the Provincial Congress for discussion. On Sunday, April 20, 1777, New York's first constitution was adopted.

During the period that Samuel Townsend worked as a member of the Provincial Congress, the Declaration of Independence had been written and ratified by the Continental Congress. As a result, American Whigs, and Samuel Townsend included, now considered themselves citizens of a free and independent country. Unfortunately the concept of freedom and independence must often overcome reality. While Samuel and his colleagues in the New York Provincial Congress were writing a constitution for what they considered their sovereign state, the war brought the might of the British Empire to New York. Instead of being free and independent citizens, Americans both in the city and on Long Island soon found themselves totally under British control and completely at the mercy of an occupying army for the next seven long years.

4

The Capture of Long Island and New York

The British army and navy arrived in the New York area during the summer of 1776 and set up massive encampments on Staten Island. The number of ships bringing troops and equipment appeared overwhelming to the Americans, and the influx of British regulars bolstered by German mercenary regiments seemed unending. The British government contracted with German principalities to hire mercenaries to bolster the British army. Quite simply it was a more expeditious way of amassing a large army on short notice. The more than 30,000 German mercenaries who fought in the American Revolution came from several different German principalities, including Hesse-Cassel, Hesse-Hanau, Anhalt-Zerbst, Ansbach-Bayreuth, Brunswick-Wolfenbüttel, and Waldeck. Actually, the term "Hessian" specifically refers to those troops from Hesse; however, since more than half or about 16,000 of the Germans came from the Hesse principalities, it wasn't long before most people began to refer to all Germans as "Hessians," and the two terms became somewhat synonymous.

With the British concentrated on Staten Island, it was apparent that they would soon invade Long Island, which was a very desirable target. One of General William Howe's officers wrote, "In this fertile Island the army could subsist without succor from England or Ireland. Forming their camp on the plain, 24 miles long, they could in five or six days invade or seduce any of the colonies at pleasure."[1]

Howe's attack on Long Island came as anticipated on Thursday, August 22, 1776. After a furious naval bombardment, a force of over 32,000 men swarmed across the "Narrows"[2] onto Long Island. Washington had about 10,000 troops on Long Island, but most were dug in on the Heights of Guan, a series of hills stretching east and west across the center of western Long Island. Only a few regiments of American riflemen were positioned near the Narrows to oppose the British and German landings. Howe's army poured onto Long Island and easily brushed aside the few American units who attempted to stop them from establishing a foothold. Once Howe's army was securely on Long Island, Howe took the next four days to leisurely plan his assault against Washington's army on the Heights of Guan.

On Saturday, August 24, 1776, during the time Howe consolidated his forces on Long Island, the New York Provincial Congress appointed Samuel Townsend's son Robert as commissary to General Nathaniel Woodhull (1722–1776), who was commander of the Suffolk and Queen's County militia on Long Island. With his appointment as commissary, Robert Townsend was directed to ensure that General Woodhull's force received adequate provisions and supplies, and Robert was given a letter of introduction to Woodhull on Monday, August 26, 1776, that confirmed his appointment. The letter read as follows:

> August 26th, 1776
>
> Sir—Your's of yesterday is just come to hand, in answer to which we would inform you, that Robert Townsend, the son of Samuel Townsend, esq. is appointed commissary for the troops under your command, of which we hope to give him the earliest notice; and that we have made application to General Washington for the regiments under the command of Cols. Smith and Remsen, to join you. He assured our committee that he would issue out orders immediately for that purpose, and we expect that they are upon the spot by this time. Confiding in your known prudence and zeal in the common cause, and wishing you the protection and blessing of heaven.
>
> We are, with respect, your very
> humble servants.
> By order, &c. ABRAHAM YATES, Jun.
> To Gen. NATHANIEL WOODHULL.[3]

Robert likely received his commission as commissary because of his father's stature as a successful merchant, but also because Samuel Townsend had been a member of the New York Provincial Congresses of which General Woodhull had been president. Woodhull also happened to be a close friend of the Townsend family.

Woodhull's militia force was located at Jamaica, and their main duties were to protect the cattle and other American supplies that were located in the area. Robert Townsend rode to Jamaica on Tuesday, August 27, 1776, and personally presented his letter of appointment to General Woodhull. Coincidentally, it was the very day that General Howe launched his assault against the American positions on the Heights of Guan. As events unfolded, Robert never got the opportunity to fulfill his function as commissary. Instead, Robert rode back to Oyster Bay, carrying a letter from General Woodhull to the Provincial Congress in which Woodhull stated the precariousness of his situation:

Jamaica, August 27th, 1776

Gentlemen—I am now at Jamaica with less than 100 men, having brought all the cattle from the westward and southward of the hills, and have sent them off with troops of horse, with orders to take all the rest eastward of this place, to the eastward of Hempstead Plains, to put them into fields and to set a guard over them.

I have now received yours, with several resolutions, which I wish it was in my power to put into execution; but unless Cols. Smith and Remsen, mentioned in yours, join me with their regiments, or some other assistance immediately, I shall not be able, for all the people are moving east, and I cannot get any assistance from them. I shall continue here as long as I can, in hopes of reinforcement; but if none comes soon, I shall retreat and drive the stock before me into the woods. The enemy, I am informed, are entrenching southward, and from the heights near Howard's.

Col.s Smith and Remsen, I think, cannot join me. Unless you can send me some other assistance, I fear I shall soon be obliged to quit this place. I hope soon to hear from you.

I am, gentlemen, your most humble serv't.
NATHANIEL WOODHULL
To the Hon. Convention of
The State of New-York[4]

Howe launched his attack on the Heights of Guan on Tuesday, August 27, 1776. During the previous night, Howe led a strong force through the undefended Jamaica Pass to the east of the American line, and by morning they were in position behind the Americans. At nine o'clock in the morning, Howe ordered two cannons fired, which signaled a massive combined frontal and flanking attack against the American lines. The Americans were in danger of being completely surrounded and many units broke and ran in panic. By early afternoon Washington's army was in full retreat across the Gowanus Marshes toward Brooklyn, and the British and Hessian troops shouted fox-hunting cries as they chased the routed and humiliated Americans. However, not all the Americans ran. The main portion of Washington's army was barely able to escape, because of an incredibly brave delaying action fought by General William Alexander (1726–1783) (Lord Stirling)[5] with Smallwood's "Marylanders" and Haslet's "Delawares." In order to cover the retreat of the main American Army, 400 Marylanders charged over 2,000 redcoats and fought them to a standstill in bloody hand-to-hand fighting, from which only ten Marylanders survived to straggle across the Gowanus Marshes to join the American army at Brooklyn. Washington observed the unbelievably gallant delaying action and remarked, "Good God, what brave fellows I must lose."[6]

Near Jamaica, General Nathaniel Woodhull was in the path of Howe's flanking force and he immediately ordered his small militia unit to drive the

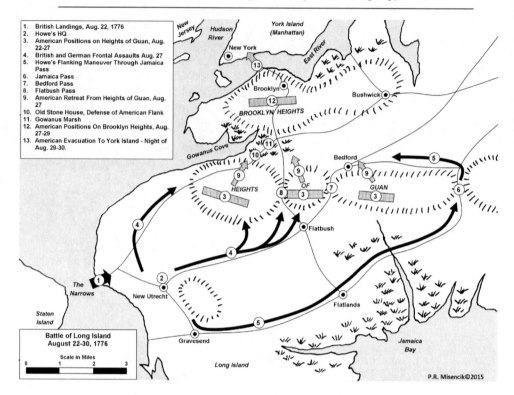

1. British Landings, Aug. 22, 1776
2. Howe's HQ
3. American Positions on Heights of Guan, Aug. 22-27
4. British and German Frontal Assaults Aug. 27
5. Howe's Flanking Maneuver Through Jamaica Pass
6. Jamaica Pass
7. Bedford Pass
8. Flatbush Pass
9. American Retreat From Heights of Guan, Aug. 27
10. Old Stone House, Defense of American Flank
11. Gowanus Marsh
12. American Positions On Brooklyn Heights, Aug. 27-29
13. American Evacuation To York Island - Night of Aug. 29-30.

Battle of Long Island, August 22–30, 1776.

cattle out of reach of the advancing redcoats. A sudden rain shower caused him to take refuge at Increase Carpenter's Inn,[7] about two miles east of Jamaica in present Hollis, Queens, New York. While at the inn, Woodhull was surprised and taken prisoner by a troop of British dragoons under the command of 27-year-old New York Loyalist Captain Oliver DeLancey Jr. (1749–1822).[8] According to popular legend, after Woodhull surrendered his sword, DeLancey ordered the defeated general to shout "God save the King," but Woodhull instead supposedly replied, "God save us all." DeLancey, enraged at Woodhull's defiance, struck the general repeatedly with his saber, grievously wounding him and almost completely severing Woodhull's arm when the poor man raised it to shield his head. DeLancey would have murdered Woodhull outright if another officer had not stepped between them and intervened. The badly wounded American general was thrown into prison at New Utrecht, where he died from his wounds on Friday, September 20, 1776.

After Howe's assault drove the Americans from the Heights of Guan, Washington and his troops retreated to the northwest corner of Long Island near Brooklyn where they were trapped with their backs to the water. General Howe could have easily rounded up Washington's army that was penned along the Brooklyn shore, but for some reason Howe delayed his attack. The Americans grimly awaited the attack they were certain would come the following day, but throughout the morning and early afternoon of Wednesday the 28th, Howe's army stayed put. In the meantime, Washington's troops worked furiously to improve their defensive positions, but around mid-afternoon a steady rain began to fall. By nightfall the rain became torrential, and almost continuous thunder and lightning tore the night. The positions of both armies became quagmires that made any sort of coordinated movement impossible. Then on the morning of Thursday the 29th, an impenetrable fog blanketed the area.

During the afternoon of the 29th, Washington called a council of his officers and informed them that he intended to evacuate his entire army across to Manhattan during the coming night. To do so, he called upon two regiments of expert sailors from Marblehead and Salem, Massachusetts, under the respective commands of John Glover (1732–1797) and Israel Hutchinson (1727–1811). That night, while three regiments of rearguard troops tramped around, stoked campfires, and in general created a diversion as if they were preparing for an assault, Washington's army of about 10,000 troops were ferried across the narrow strait to Manhattan Island.

Around four o'clock in the morning on Friday, August 30, 1776, the fog thinned somewhat and British pickets reported a noticeable lack of troop activity in the American positions. Patrols were ordered forward and as they cautiously entered the American lines they found only campfires burning brightly and some deserted equipment lying about, but there was no sign of the rebel army. The alarm was raised and the British and Hessian troops raced after the Americans, but they reached the Brooklyn shore only in time to see the last of the Americans a short distance off as they were ferried toward Manhattan. The British and Hessians fired several volleys at the departing Americans, wounding four soldiers. They were the only casualties suffered during the evacuation.

The British were now the masters of Long Island, and it was only a matter of time before General Howe would hurl his enormous force against the outnumbered Americans on Manhattan. Washington knew the assault was inevitable, and he pondered where best to deploy his army to meet the redcoats. It was an impossible task, because Howe could land almost anywhere on Manhattan. So Washington divided his army and placed about one half on Harlem Heights about two thirds of the way up Manhattan. They were in position there to protect an escape route north across the Harlem River

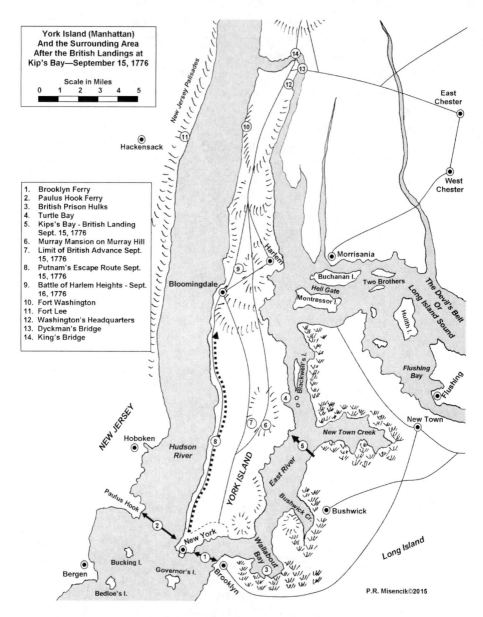

York Island (Manhattan) area during and after the British landings at Kip's Bay on September 15, 1779.

Map legend:

York Island (Manhattan)
And the Surrounding Area
After the British Landings at
Kip's Bay—September 15, 1776

Scale in Miles
0 1 2 3 4 5

1. Brooklyn Ferry
2. Paulus Hook Ferry
3. British Prison Hulks
4. Turtle Bay
5. Kips's Bay - British Landing Sept. 15, 1776
6. Murray Mansion on Murray Hill
7. Limit of British Advance Sept. 15, 1776
8. Putnam's Escape Route Sept. 15, 1776
9. Battle of Harlem Heights - Sept. 16, 1776
10. Fort Washington
11. Fort Lee
12. Washington's Headquarters
13. Dyckman's Bridge
14. King's Bridge

P.R. Misencik©2015

toward Westchester. The other half of the army under General Israel Putnam was deployed in and around New York City at the southern end of the island.

The British invasion of Manhattan occurred on Sunday morning, September 15, 1776. It began with a tremendous bombardment from Royal Navy ships, and then Howe's troops stormed ashore at Kip's Bay[9] about a third of the way up Manhattan Island. The British and Hessian forces rapidly moved inland and could easily have penetrated across the island to the Hudson River shore, sealing off the southern portion of Manhattan and trapping the American troops in and around New York City. General Howe, however, inexplicably stopped his advance in order to enjoy tea, claret and cakes served by the charming Quaker, Mary Lindley Murray (1726–1782), and her daughters Beulah (1762–1800) and Susanna (1764–1808) at "Inclenberg," their home on Murray Hill.[10] While Howe and his officers needlessly wasted away the afternoon, American General Israel Putnam (1718–1790) and his force of 3,500 men were able to escape up the narrow route that remained open along the western shore of Manhattan Island. By nightfall Putnam's force joined the rest of Washington's army at Harlem Heights. There has been considerable speculation about whether Mrs. Murray deliberately distracted and delayed General Howe and his army to help the Americans, or whether she engaged the general and his staff in entertainment merely as a manifestation of 18th-century hospitality. There is some evidence that Mrs. Murray may have been a "warm Whig" or someone who generally favored the patriotic movement, while her husband Robert was considered to be a Loyalist. At any rate, Mrs. Murray was certainly acquainted with George Washington, who established his headquarters at "Inclenberg" just for the day of September 14, 1776,[11] the day prior to the British invasion. Whatever the true reason for her detaining Howe, there is a plaque at the site of the Murray mansion which reads in part: "In honor of Mary Lindley Murray for services rendered her country during the American Revolution, entertaining at her home, on this site, Gen. Howe and his officers, until the American troops under Gen. Putnam escaped. Sept. 15, 1776."

5

The British Come
to Oyster Bay

Some months prior to the British arrival in the New York area, frenzied patriotic emotions erupted in Oyster Bay when the more strident Whig elements began to persecute their Loyalist neighbors. Members of the Sons of Liberty and other overzealous patriots directed acts of vandalism, arson and personal attacks against Loyalists, including those who had been long-time friends, neighbors and acquaintances. Roving bands of patriots ransacked the homes of suspected Loyalists ostensibly to confiscate any weapons that might be used in support of the king. Queen's County established a "Black List" of suspected Tories, and in January 1776, Congress passed the "Tory Act," which called on committees to round up suspected Loyalists for "safekeeping."[1] Some Loyalists went into hiding, seeking refuge in forests, swamps, or other remote areas on and off Long Island. Most of those who didn't run were summarily jailed.

Samuel Townsend publically spoke out against the persecution of his Loyalist neighbors with little result. Interestingly, it wasn't the first time that Samuel had spoken out in support of people that he felt were victims of injustice. In 1758, during the French and Indian War, Samuel had publically advocated justice for neutral French citizens and other detainees that had been interned in King's County. As a result, he was incarcerated for several days and heavily fined by the general assembly of New York for writing a letter that was a "high misdemeanor and most daring Insult on the Honour, Justice and Authority of this House [the general assembly]."[2]

Although Samuel Townsend advocated restraint in dealing with Loyalists, not all members of his extended family were so inclined. The chairman of the Queen's County Committee of Safety was one George Townsend (1720–1802), a cousin of Samuel. George was a strident and fanatical anti–Loyalist, who, in spite of Samuel's calls for restraint, was determined to purge society of anyone suspected of harboring Loyalist sympathies. On Monday, August

12, 1776, George Townsend and members of the local Committee of Safety arrested approximately twenty Oyster Bay Loyalists. The Loyalists were spirited across Long Island Sound to Connecticut and thrown into prison there. During the colonial period, Long Island Sound was commonly referred to as the "Devil's Belt," which got its name from the reefs in the Sound known as the "Devil's Stepping Stones."[3]

The harsh behavior of the strident patriots against their former friends and neighbors created a great deal of resentment that predictably resulted in reprisals as soon as the British became masters of New York and Long Island. Now that the British army was there to support them, the Loyalists began to retaliate against their former persecutors and also against anyone suspected of harboring Whiggish sympathies. Lists of disloyal Whigs were drawn up, and not surprisingly the militant George Townsend and another Oyster Bay neighbor, John Kirk, were included on all of the lists. It was understandable that George Townsend and John Kirk were targeted, since they were among the more fanatical anti–Loyalists in the Oyster Bay area and were responsible for a great deal of the committee's actions against Loyalists. The two had personally led most of the assaults on Long Island Tories during the summer of 1776. However, it came as a shock to the Townsend family to learn that Samuel Townsend's name was also included on many of the blacklists. In spite of the fact that Samuel Townsend often spoke out publicly against the persecution of Loyalists, his family relationship to George Townsend as well as Samuel's membership in the Provincial Congress was apparently sufficient reason for some of his Loyalist neighbors to denounce him. It would not be long before the inclusion of his name on the list would cause him and his family considerable difficulties.

After the Americans were defeated in the Battle of Long Island on Tuesday, August 27, 1776, the members of the New York Provincial Congress realized that it was only a matter of time before New York City would fall to the British. In anticipation of the British assault on New York, the Provincial Congress decided to relocate about 55 miles north to Fishkill, New York, where they could continue their legislative activities unimpeded. Samuel Townsend was preparing to join his Provincial Congress colleagues at Fishkill when he was arrested by the British authorities.

One afternoon, early in September 1776, a British troop of the 17th Light Dragoons clattered into Oyster Bay and stopped at the home of Jacob Townsend, whose daughter Almy had married Thomas Buchanan in 1765. The officer enquired for Mr. Samuel Townsend and was directed to the Townsend home just next door where they found Samuel seated on the stoop.[4] The dragoon officer placed Mr. Townsend under arrest, "with great discourtesy—accompanied by an oath"[5] and told him "to get himself ready to accompany them to the Provost at New York."[6] During the wait, the officer reportedly took pleasure in informing Townsend and his family that Samuel would be taken to the local British headquarters at Jericho and from there transferred to a prison in New York or possibly one of the prison hulks in Wallabout Bay. At the same time another party of redcoats was in the process of arresting George Townsend and John Kirk. Interestingly, both men had been warned of their impending arrest, and were advised to flee, but they refused. The dragoons found John Kirk at home, and George Townsend working in his cornfield, "stouting top stalks."[7]

When the British occupied New York, a number of derelict ship hulks were hastily set up as impromptu prisons for prisoners of war and civilians who were considered disloyal to the king. The most infamous were the decommissioned derelict ships that were moored in Wallabout Bay on the Long Island side of the East River. During the war, a total of sixteen derelict hulks were moored in Wallabout Bay to be used as floating prisons. The Wallabout Bay ships included the *Hope*, the *Falmouth*, the *Stromboli*, the *Hunter*, and others, but the most infamous was the HMS *Jersey*. The conditions aboard the decaying hulks were incredibly deplorable. Inmates were kept below decks in foul fetid conditions and fed meager rations that only served to delay, but not prevent starvation. An estimated 12,500 prisoners died on the Wallabout hulks, and only about 1,500 sick and emaciated prisoners survived them. The conditions aboard the prison hulks were notoriously inhumane, and being imprisoned aboard them was tantamount to a death sentence. Understandably, the threat of Samuel's being sent aboard the *Jersey* or one of the other prison hulks caused his family great distress.

In spite of the seriousness of his arrest and possible captivity in the living hell of a prison hulk, Townsend remained calm and agreed to peacefully accompany the soldiers, but he asked for time to have his horse saddled and to gather some personal effects to take with him. The officer grudgingly allowed Townsend a few extra minutes, and while he waited, the officer walked around the house obviously looking for any other evidence that would confirm the Townsend family's disloyalty. When the officer walked into the parlor, he noticed a fine fowling piece[8] hanging over the mantle. Cursing loudly, he took the weapon down from its hooks and smashed it repeatedly against the floor until the stock was shattered and the fine barrel was bent. Throwing aside the remains of the fowler, he told the astonished Townsends that rebels did not have the right to possess such a weapon. Next, he noticed a hanging portrait of Captain Solomon Townsend that had been painted in Portugal in 1772 during one of Solomon's voyages. The officer approached it menacingly, but fortunately refrained from damaging the painting. He only stated angrily that he was sorry it was not in his power to also wreak vengeance on Solomon. Ironically, at that time, Solomon was engaged on convoy duty with the *Glasgow* in support of the British army.

Outside her home, Sally saw that a crowd had been drawn by the squad of redcoats that invaded the Townsend home. When the townspeople learned that Samuel was being arrested, it was apparent that some were inclined to offer support to the beleaguered family but were intimidated by the martial demeanor of the redcoats, so they stood silently in the yard, not willing to express themselves in any way. It was obvious to Sally that while some of the neighbors appeared saddened by the Townsends' misfortune, others obviously approved of her father's arrest. It was common knowledge that many of their neighbors were Loyalists, but Samuel Townsend had always treated them fairly and courteously, and it was surprising that they would go so far as to denounce him to the British.

Some of his neighbors had indeed denounced Samuel for his Whiggish leanings and his activities in the rebel congress. However, most had pangs of conscience when they saw their gentle and popular neighbor being roughly hauled off to prison. One witness to the arrest, Elizabeth Wooden, whose family were Loyalists, said she knew that some Oyster Bay Tories informed on Townsend, because by serving in the rebel Provincial Congress, Samuel had not honored his pledge to remain neutral. However, when they saw the manner in which he was torn from his family, they openly regretted that their political animosity had caused such a sad result.[9]

Anecdotal Oyster Bay and Townsend family lore describe Sally's reaction to her father's arrest. Realizing that her father's predicament was caused by Tory accusations, Sally quickly concluded that the family would need the influence of a respected Loyalist to help her father. One person who had the stature and required level of influence was Thomas Buchanan, the husband of her cousin Almy. Thomas Buchanan, who did not keep it a secret that he was a steadfast Loyalist, was liked and respected by the large Tory population of Long Island. Ironically, the openly honest, honorable and congenial Buchanan was also well liked and respected by most of the Whigs in the area. However, more importantly, as a result of his large, successful and increasingly important shipping business, Buchanan had the respect and friendship of many of the most powerful Loyalists in New York City. Buchanan was one of her father's best friends, and Sally was certain that if anyone would be willing and able to help her father, Thomas would be that person. The fact that Samuel's son Solomon was captaining a Buchanan ship in support of the British military could only help Samuel's cause. The Buchanans lived in Oyster Bay, but Sally knew that Thomas and Almy had taken a carriage ride to Norwich that morning. In fact Sally's older sister Audrey had decided to ride her horse and accompany them on the day's ride. Norwich was on the road to Jericho, and Sally calculated that if she could find Thomas quickly enough, he might be able to use his influence to free her father from the dragoons before he was taken to British military headquarters in Jericho or, worse, to a prison in New York.

Without telling anyone, Sally slipped unnoticed from the house and ran to the stable where she quickly saddled her horse and led it around the far end of the meadow to keep out of sight of the redcoats around her house. Then she climbed onto the horse's back and raced out the back meadow to avoid the dragoons, who were mostly on Main Road. From there, she circled back on Front Street and urged her horse into a ground-covering gallop in the direction of Pine Hollow on the road to Norwich. In the meantime, Samuel Townsend, who had packed his meager kit, was only allowed time for a brief farewell with his family before he was led away by the redcoats. Samuel did not give any indication that he noticed Sally was not there to bid him goodbye. The red-coated detachment and their prisoner rode south on South Street toward Jericho, but before they had progressed very far, they were joined by another party of mounted cavalrymen who had George Townsend and John Kirk in their custody.

Sally cantered down Front Street and turned south on Pine Hollow Road. Looking back up South Street she would have seen that the dragoons had started out toward Jericho with her father as prisoner and that she was well ahead of them. Now if she could quickly find Thomas Buchanan, he might be able to do something to help her father before the dragoons took him all the way to Jericho.

Covering distance quickly, she sped through Pine Hollow and urged her horse up Great Hill and was eventually rewarded by the sight of the Buchanans' approaching phaeton with her sister Audrey riding alongside. Sally raced toward the party who had stopped when they saw her speeding down the road toward them, and even before she stopped, Sally began to gasp out the story of her father's arrest. She told them that the dragoon patrol with the captive Samuel Townsend was approaching behind her along this very road toward Jericho, and she begged Thomas Buchanan for his help in securing her father's release.

Thomas listened to Sally's story and said that he would certainly meet the soldiers and try to negotiate Samuel's release. Since the British might recognize Sally, it was decided that she would trail behind the phaeton, and when the redcoats were spotted Sally would ride into the woods out of sight of the British. That was okay with Sally since she didn't really want to be near the obnoxious dragoon officer who had arrested her father. They all proceeded toward Oyster Bay with Sally and Audrey riding alongside the Buchanans' phaeton, and within a short time, they spotted the approaching British patrol. Sally immediately rode into the dark woods bordering the road and watched from the shadows as Thomas hailed the dragoon officer.

Sally noticed that the dragoons were more numerous than had stopped at her house and was somewhat surprised to see that her cousin George and neighbor John Kirk had also been arrested. She observed Thomas Buchanan politely converse with the officer in charge, but the dragoon officer was argumentative and refused to consider negotiating the release of his prisoners. He gesticulated dismissively and summarily ordered his detachment forward toward Jericho. Thomas realized that he had no recourse but to meekly accompany the patrol to their headquarters and hope to find a more understanding superior. He told Audrey that she should give him her horse, and he would follow the dragoons to Jericho, where he hoped to appeal to the officer commanding there. Audrey quickly dismounted and handed the reins to Thomas. He helped Audrey into the phaeton with Almy, then mounted Audrey's horse and galloped off after the departing dragoons.[10] When the patrol disappeared, Sally rode out and joined the other two women, and the three sat motionless for some time. After a while they sadly started on toward Oyster Bay. Now that Sally had found the Buchanans and obtained Thomas's assistance, the reality of Samuel's predicament sunk in. All that any of them could do now was hope for the best, but they were not at all certain that Thomas would be able to free Samuel. The three women rode back to Oyster Bay wondering when and if they would ever see their captive relatives again. They tried to reassure and console each other, but all were sobbing and tear-streaked when they finally arrived at the Townsend home.

When they reached the Townsend home, they found the family understandably upset at the arrest of Samuel, but Sally was surprised to find that she was praised for her quick-witted resourcefulness in racing to locate their influential Loyalist friend Thomas Buchanan and obtain his intervention in Samuel's behalf. Even her brothers complimented their sixteen-year-old sister for her cool decisiveness and clearheaded action when everyone else seemed to be stunned into immobility. Sally didn't feel that she did anything out of the ordinary; she just tried to do something to save her father. But now she couldn't think of anything else to do other than join the rest of her family in praying that Thomas Buchanan would succeed in gaining her father's release.

As it turned out, Sally's efforts were not in vain, for Thomas Buchanan did indeed secure the release of Samuel Townsend. However, it cost him dearly. The commanding officer at the Jericho headquarters demanded a surety of several thousand pounds, a king's ransom, before he would consider allowing the Oyster Bay merchant to return home. In addition both men had to swear that when summoned, Samuel would be produced within six hours' time,[11] otherwise Samuel would be declared an outlaw, and Thomas Buchanan's loyalty would not only be tainted, but he would forfeit the large surety bond he posted to obtain Samuel's release. Thomas also attempted to secure the release of George Townsend and John Kirk, but in spite of Buchanan's offer of a very large surety, the officer would have none of it. George Townsend and John Kirk were too well known as rebel firebrands to be released on bond. While Samuel was allowed to return to his home and wait there for a hearing before a magistrate, George Townsend and John Kirk were sent under guard to New York and placed in the Provost Prison where they were at the mercy of the notoriously sadistic Provost Marshal, William Cunningham (1738–1791).[12] The two men remained in the Provost Prison for over nine weeks, but were released when John Kirk contracted smallpox. Rather than have Kirk treated or even quarantined, the devious Cunningham released the two men and sent them back to Oyster Bay, no doubt hoping that they would spread the disease among other Long Island Whigs. In the case of John Kirk, Cunningham's plan was successful. When Kirk returned home he infected his wife and infant child, and within a short time all three were dead from the disease. George Townsend did not contract the smallpox, but the cruel treatment he received while in the Provost Prison, along with Cunningham's role in the death of John Kirk and his innocent family, caused George to have an even more extreme hatred of Loyalists.

Realizing that their father would soon be summoned before a Loyalist magistrate who would interrogate him about his service with the Provincial Congress, Sally and her brother Robert appealed to their father to sign the oath of allegiance to King George. Signing the oath would provide Samuel with a measure of defense against the expected charge of sedition. At first Samuel refused to sign, because as a Quaker he was averse to taking any sort of oath. In addition, as a man who considered honesty and honor inviolate, the merchant argued that he could not in good conscience swear allegiance to a monarch or a government that he considered unjust. The family considered that if Samuel failed to take the oath, he would not only be torn from his family and possibly sent to suffer the horrors of the prison hulks, but it would likely subject the rest of the family to hardship and place them at the mercy of the more extreme Tory factions. Samuel briefly considered fleeing to Connecticut, but realized that doing so would cost his friend Thomas Buchanan the small fortune he pledged in bond, and it would also likely implicate Thomas and Almy in his escape. Robert finally convinced his father that if necessary, he should sign the loyalty oath. Robert's argument was that an oath given under duress was not binding either before God or man.

Less than a week later, Samuel was summoned by the British authorities to appear on Tuesday, September 10, 1776, before a magistrate in the superior court. In court, Loyalist Judge Whitehead Hicks (1728–1780)[13] began to question Samuel regarding his reported activities, especially those that could be construed as showing disloyalty to the royal government. To the Townsend family's surprise however, it was apparent that Judge Hicks was inclined toward leniency for Samuel. Hicks was noted for his integrity, courtesy, and professional conduct toward all parties, but even so, he was likely responding to recommendations of powerful New York Loyalists who had been lobbied by the unimpeachable Loyalist Thomas Buchanan. For whatever reason, Samuel was offered amnesty. Hicks read the Proclamation of Pardon, which General Howe issued on Friday, August 23, 1776, that pardoned anyone deemed to be in rebellion if they would swear allegiance to King George III. Judge Hicks offered Samuel the opportunity to take the oath of allegiance, and the merchant signed the oath without any apparent reluctance. As a measure of protection, Judge Hicks gave Samuel a certificate as proof of his allegiance.

Certificate from Judge Hicks

This is to certify that Samuel Townsend hath submitted to government and taken the oath of allegiance to his Majesty King George this 10th of Sept. 1776 before me.

Whitehead Hicks
One of the Judges of the Supr. Court

Sally and her brother Robert accompanied their father to the court and both were moved by the sadness and dejection they knew their father felt at being forced to sign the oath. The defeated demeanor of her father, who had always advocated resolve and resourcefulness and who had always remained strong in the face of adversity, undoubtedly affected her profoundly. Only a tyrannical government would force people to swear allegiance to a system that treated them so cavalierly. Because of the injustice of Samuel's arrest and his being forced to swear allegiance to the Crown, which was contrary to his personal code of honor as well as to his religious beliefs, Sally and her closest brother Robert began to feel a greater affinity to the Whiggish viewpoint, if not to the concept of an independent America that was not controlled by a red-coated army of occupation. At the time, however, Sally had no idea how they could resist British oppression without further jeopardizing their family.

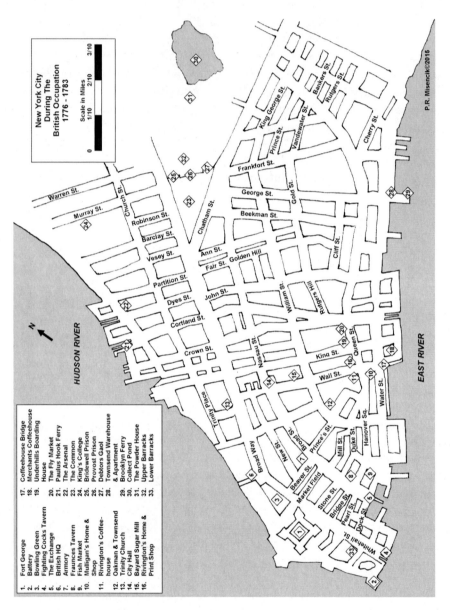

New York City during the British occupation, 1776–1783.

Unbeknownst to Sally, or the rest of the Townsend family for that matter, Robert had some previous experience working for the American cause against the British. There are indications that during the years 1772–1774, Robert held the funds of the Sons of Liberty[14] by burying their monies deep within the Townsend mercantile accounts. Robert never told any family member about his previous association with the patriot group. At any rate, the Sons of Liberty would not be of much help to them now. Though Robert undoubtedly had contacts within the Sons of Liberty, the fact is that after the British occupation of New York and Long Island, most of the contacts he had in the patriot organization had fled the area and the rest had gone to ground. There didn't seem to be any other way to resist the British and Loyalists in Oyster Bay. All they could do was watch and listen for any information that might benefit the patriots, and if the opportunity arose, somehow hope to forward that information to the Americans.

The one thing they were certain of was that because of Samuel Townsend's experience, the entire Townsend family would be under scrutiny, so everything they did would have to appear normal and innocuous. Any action by any family member that was construed as suspicious could bring disaster to the Townsend family. Whatever Robert and Sally did to resist the British or aid the Americans would have to be their secret alone. Their first tentative steps toward espionage would later pay dividends. Robert Townsend as "Samuel Culper Junior" would become one of the leaders of the "Culper Ring," perhaps the most successful American spy network during the Revolutionary War, and Sally would assist the American cause as a spy while playing a very dangerous game as the romantic interest of a very intelligent and capable British spy hunter.

The humiliation of being forced to make a public denial of his Whiggish inclinations continued to plague Samuel Townsend. On Monday, October 21, 1776, a petition that affirmed loyalty to the British government was addressed to Governor Tryon. More than 1,300 freeholders from Queen's County signed it, and Samuel Townsend was one of the signatories. Not altogether surprising is that his son Robert also signed the petition. Robert asserted that it would be an unnecessary risk for the family if he and his father refused to sign.

Even though Samuel had signed the loyalty pledge, the Townsends knew it would take some time for the taint of his arrest on suspicion of disloyalty to abate. So to allow the dust to settle, they decided that the quiet, uncontroversial Robert would become the face of the Townsend mercantile business and he would take over the higher-profile duties associated with the trade. It was a good choice. Robert indeed had a knack and a flair for business. Around 1769–1770, when Robert was still in his teens, Samuel had arranged for Robert to be apprenticed to the mercantile firm of Templeton & Stewart, which was located in an area of New York called the "Holy Ground." The Holy Ground was in the northern section of the city in the area of Church, Barclay, and Vesey Streets near King's College,[15] and the roughly two-block area was perhaps the largest and most expensive "red light district" in North America. Because of its proximity to the city's docks where the majority of the deep-water ships unloaded their cargoes, many of the reputable mercantile and trading companies were located in and around the area of the Holy Ground. However, that same proximity to the waterfront also provided grog shops and bordellos readily available to sailors who were eager for entertainment and female companionship after a long sea voyage. Before the Revolutionary War and particularly prior to the British occupation, the Holy Ground had an erotically adventuresome reputation; however, its clientele were for the most part well-behaved citizens merely looking for a good time. There were high-class bordellos as well as more earthy "trugging" houses or brothels that catered to sailors and lower class clients. It was a vibrant and dynamic area that was relatively safe and had sufficient resources to provide adequate entertainment opportunities for the crowds of enthusiastic clients who visited the neighborhood. For example, within the area owned by the Anglican Church, and adjacent to St. Paul's Chapel near the entrance to King's College, over 500 prostitutes maintained their lodgings and workplaces.[16]

After the great New York fire of Saturday and Sunday, September 21–22, 1776, which destroyed many of the buildings in the Holy Ground, the nature of the area changed dramatically. The shells of burned-out buildings were hastily patched up in jury-rigged fashion to provide any sort of shelter for the basest of entertainments. Piles of debris were cleared only enough to accommodate passage, and the most common type of roofing and window coverings was simple canvas or sailcloth. The more industrious doxies, confidence men, and villains of every ilk erected tents or rudimentary canvas-covered shelters in almost every available space where they could live and ply their trade. The area catered to every taste or inclination. Homosexual prostitutes or "mollies," known for their garish makeup, female dress, and effeminate ways, carried on a brisk trade in mostly canvas-covered "molly houses," which were interspersed throughout the area. Crooked gambling houses, low grog shops, and almost every sort of "entertainment" designed to separate a person from his money populated the dismally seedy area. Because of the prevalence of canvas and sailcloth that was used to provide shelter or a modicum of privacy, the area became known as "Canvass-Town" or "Topsail Town." One William Duer (1743–1799) described Canvass-Town as "cheap and convenient lodgings for the frail sisterhood, who plied their trade most briskly in the vicinity of the shipping and the barracks."[17] Gone with the fire were the former well-behaved clients of the Holy Ground. Now, the rough shelters that housed coarse, well-worn prostitutes, grimy pawnshops, filthy flophouses and murky rotgut bars took on a more sinister and violent nature. The clientele were now predominantly hard-bitten, belligerent soldiers and sailors of the occupying British and German military. Robberies, muggings, and murders were commonplace, and often corpses were left where they lay until their stench began to discourage potential customers.

Fortunately Robert Townsend had left the employ of Templeton & Stewart around 1773, years prior to the British occupation and the great fire of New York. But even so, Robert, who worked there between the ages of sixteen and twenty, certainly was aware of the reputation and the activities carried on in the bawdy houses of the Holy Ground. For the young and virile Robert, the lure of erotic adventure must have been present, but there is no evidence that the reserved Quaker youth succumbed to the various temptations. Instead Robert distinguished himself at Templeton & Stewart, where he learned how to run a business, and more importantly, he concentrated on how best to turn a good profit and acquire financial independence. He learned well. For example, between May 1781 and July 1783, Townsend grossed £16,786, and his expenditures were £15,161.[18] This meant that during that twenty-six-month period, Robert netted £1,625, or £62.5 per month. By the standards of the day he was making a considerable amount of money.

To preclude Samuel from taking part in higher-profile activities that could arouse any further suspicion by the British authorities, Robert took on more of the direct management of the Townsend mercantile business. To do so, he decided to move to New York City, from where he would supervise the Townsend enterprise. Sally was sad to learn of Robert's decision to move to New York and she knew that she would miss her brother very much.

In New York Robert took residence at Underhill's boardinghouse on Queen Street. He and his father had previously used the boardinghouse when they came to New York on business, primarily because they were acquainted with the owners, Amos and Mary Underhill. Mary happened to be the sister of Abraham Woodhull, an acquaintance who lived in Setauket on Long Island. Robert also kept a small temporary apartment that was located at the Townsend warehouse at number 41, Peck's Slip, at the foot of Ferry Street. Robert generally used the Peck's Slip apartment when his continued presence was required, such as when a ship's cargo was being loaded or unloaded. In the city Robert was well placed to look after the inventory at the Peck's Slip warehouse and also oversee the Townsend trade through his family's association with Templeton and Stewart and other trading companies.

6

Living with the Enemy

During the autumn of 1776, when both armies were going into winter quarters, the Loyalist Colonel Oliver DeLancey (1718–1785)[1] brought his brigade onto Long Island and established his headquarters at Huntington. DeLancey's 1st Battalion was assigned to bivouac in Oyster Bay, and soon after, Samuel and Sarah Townsend were summarily informed that they were required to provide quarters, including room and board, for one of DeLancey's officers. That October, a Major Joseph Green[2] (1746–1830), who was commander of the 1st Battalion, appeared at the Townsend's door and politely informed them that he had been assigned to live with them. While it galled the Townsends that their house was being "invaded" by the enemy, Major Green was nevertheless welcomed into the Townsend home, and he was given Robert Townsend's now vacant ground-floor bedroom as his quarters. In addition, the Loyalist officer was invited to dine with the Townsends during their family meals, and for all intents and purposes, he was treated almost as a member of the family. Surprisingly and in spite of their early consternation at having an enemy officer forced upon them, the Townsends quickly grew fond of Major Green. He was young, handsome, very personable and disarmingly polite. In short, he was distinctly unlike most of the other officers and troops who strutted about the town like conquerors, bullying the men and making suggestive advances toward the women in the community. Sally was initially outraged that her family was required to quarter an "enemy" officer and she fully intended to have as little to do with him as possible. However, as time passed, Green's respectful and unassuming personality endeared him to the Townsends, which caused Sally to feel somewhat guilty when she realized that she rather liked the young and engaging officer.

As was the custom, the Townsends decided to host a "frolic," or party, in honor of their houseguest. Most of their friends and neighbors were invited, among whom were Thomas and Almy Buchanan, Daniel and Susannah Youngs, the Woodens, and other prominent Oyster Bay Loyalists. Daniel

Robert Townsend's downstairs bedroom used by Major Green and later by Lt. Col. Simcoe (author's photograph).

Youngs (1748–1809) was a captain in the Loyalist militia, and he and his wife, the former Susannah Topping (1752–1847), lived at the family homestead at the foot of the Cove.[3] Their home served as the local Loyalist militia headquarters. Absalom Wooden (1753–1841) attended the frolic, and he was a member of Daniel Youngs's Loyalist militia regiment. Also in attendance were Jacob (?–?) and Mercy Townsend (?–1833), the parents of Almy Buchanan, whose younger daughter Hannah accompanied them to the party. Sally felt somewhat conflicted when she found herself drawn to the "enemy officer" Major Green, who appeared handsome in his gold-laced regimentals. However, as the evening progressed she discovered that she needn't worry about becoming emotionally attached to Green, because it was soon apparent that the dashing young major was very attracted to Sally's cousin Hannah.

Hannah Townsend must have felt the same fascination for Major Green, because later that month, the couple announced their engagement. Although Sally was happy for her cousin Hannah, she felt some disappointment that her cousin was going to marry an enemy officer; one who was occupying not only their town, but also her very home. Major Green said he wanted the wedding to take place as soon as feasible, because of the possibility of his deployment from Oyster Bay. Sally immediately seized upon the opportunity to pick up any information she could with regard to Major Green's deployment. She became almost inseparable with the betrothed couple and helped them plan for their wedding.

The wedding plans for Hannah and Major Green progressed, and to accommodate Major Green's wishes for an early wedding, the ceremony was planned for Tuesday, January 7, 1777, at St. George's Church in Hempstead.[4] Whenever Green was in the Townsend home, Sally engaged him in chatty conversations that touched on his apparent haste for getting married and about his regiment's possible winter deployment. She hoped that he would provide some clues regarding a winter campaign or perhaps an indication of British plans for the regular campaign season of 1777. However, it soon was apparent that Major Green's fears of early deployment were groundless. Major Green was merely love-struck, and even though there were no plans for a winter deployment, he was so worried that something might interfere with his wedding that he wanted to marry Hannah as quickly as possible.

The previous month, Sally had a minor altercation that could have brought her loyalty into question, and it was over the lack of a red ribbon. Now that the British occupied New York and Long Island, the local Loyalists began to publicly demonstrate their allegiance to the crown by wearing red ribbons. Before the British came, the Loyalists felt they had to keep a lower profile in fear of persecution by the militant Whigs like the Sons of Liberty. But now that they had the British army to protect them, a profusion of red ribbons appeared that proudly declared allegiance to the king of England. Tory men wore red cockades in their hats and pinned red ribbons to their clothing, while women decorated their clothing in red, and wore red ribbons in their hair. Even horses' bridles were festooned with red cockades and red streamers that proclaimed their owner's allegiance to the king and the Loyalist cause. This vogue of Loyalist decorations caused Sally to come to cross-purposes with at least one member of the British military.

In December 1776, Sally was asked by her father to ride to the Youngses' home on the Cove to deliver some oznaburg linen, ginger, and sugar cones from Townsend's store. Sally liked Daniel and Susannah Youngs, even though she was disappointed that Daniel chose to side with the British as a militia officer. Regardless, she was glad for the chance to take a pleasant ride down to the Cove. On the way, she was overtaken by a red-coated dragoon who slowed his horse and attempted to strike up a conversation with her. The trooper's imposing presence, regimental coat and shining helmet brought back memories of the arrogant redcoat who had arrested her father and destroyed his valuable fowling piece, so she continued to ride along and pretended not to notice him. The obviously miffed dragoon persisted, and finally in a loud commanding voice, asked why she dared to appear thus without the red Tory badge or escutcheon adorning her horse to symbolize allegiance to His Majesty, King George.[5] The soldier's haughty and domineering manner irritated Sally and rather than meekly give an answer that would have placated him, she snapped back at the trooper, stating that obviously her horse does not wear red, because of its Whiggish leanings, and she added that she preferred to ride her filly as it was.[6] The trooper appeared to be taken aback by her scornful look and sassy reply, and he gave her a dark glare before he put spurs to his horse and sped on. The Youngses' home was only a short distance ahead, and Sally was dismayed to see that the trooper was heading there. The large dwelling served as headquarters for Captain Youngs's Loyalist militia unit, and Sally rode up just as the trooper was tying his horse to a post. When he saw her ride up, the trooper scowled at her and started up the walk toward the house, just as Captain Daniel Youngs walked out the front door. The trooper glanced darkly at Sally, and she was certain he was going to tell Daniel about her lack of respect for the Loyalist cause, but Daniel walked right past him and warmly greeted Sally. The trooper watched as Captain Youngs took Sally's parcel and helped her down from her horse. Seeing the obvious friendship between the girl and the Loyalist officer, the trooper handed Youngs the dispatches he carried, but apparently not sure of their relationship, he didn't mention his encounter with the girl. Later, when Sally was riding home, she had a momentary panic attack when she considered that word of her altercation with the trooper might get back to Major Green, who was still living in her home. She knew that even though her father and brother had publicly submitted to British authority, many Loyalists were keeping a close eye on the Townsends, and it would not be good for any of the family to arouse suspicion. In spite of her fears, nothing came of the incident; either the trooper did not mention the minor affair to Major Green and Captain Youngs or the officers had merely discounted it. For whatever reason, Sally never heard any more regarding the incident.

On Tuesday, January 7, 1777, the wedding of Hannah Townsend and Major Joseph Green took place in St. George's Church in Hempstead. Sally attended the wedding, and she thought the couple looked especially admirable: Hannah, beautiful in her gorgeous wedding gown, and Major Green, handsome and dashing in his gold-trimmed, green regimentals.[7] Sally was very happy for her cousin. She found herself wondering what her own wedding would be like and if she would ever wear a dress as beautiful as Hannah's. However, in spite of her admiration for the couple, when Hannah and Joseph repeated their vows, Sally could not help but feel a tinge of betrayal on the part of her cousin. Sally felt that with the solemn words of the wedding service, Hannah was not only marrying a British officer, but was also in some way denying America.[8]

7

The Times
That Try Men's Souls

The 1776 Christmas season approached, and the news of the war was nothing but dismal for American patriots. After repulsing a British attack in a small but sharp skirmish at Harlem Heights on Monday, September 16, 1776, the weary Americans had been beaten in one fight after another. British General William Howe was a master at flanking maneuvers, and with his superior numbers he consistently threatened to isolate and encircle Washington and the American army. It was only by constant retreats and exhausting forced marches that Washington was able to extricate his battered and dispirited forces from one potential trap after another. After the Battle of Harlem Heights, Washington barely had time to withdraw his army across the Harlem River north into Westchester before powerful British units that had landed at Throg's Neck and Pell's Point could seal off the Americans retreat. While the bulk of the American army had withdrawn from Manhattan, Washington detached about 2,900 troops to hold Fort Washington on the northwestern corner of the Island.[1] Fort Washington's defenses were very impressive. The stronghold was located on a hill called Mount Washington, which rose 230 feet above the Hudson River. The fortification mounted 34 cannons and was supported by strong outer works with ravelins[2] and redoubts.[3] Fort Washington was the last remaining stronghold on Manhattan.

Washington's army was chased across Westchester by the pursing British and German forces, and after a battle at White Plains, they again were forced to retreat to North Castle. However, Howe decided to disengage his pursuit of Washington, and on Monday, November 4, 1776, marched his force back toward New York. Washington sensed that Howe's next move would be against Fort Washington, so he dispatched a message to General Nathaniel Greene (1742–1786), warning Greene that Fort Washington was in jeopardy. Greene was at Fort Lee across the Hudson from Fort Washington, but was in overall command of the two forts. Washington was concerned that with Howe's entire army assaulting Fort Washington, the fort's defenses were untenable. While Washington advocated abandoning Fort Washington, he allowed General Greene to use his discretion. One of the primary reasons for holding the fort was that it was almost directly across the river from Fort Lee on the New Jersey side, and it was thought that the crossfire from Forts Washington and Lee would prevent any British ships from sailing past them up river. However, that thought was shattered on the morning of Thursday, November 7, 1776, when three Royal Navy frigates sailed upriver through the combined gunfire of the two forts and penetrated upriver with a minimum of damage and casualties. The fact that the forts could not prevent British ships from sailing up river eliminated any strategic need to hold Fort Washington.

After detaching General Charles Lee with about 11,000 men on the east side of the Hudson, Washington crossed the river with a smaller force of about 5,000 troops and arrived at Fort Lee on Friday, November 15. There he learned that Greene had decided to hold Fort Washington, and that the British and Germans had invested the fort, isolating the 3,000 defending troops. Greene told Washington that in a council of war, Colonel Robert Magaw, the commander of Fort Washington, said he was certain that he could hold the fort against the entire British army at least until December.

Unfortunately, Magaw's adjutant, Lieutenant William Demont of the 5th Pennsylvania Regiment, had slipped away and deserted to the British during the night of Saturday, November 2, 1776. Demont took with him the complete plans of the fortifications as well as comprehensive descriptions of the numbers, armaments and disposition of the defending troops. In addition, Demont had been involved in the construction and armament of the fort, and was perhaps one of the most knowledgeable officers regarding its strengths and weaknesses. Demont's defection sealed the fate of the fort and its defenders, and he went down in history as the first known traitor to the American cause.

After a powerful assault supported by a massive artillery bombardment, Fort Washington fell in one day. Over 2,800 Americans were marched into captivity, where a great number of them languished and died under atrocious conditions in makeshift prisons or on the prison hulks in Wallabout Bay.

The loss of Fort Washington made the defense of Fort Lee across the river untenable, and Washington began to evacuate men and supplies while he still had the opportunity. However, before he was able to withdraw the bulk of his arms and equipment, the British moved against the fort. During the night of Tuesday, November 19, 1776, under cover of heavy rain, the British ferried a strong force of about 5,000 men under General Cornwallis across the Hudson River and landed them at Lower Closter Landing[4] about six miles north of Fort Lee. As soon as they landed and formed up, they dragged their guns and equipment to the top of the palisades and marched south.[5] Fortunately, an American patrol spotted the British force on the New Jersey side of the Hudson and rushed the alarm to Washington at Fort Lee. When Washington and Greene learned that the British were on the west side of the Hudson and only a short distance away, they quickly roused the garrison and immediately fled the fort, abandoning large quantities of arms and materiel. The Americans had not been gone very long when Cornwallis marched his men into the abandoned Fort Lee, where they found tents, military baggage, 50 cannon, huge stores of flour, ammunition, and vast quantities of other supplies that were left behind. Cornwallis's troops also captured or killed over 100 skulkers who had lagged behind Washington's withdrawing army.

Realizing that the Americans were on the run, Cornwallis set off in immediate pursuit and chased after Washington, who was moving south into central New Jersey. The British caught up and skirmished the Americans at Hackensack, Newark, and New Brunswick, routing them each time. The weary and dispirited Americans continued to flee further south to Princeton, desperately trying to stay out of reach of the pursuing redcoats. Since their expulsion from New York and their retreat across New Jersey, the Americans had not put up much of a fight against the enemy. Washington realized that his exhausted and discouraged troops were no match for the veteran British and German forces, and he refused to risk his small army in a major battle.

With the American army in headlong retreat, most British and many Americans concluded that it was just a matter of time until the war ended with the capitulation of Washington and his army. Since evacuating New York, the American losses in men and materiel were enormous. They had lost over 146 cannon, 3,000 muskets, and one-half million cartridges, and worse yet, they had lost tents, supplies, and food that were essential for their survival, especially with winter approaching. Of a deeper concern was the unmistakable fact that the series of defeats and constant retreats had deeply shaken the confidence of both the American soldiers and civilians. As a result, recruitments dried up, enlistments were expiring and men were deserting in droves. Washington's army was melting away. Most of the militia had disappeared, and another large number of enlistments would expire at the end of the year, merely five weeks away. To add to Washington's exasperation, General Charles Lee refused to respond to Washington's orders to bring his force south to New Jersey. Lee still had a full Division under his command in New England, and Washington desperately needed them now. Washington sent messages to Lee almost daily, first asking, then ordering Lee to bring his forces south, but for some reason Lee chose to ignore him.

On Monday, December 2, 1776, Washington and his worn-out force of 3,000 men limped into Princeton, New Jersey, with Cornwallis's army in New Brunswick. Cornwallis had been pushing his army across New Jersey in pursuit of Washington, but now that the Americans were hemmed in by the Delaware River, Cornwallis felt that there was no longer a need for a forced march to round up Washington's bedraggled army. The British general stopped in New Brunswick and allowed his army to rest until Saturday, December 7, 1776, before he again set off in pursuit of Washington. Washington, however, did not intend to be trapped, and while Cornwallis was in New Brunswick, the American commander-in-chief moved his army across the Delaware River into Pennsylvania. It was a prodigious undertaking. The troops were ferried night and day across the river, and the last of the troops crossed on Sunday, December 8, just as Cornwallis's army approached. Interestingly, the leading elements of British and German troops approached the river just as the last boatloads of Americans reached the far side. The British and Germans shouted taunts and jeers at the escaping Americans, but they were quickly answered by a few American artillery pieces that were positioned to protect the crossing point. The Americans effectively silenced the taunting British and Germans by scattering them with a fusillade of grape shot. When Cornwallis arrived at the river, he found that Washington had not only successfully crossed the Delaware, but he had also taken or destroyed every boat for a distance of seventy miles, which effectively prevented Cornwallis and his army from following the Americans into Pennsylvania.

Loyalists were elated and the Whigs were devastated at the news that Washington and his defeated army had been chased the length and breadth of New Jersey and were now seeking a tenuous refuge across the Delaware River in Pennsylvania. It appeared to almost everyone that the beleaguered Americans would not be able to hold out much longer.

Despite Washington's series of successful retreats and his ability to keep his troops intact, many Americans felt that Washington's defeats during the preceding three months were indications that America's Declaration of Independence, barely six months old, was hopeless and that the war would soon end with an American surrender. The impact of these attitudes was immediate and profound. Militia units refused to turn out in support of Washington, General Lee felt justified to continue ignoring Washington's orders to bring his troops south, and worse, many Americans were accepting Howe's offer of amnesty. Washington would later write that these were "the dark days of America."[6] On Wednesday, December 18, 1776, Washington wrote to his brother that "if every nerve was not strained to recruit this new army, the game was pretty nearly up." He added, "You can form no idea of the perplexity of my situation. No man, I believe, ever had a greater choice of difficulties, and less means to extricate himself from them. However, under a full persuasion of the justice of our cause, I cannot entertain an idea that it will finally sink, though it may remain for some time under a cloud."[7]

In Oyster Bay, the Townsend family was well aware of the sad plight of the American army, which had been savaged and chased the length of New Jersey and was now believed to be cowering across the Delaware River in Pennsylvania. But just when American morale was at its lowest ebb, Washington and his ragged army struck back and won two very stunning and improbable victories. On the night of Christmas Eve, Washington stealthily sent his army back into New Jersey, and in a dawn attack, struck the Hessian outpost at Trenton, where he captured the town and almost the entire garrison. A week later, Washington once again launched his army on a daring attack into New Jersey. The Americans crossed the Delaware and slipped around Cornwallis's army, which was approaching Trenton. And while Cornwallis and his army surveyed the carnage left by the American attack on Trenton, Washington's army smashed into Princeton, where after a hard-fought engagement, the Americans captured the town and almost its entire British garrison. In Trenton, Cornwallis heard the sounds of the Battle of Princeton, and rushed toward the sound of the fighting, but he and his army arrived too late to be of any use. The victorious Americans had slipped off like phantoms toward the northwest to establish their winter quarters near Morristown, New Jersey. The news of Washington's miraculous victories elated the Whigs, and now it was the turn of the Loyalists to be concerned. Washington and his army had somehow risen from the dead and had proven themselves capable of fighting and winning battles against the most powerful military force on earth.

8

The Jägers Come
to Oyster Bay

Later, during January 1777, Oyster Bay residents were startled to see a contingent of green-coated troops marching into town from the west. They were quickly identified as German troops, and the townsfolk were terrified to see mercenary forces so near, especially after hearing tales of the Hessians' savage and barbaric behavior during the battles for Long Island and New York. Stories abounded of Hessians pinning American troops to trees with bayonets and slaughtering American troops as they tried to surrender. In actuality, atrocities committed by the German troops were the exception rather than the rule, but the stories nevertheless continued to gain traction among the American populace. It wasn't long before all German troops were regarded as barbaric mercenaries.[1]

The Oyster Bay residents were especially concerned, because they were aware that German troops had been severely mauled by the Americans at Trenton the previous month, a battle in which their commander Oberst (Colonel) Johann Gottlieb Rall had been killed. It was feared that the Germans would likely vent their rage on the local citizenry. The stunned and terrified residents watched silently as the dreaded Germans entered Oyster Bay with the obvious intent of establishing winter quarters there. Very few women ventured outside, and most of the men rushed to ensure the security of their homes and families. Sally and her sisters watched from her upstairs bedroom window as the Hessian regiments paraded by on Main Road in front of their home. The girls noticed that in response to shouted orders, one green-coated unit swung out of line and formed up along the side of the road. It could only mean that those German mercenaries would be bivouacked in the immediate area, perhaps in their very home.

From her vantage point, Sally closely scrutinized the troops and noticed that while some of the men were mounted, most were not. She also saw that their green jackets were faced with crimson and the men were all armed with

Sally Townsend's upstairs bedroom (author's photograph).

curious-looking, short, stubby firelocks that were slung over their shoulders. Sally and her neighbors did not realize it at the time, but the short-jacketed, green-clad Germans with the unusual firelocks were Jägers, which meant "huntsmen." They were special light-infantry units recruited from among the German foresters, gamekeepers, and expert hunters. The stubby weapons they carried were large-bore rifles, as opposed to the more conventional smoothbore muskets that infantrymen carried. The rifling, or spiral grooves on the inside of the gun barrels, gave the weapons far greater accuracy over longer distances than muskets. While the maximum effective range of a musket was approximately 80 yards, a rifleman could easily hit his target at twice that range or even considerably farther depending on the skill of a rifleman. The Jägers, for the most part, were skilled marksmen who were able to shoot their rifles with deadly accuracy.

Because of their uniforms, the Jägers were frequently referred to as "greencoats," and they were usually deployed in small detachments for scouting and reconnaissance missions or to serve as long-range snipers against American units. They were all marksmen and woodsmen and were the European equivalent of American frontier riflemen. The Jägers that were assigned to bivouac in Oyster Bay were the 1st Battalion Jäger Korps commanded by Oberstleutnant (Lieutenant Colonel) Ludwig Johann Adolphus von Wurmb (1736–1813). They were an elite unit who considered themselves superior to the rest of the German line troops, and even superior to other Jäger regiments. Wurmb was a highly competent and distinguished officer who had an exceptional military record and who was in overall command of the Jäger troops from Hesse-Cassel, Hesse-Hanau, and Anspach that were serving in America.[2] The first Jäger units had arrived in New York in August 1776, and additional units arrived in October of that year. Now the Jägers were establishing their winter quarters on northern Long Island.

The residents of Oyster Bay viewed the influx of the dreaded Germans with trepidation. Because these fearsome foreign troops were garrisoned in the vicinity, women remained indoors where they felt safer, and anyone, including men, whose business took them out-of-doors, tried to avoid contact with whatever Germans there were about the town. However, as the days passed into weeks, and in spite of their fears, the Townsends and their neighbors found that there was little if any friction or difficulty between the townspeople and the Jägers. They also learned over time that there was no real reason to be frightened of the Germans In fact, the townspeople had experienced far more egregious and numerous instances of ill treatment and abuse by the occupying British and Loyalist troops.

For example, Elizabeth Titus of Oyster Bay related how thirty or forty of Captain Oliver DeLancey's 17th Light Horse Regiment turned their horses loose to graze in her father's meadows, and then arrogantly invaded their house and kitchen without even saying a word. When soldiers from that same unit began digging potatoes from Joseph Lawrence's garden, he objected and was arrested and sent under guard to New York, where a Judge had him jailed so that he would learn to exhibit proper politeness and deference toward British troops. In fairness, many British officers treated civilians correctly and tried to ensure that the men under their command did likewise. In fact, many British officers maintained appropriate discipline among their troops, which was much appreciated by the citizenry. Some British officers were so highly regarded by members of the community that they were regularly invited to Oyster Bay homes to share dinner with the families. For some reason, however, American Loyalist troops seemed more inclined toward cruelty toward their countrymen, and most acts of looting or brutality appeared to come from American Loyalist soldiers.

Under martial law, members of DeLancey's Loyalist brigade had a reputation for treating their fellow Americans harshly regardless of whether they

Jäger Corps of Hesse-Cassel, 1776–1783 (© New-York Historical Society).

were Whigs or Loyalists. British regulations required that citizens' provisions and livestock had to be surrendered without question when they were requisitioned by the army. However, the British authorities had determined fixed prices to somewhat compensate the local inhabitants for the loss of their food

and property. It was also British policy to attempt to spread their requisitioning among the citizenry so that no one family would suffer unduly. The loss
of a significant portion of their fuel, wagons, food, seed grain, or livestock
could be devastating to a family. In spite of this policy, DeLancey's Loyalist
soldiers foraged excessively without any regard to local necessity or whether
the families they plundered had enough remaining on which to subsist. In
many instances, farmers were not paid fully for what was requisitioned, and
in some cases when the farmers were paid, they were often robbed by thugs
who were in league with the requisitioning soldiers. Whig farmers were frequently plundered with no pretense of payment. Marauding soldiers often
visited outlying farms and pillaged anything usable or saleable, regardless of
the farm family's political loyalty. Out-of-the-way families were regularly ter-
rorized, and women and even young girls were frequently molested and often
gang-raped. Females were abducted from remote homesteads and taken to
soldiers' camps where they were raped over periods of several days.[3] It did
not take long for American Loyalist officers and their troops to become uni-
versally feared and detested by almost all Long Island residents, including
those who considered themselves Loyalists and supported the British cause.

Having experienced the oppressive presence of DeLancey's Loyalists,
Oyster Bay residents were surprised that as time passed, no one seemed to
have any complaints about the behavior of the Jägers. In fact, the families
that had Jäger officers billeted with them were often complimentary about
their houseguests. Indeed, the Jägers' commanding officer, Oberstleutnant
von Wurmb, made it a practice to respond to requests or complaints from
townspeople politely, quickly and effectively. The Jäger officers and men in
the ranks continued to impress the local inhabitants with their unpretentious
and chivalrous demeanor, particularly in their contacts with the women of
Oyster Bay.

Within a relatively short period of time, the German soldiers became
popular with the residents and were frequently invited as guests at a family's
dinner or to attend the various entertainments and frolics that were held in
the town. The German troops were entertained by the townspeople, but in
return they also provided the residents with welcome entertainment. For
example, British regiments contained musicians who played fifes and drums
and the occasional bagpipe; however, the Germans had fifes and drums, but
they also had oboes, trumpets, and French horns with which they played a
vast assortment of martial as well as popular European tunes. German bands
acquainted American citizens with some of the first brass music heard in
America.[4] In some cases the Germans troops were able to get along better
with the American civilians than they were able to get along with their British

allies. Many British officers believed that the hired German mercenaries were preventing them from more rapid wartime advancement. In one incident a British officer accosted a German officer shouting, "God damn you, Frenchy, you take our pay!" The German mercenary stiffened and calmly replied, "I am a German and you are a shit."[5] Both men drew their swords and the English officer was killed in the brief duel that followed.

Like soldiers everywhere, it wasn't long before the Jägers became acquainted with the local females of Oyster Bay and the neighboring locales. The young ladies also enjoyed socializing with the dashing Jägers, and while German officers courted all of the Townsend girls, Sally apparently became their favorite. Elizabeth Titus, a young neighbor who also took part in the flirtations, recalled that while each of the young women had at least one suitor, Sally Townsend, with her large, flashing eyes, "was beloved by every one."[6] Two Jäger officers who were billeted near the Townsend residence were Oberleutnant (1st Lieutenant) Ernst Wintzingerode and Leutnant (2nd Lieutenant) Ochse. Records indicate that Wintzingerode was quartered in the home of T. Townsend[7] while Ochse shared space with a number of other junior officers at the farm of D. Mudge.[8] Sally's niece, Sarah Thorne, recalled that Wintzingerode formed a close friendship with Sally Townsend, and Elizabeth Titus said that Lieutenant Ochse was greatly attracted to Sally's younger sister Phebe. Ochse once wrote a verse to cheer Phebe up when she lost a ribbon bow from her shoe. For the first time since the war began, the winter passed fairly pleasantly for the people of Oyster Bay.

Spring and Summer of 1777

Once spring arrived and the campaign season was about to begin, most of the military units that had spent their winter quarters in the area prepared to depart and join the main British army. Only a few Loyalist militia regiments remained to defend against rebel raiders from across the Devil's Belt. During the time the Jägers prepared to quit their winter quarters, Sally intensified her efforts to gain information about British and Hessian plans for the coming campaign season. However, she soon became frustrated; either Wintzingerode was not privy to plans regarding his regiment, or more likely the young officer was not willing to share military information with local civilians, regardless of how attractive they might be. Sally even visited the Loyalist militia headquarters at the Cove to strike up conversations with her old friends, Captain Daniel Youngs and Absalom Wooden, who would remain as part of the Loyalist defense network on Long Island. No one seemed to know anything about the coming campaign season, or else they were not sharing whatever information they had. Sally had hoped to discover something worthwhile to give to Robert the next time she saw him, if for no other reason than to let him know she was still serious about helping the American cause.

From time to time during the winter, Robert had returned to Oyster Bay to visit with the family and discuss business with Samuel. Whenever he did, Sally would secretly give him whatever information she had been able to gather, but now Robert seemed more concerned about the potential danger of being suspected of spying or even passing along British military intelligence. Sally was aware that such activities could be considered spying, and spies were likely to be summarily executed. Just recently, she had heard the story of Tunis Bogart (1720–?) and Andrew Hegeman (c. 1760–?) of Staten Island who had been ordered to haul supplies for the British. They had been in New York the previous September 26th where they witnessed the hanging of young Captain Nathan Hale for spying. Sally didn't really consider chatting with Loyalist and German officers as spying and didn't think anyone else would either, but it filled her with dread when she considered that if Robert were caught with military information she had given him, he would likely be accused of spying. The thought of her brother Robert being hanged was too horrible to contemplate. Nevertheless, she wanted to do something for the American cause, but she realized that to keep from implicating herself or Robert, she would have to be very careful indeed.

During the first week of May 1777, Sally visited Susannah and Daniel Youngs at the Cove, where she overheard Daniel talking with one of his officers about a British raid on a rebel depot in Connecticut. Sally listened intently, thinking she would learn of an impending action; however she soon learned that the raid had already occurred. On the evening of Friday, April 25, 1777, Governor William Tryon and about 2,000 men with a detachment of artillery landed from ships at Fairfield, Connecticut. The next day, they marched the twenty-three miles to Danbury to destroy a rebel supply depot there. The redcoats reached the town unopposed at three o'clock in the after-

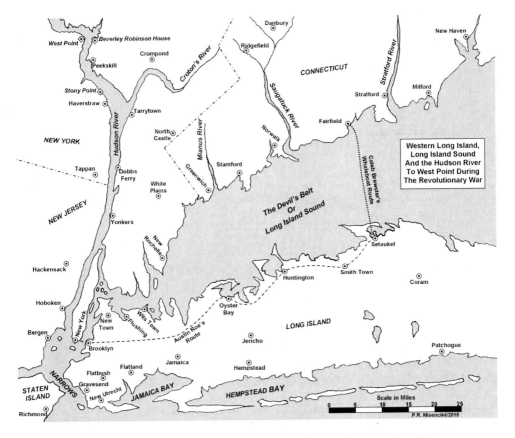

Western Long Island, Long Island Sound, and the Hudson River to West Point.

noon and set fire to most of the barns and dwellings in the town. By next morning, nineteen homes and twenty-two barns had been burned to the ground. Most of the buildings destroyed were not used as military storehouses, but in those that were, the American army had lost critical provisions, clothing and over 1,700 tents.

General Benedict Arnold happened to be on leave and visiting in the area when the British attacked Danbury. He immediately rallied all available American forces in the vicinity, and went after the British, who were returning to their ships. By Sunday April 27, 1777, Arnold had gathered about 150 Continental troops near Danbury and another 150 Continentals and about 500 militia troops in nearby Bethel, Connecticut. Then he convinced sixty-six-year-old Major General David Wooster, who was in command of the Connecticut militia, to take 200 men in pursuit of the withdrawing British, while Arnold hurriedly led the remaining 500 troops to Ridgefield to block Tryon's withdrawal route. Wooster and his force struck the British rear and captured about forty prisoners; however, Wooster was killed in the skirmish. The redcoats pressed on toward their ships, but when they reached Ridgefield, they ran into Arnold's force, which had just managed to get ahead of them. The larger British force formed along the American front and with their superior numbers were able to extend their line beyond the American flanks. As they advanced, the British flanks began to curve inward and threatened to envelop Arnold's smaller force. Aware of the danger of encirclement, Arnold ordered a fighting withdrawal, but was fired on by a squad of redcoats that had penetrated to his rear. Arnold was not hit by the fusillade, but his horse was shot out from under him, and he was momentarily pinned to the ground. A redcoated soldier seeing the vulnerable American commander, rushed forward with brandished bayonet. Arnold drew his pistol and shot the redcoat, and then he extricated himself and made his escape. In spite of Arnold's heroic attempt to cut off the British withdrawal, the redcoats succeeded in returning to their ships, but Arnold's quick response and relentless pursuit caused the British to lose about 155 men killed and wounded. The much smaller American force suffered twenty killed and about eighty wounded. In recognition of Arnold's leadership, Congress promoted him to major general and corrected an earlier injustice by predating his commission to give him seniority over five generals who had previously been promoted over his head. In addition, Congress awarded him a horse and tack to replace the one he lost in the engagement.

Sally listened as Daniel Youngs remarked that Governor Tryon was lucky to get away at all. The red-coated force barely avoided another bloody retreat like the one from Lexington and Concord only because a local Tory guided

Tryon and his main force around Arnold's doggedly redeploying army. As she listened, Sally wished that she had known of Tryon's raid in time to somehow get word to Robert, who might have been able to get the information to the Americans. She mused that if she had been able to provide a timely enough warning, the Americans might have mustered enough troops to capture Governor Tryon and all of his 2,000-man force.

10

Oppressive Occupiers

During the spring and early summer of 1777, not much news of the war reached Oyster Bay. There were some rumors that Howe was going to launch his army on a major campaign to capture Philadelphia, and in fact Howe, in an attempt to lure the Americans into a decisive battle, had made some feints in the vicinity of Middle Brook, New Jersey. A sharp action was fought at Short Hills, New Jersey, on Thursday, June 26, 1777, but Washington withdrew his army before a general engagement could develop. Finally, on Wednesday, July 23, 1777, Howe loaded 17,000 men onto a fleet of transports and sailed off toward the south. Some of Washington's officers believed that Howe's goal was Philadelphia by way of the Delaware or Chesapeake, while others believed Howe's objective was Charleston, South Carolina. To complicate matters, some officers were concerned that Howe's initial course to the southward was merely a feint to draw the American army in that direction. Once his ships sailed over the horizon, Howe could reverse course to the north and either sail up the Hudson toward Albany or possibly recapture Boston. Howe's fleet did indeed vanish over the horizon and did not appear for about a week, but when they were spotted off the Delaware Capes, Washington now was certain that Howe's objective was Philadelphia.

In the third week of August 1777, the war came closer to home for Sally with an American attack on the British garrison at Setauket, just 25 miles to the east. Since the British conquest of New York and Long Island a year prior, approximately 250 Loyalist troops of the 3rd battalion of DeLancey's Brigade under Lieutenant Colonel Richard Hewlett (1729–1789) were garrisoned in Setauket. They were every bit as oppressive as the other Loyalist units that were scattered around Long Island. For the most part they made no distinction between those citizens who favored the king or those that espoused the rebel cause. They treated everyone as a conquered and occupied people, and arrogantly took whatever they wanted, whether it was furniture, food, crops, equipment, or animals. They pillaged the homes and farms of the citizenry, by ripping the siding off homes, tearing down fences, and even taking the pews and pulpits from churches to use as firewood or in the construction of their makeshift camps. Any form of protest was often treated with unnecessary brutality. Since most of the Loyalists and Loyalist troops favored the Anglican Church of England, the Loyalists in the Setauket area worshipped at Christ Church or the "Caroline Church" as it was popularly called, because an altar cloth and communion service had been given to the congregation by Queen Wilhelmina Karoline of Brandenburg-Anspach, who was the wife of King George II. Even so, the Tories who worshipped at Christ Church, including its minister, were not spared from being plundered by the occupying troops. During a Sunday service in 1777, the Reverend James Lyons (c. 1701–1790) was preaching the sermon from the high pulpit in Christ Church when he saw through the windows that redcoat troops were busy stealing vegetables and digging up potatoes from his garden. Lyons, who was born in Ireland and was known to have a sharp wit and a volatile Irish temper, immediately stopped the sermon and shouted, "Here I am preaching the blessed Gospel to you, and there are your damned redcoats in my garden stealing my potatoes!"[1]

However, by comparison, the Setauket Presbyterian Church on the adjacent corner of the village green fared even worse. Considered a rebel church, because most of its congregation favored the Whig faction, the church was taken over by British troops. It was stripped of its pews and even the pulpit to provide firewood for the Loyalist soldiers. Fortified breastworks were thrown up around the church, and the building itself was used as a garrison and also as a stable for the unit's horses.

In August of 1777, General Israel Putnam authorized a raid on Setauket. General Samuel Holden Parsons (1737–1789) was given command of the expedition, which included Colonel Samuel Blachley Webb (1753–1807) and his "Additional Continental Regiment."[2] During the night of Thursday, August 21, 1777, Parsons and Webb with about 500 men crossed the Devil's Belt in whaleboats from Fairfield, Connecticut. Unfortunately spies in Connecticut informed Hewlett of the imminent American attack, and he was able to improve the fortifications around the Setauket Presbyterian Church. The troops stripped siding from the church and neighboring homes, hauled in split rail fences from all around the area, and even dug up the gravestones in the church cemetery to construct a six-foot-high breastwork around the church. Dirt was moved from around the property, and many graves in the Burying Ground were unearthed in the process. Hewlett's fortification circled the church at a distance of about 30 feet from the building. It was a formidable parapet that was protected by the addition of four swivel guns[3] mounted on the works.

Parsons, Webb, and their troops landed at Crane's Neck near present Old Field, New York, early in the morning of Friday, August 22, 1777. From there they marched the two-and-a-half miles or so to Setauket Green, where they found Hewlett and his Loyalist troops ready and waiting, strongly entrenched behind their earthworks. Parsons demanded the surrender of Hewlett and his troops, and when the Loyalist commander refused, the Americans opened fire, which began a three-hour skirmish. One American soldier was wounded in the firefight, and the only other significant casualties were the Caroline and the Presbyterian Churches, which were pierced by numerous balls in the exchange of musketry. The old Presbyterian Church was struck by lightning and burnt in 1811, but the Caroline Church still proudly displays the musket ball damage from that long ago engagement. The American light artillery failed to make any significant impression on the Loyalist earthworks, and the Americans were not inclined to attack a well dug-in enemy. After three hours of fruitless gunfire, Parsons decided that it would be prudent to withdraw before British ships on the Devil's Belt could cut off their retreat. The Americans successfully recrossed to Connecticut, taking with them about a dozen captured horses. Lieutenant Colonel Hewlett was praised for his defense of Setauket. While there were no future major expeditions against the town, it was frequently the target of smaller scale raids. To assist in the defense of Long Island British and Loyalist outposts, a system of signal beacons was devised to provide an early warning and to facilitate a rapid response against attacking rebel troops.

Washington moved his army to defend Philadelphia, but late in October, Sally learned that the British had captured the American capital on Friday, September 26, 1777, after defeating Washington in skirmishes near Wilmington, Delaware, and in a major battle on Thursday, September 11, 1777, at Chads Ford[4] on the Brandywine Creek in Pennsylvania. Just prior to the British capture of Philadelphia, the American Congress packed up and abandoned the city, and moved to York Town, Pennsylvania (present York, Pennsylvania). In essence, York Town, Pennsylvania, became the capital of the United States as long as the British occupied Philadelphia.

Washington struck back at the British at Germantown outside of Philadelphia on Saturday, October 4, 1777, but once again the Americans were forced to retreat after a bloody and hard-fought battle. In addition to the gloomy news from Philadelphia, Sally was disheartened to learn that a powerful army of British, Hessians and Indians under General John Burgoyne had captured the strategic outpost Fort Ticonderoga and was advancing south along Lake Champlain and the Hudson River toward Albany.

In early November 1777, reports reached Long Island that electrified the

Whigs and shocked and dismayed the Loyalists. General John Burgoyne surrendered his entire army to the Americans at a place called Saratoga on the Hudson River, just a few miles short of Albany. Sally could hardly believe the news, and at first she doubted it as an unfounded rumor until she read about Burgoyne's surrender in Rivington's *Royal Gazette*. That convinced her that the story must be true. Rivington was so blatantly Tory that even though the story of Saratoga was printed earlier in the *New-York Mercury* and *Universal Register* newspapers, Sally did not fully believe it was true until James Rivington finally verified the British defeat in his newspaper some weeks later.

The campaign season of 1777 ended with Howe's Army in winter quarters in Philadelphia, while Washington's army hacked out a winter encampment at Valley Forge, a scant eighteen miles from Philadelphia. Long Island was once again under the oppressive control of Loyalist regiments. While the civilians on Long Island had previously suffered under Oliver DeLancey's occupation, it was nothing compared to the rape and pillage they now experienced when Colonel Edmund Fanning's[5] King's American Regiment or "Associated Refugees" also established their winter quarters in the area. To both Whigs and Tories, Fanning's regiment was nothing more than a band of vicious thugs. They preyed on the citizenry without mercy, confiscating anything of value and destroying fences, buildings and even furniture for firewood. Anyone who protested was treated harshly, and severe punishment was inflicted on citizens at the slightest provocation. In one account, some of Fanning's men invaded a home and demanded everything of value. When the resident resisted, they tied him to his bedpost and held a lighted candle under his fingertips until he told them the hiding places of the family's valuables. Even places of worship were not safe from Fanning's men. They took over a local church and used it as a barracks, and a Quaker meetinghouse was confiscated as a storehouse. A strict nine-o'clock-p.m. curfew was imposed, and guards were posted to enforce it. One night after curfew, Oyster Bay resident John Weeks (1741–1807) was out after curfew, and when challenged he ran. He was quickly captured, given a summary hearing and sentenced to be whipped. Weeks was tied spread-eagle to the large locust tree in front of the Townsend's home and was mercilessly flogged. Even the sobbing screams from his mother and sister could not put a stop to the terrible punishment.

It seemed as though the news of the American victory at Saratoga had caused the American Loyalists to react with increased fury and brutality toward their American countrymen. Francis Edward Rawdon-Hastings, 1st Marquess of Hastings or Lord Rawdon (1754–1826), as he was more commonly called, believed that the war should naturally extend to all of the civilians, especially to women and girls. Earlier in the campaign he gave tacit approval for his men to rape what he called the "fair nymphs" of Staten Island, and publically stated that officers should "give free liberty to the soldiers to ravage it at will, that these infatuated wretches may feel what a calamity war is."[6] To many British officers, there was no real distinction between American Rebels and American Loyalists. They were all "a Levelling, underbred Artful race of people,"[7] and all should be treated as enemies.

On Sunday, December 14, 1777, Sally was surprised to see Major Joseph Green hurriedly mustering about 100 men from the 1st Battalion. Sally knew this was unusual, since midwinter deployments only occurred for matters of some significance. By their packs, provisions, and accouterments, it was evident that they were getting ready to march, so Sally asked the major where he and his men were off to. Green answered directly that the signal beacons reported that a force of rebels had come on a raid across the Devil's Belt and had landed near Setauket. He added that he was leading his force to join 200 Hempstead militia along with Colonel Hewlett's force at Huntington, and would march directly for Setauket. Supposedly Colonel Hamilton, with a troop of horse, was already in pursuit of the rebels. Green said that he hoped they would arrive in time to catch the raiders and properly deal with them but surmised that by the time he marched the 25 or so miles to Setauket, the raiders would have escaped back toward Connecticut on their whale-boats.

Major Green's reference to "signal beacons" piqued Sally's interest and she was determined to find out more about them. During the next several days, she purposely struck up conversations with members of Green's battalion and was able to piece together items of information regarding a British system that transmitted signals along the length of Long Island all the way to New York. The various transmitting stations were apparently closely guarded, but she was able to deduce from some of the soldiers of DeLancey's battalions that the British had a signal-transmitting installation on Norwich Hill just south of Oyster Bay. Sally also learned that the method for transmitting signals was to ignite a large pile of wood, which was about twenty feet high. The ensuing fire made a bright blaze that could easily be seen at night by adjacent signaling stations. If signals were required during the day, another large pile of brushwood and dried leaves would transmit signals by means of very thick smoke. Militia units guarded the signal stations to prevent sabotage or malicious firing by rebels.[8] When Robert next visited Oyster Bay, Sally told him what she knew of the signal beacons.[9] Robert appeared pleased at receiving that information, but once more he impressed on her the need to be very careful in her conversations with the British and Loyalists. It would be very dangerous for the Townsend family if any of them were accused of spying.

During the early months of 1778, the impact of Burgoyne's surrender continued to be felt in North America. The news that the new United States had negotiated an alliance with France swept like wildfire across America. A Franco-American treaty was signed on Friday, February 6, 1778, and ratified by the Continental Congress on Monday, May 4, 1778. That meant that the American army, which had somehow survived three years of war against the might of the British Empire, was about to be strengthened by a powerful ally. The French would provide desperately needed troops, equipment and more importantly, a first-rate navy. Once again New Yorkers verified the news of the American alliance with France by reading about it in James Rivington's *Royal Gazette*. If the blatant Tory propagandist Rivington printed news of something harmful or detrimental to the Loyalist cause, it had to be true. However, Rivington buried the news of the alliance among other Rivington propaganda stories that included warnings of the dire consequences if Britain should fail to win the war. Rivington's articles outlandishly predicted that Louis XVI of France would be crowned King of America; women would be forced to wear cosmetics or "paint for ladies' faces" and that American citizens would be required to convert to Catholicism.

The British commander-in-chief, General Howe, was aware of the impact Burgoyne's surrender would have on the outcome of the war. Even before the news of the French alliance was announced, Howe realized that it was just a matter of time before France entered the war against Britain. Now faced with the increasing, unattractive likelihood of an unwinnable war, Howe requested to be replaced as commander-in-chief. His resignation was accepted, and General Sir Henry Clinton took command of the British Army in May of 1778.

Realizing that he could not effectively defend both Philadelphia and New York against the power of the French Navy and a combined Franco-American army, Clinton decided to abandon Philadelphia and concentrate his army in New York. On Thursday, June 18, 1778, Clinton marched his troops out of Philadelphia and headed across New Jersey toward Sandy Hook, from where they would be ferried to New York.

The news of the British evacuation of Philadelphia once again cheered the Whigs and cast a pall over the Loyalists. While General Howe had been beloved by his troops, American Loyalists, on the other hand, were exasperated by his repeated failure to press Washington and bring the rag-tag American army to a decisive battle. They condemned his lethargic method of waging war, blamed Burgoyne's disaster at Saratoga on Howe's failure to support him, and cursed what they believed was the main reason for Howe's inexplicable inactivity: his dalliance with Elizabeth Lloyd Loring (1752–1831), the wife of his commissary of prisoners, Joshua Loring, Jr. (1744–1789). Satirists ridiculed Howe and his mistress in verse with bawdy doggerel.[10] An unknown Loyalist wrote:

> Awake, arouse, Sir Billy,
> There's forage in the plain,
> Ah, leave your little Filly,
> And open the campaign.
> Heed not a woman's prattle
> Which tickles in the ear,
> But give the word for battle,
> And grasp the warlike spear.[11]

Whigs also ridiculed Howe and his mistress. In his famous satire known as the "Battle of the Kegs,"[12] Francis Hopkinson, a signer of the Declaration, included a doggerel stanza alluding to Howe's preference for Elizabeth Loring over martial activity:

> Sir William he, snug as a flea,
> Lay all this time a-snoring
> Nor dreamed of harm as he lay warm,
> In bed with Mrs. Loring.[13]

James Rivington, in his *Royal Gazette*, also made several disparaging comments regarding Howe's lack of performance as commander-in-chief. Several officers loyal to Howe took exception to Rivington's articles, and one ranking officer in particular condemned the printer for his criticism of the army's beloved Howe. Rivington responded with this editorial:

> I shall seize the earliest opportunity to evince to this tool of our late general that my press shall never exist under the influence of any individual of that faction which has ever since the arrival of the Army from Halifax, in many instances betrayed the King and his Ministers, and aggrandized the military abilities of Mr. Washington who had none to boast of before S. W. H. [Sir William Howe] landed on Long Island.[14]

No sooner had Clinton's troops departed Philadelphia when Washington launched his army in pursuit, intending to bring Clinton's army to battle before they crossed New Jersey and reached the safety of New York. Clinton's force numbered about 10,000 men, while Washington had about 13,500 troops who had spent the previous several months in rigorous training under the direction of the Prussian Major General Friedrich Wilhelm Ludolph Gerhardt Augustus von Steuben (1730–1794).[15] Steuben started his training regimen with a company of 100 picked men, who in turn each trained another 100 until the entire army could march and fight with precision in the European style of linear tactics. Steuben's colorful personality quickly endeared him to the troops. He spoke German and French, but did not have a grasp of English. His instructions were given in French and translated into English by his bilingual aide, Captain Benjamin Walker (1753–1818). According to folklore, Steuben frequently grew frustrated when the Americans soldiers did not understand his curses in German or French, so he would call on Captain Walker to curse for him in English. By June of 1778, the Americans were anxious to try their newly learned martial skills against the British regulars. Washington was more than happy to oblige them, and as he raced his army across New Jersey, it was evident that his troops were not only tired of being on the defensive, they were spoiling for a fight with the redcoats.

The speed with which the American army moved across New Jersey in pursuit of Clinton's army is further testimony to the training they received from General von Steuben. The Americans caught Clinton's force on Saturday, June 27, 1778, near Monmouth Courthouse,[16] and Washington began to deploy his army for a general engagement. Washington offered command of the attacking force to his senior officer, General Charles Lee. Lee was not a good choice to lead the attack, because four days earlier in a council-of-war, he argued against sending the amateur American army against Clinton's battle-hardened veterans. Lee's opinion that the Americans were no match for the Britons was so forceful that some of the other generals sided with Lee. As a result the council-of-war issued a recommendation to avoid a general engagement with the British. However, Lee did not persuade all of the American generals. Generals Wayne, Lafayette, and Greene were appalled by Lee's timidity toward the British, and they refused to sign the recommendation. Alexander Hamilton (1755–1804) commented that the council-of-war's recommendation "would have done honor to the most honorable body of midwives and to them only."[17] Washington decided to disregard Charles Lee and the council-of-war's recommendation to avoid battle. He sided with the minority of his general officers, and planned to launch the Americans against Clinton's army at Monmouth Courthouse.

The redcoats were bivouacked around Monmouth Courthouse on their march to New York. Washington ordered Lee to attack as soon as the British began to resume their march, but Lee replied that he expected the enemy to attack him. Worse, Lee had not reconnoitered the British positions, even though he had been ordered to do so. He had no idea what Clinton's force was doing. Lee unbelievably told his officers that if he did not receive adequate intelligence concerning the enemy, he would not prescribe a plan of action, but rather would move cautiously and make his plans on the fly. His officers were stunned to realize that Lee was going to enter a major battle without any knowledge of the disposition or strength of the enemy force and without any sort of a battle plan at all.

When dawn broke on the morning of Sunday, June 28, 1778, Lee had no knowledge of the disposition of the British force and was not certain whether Clinton was still encamped or had taken his army on the move. In fact, Clinton's main army had left Monmouth at about four o'clock in the morning, but Clinton himself remained behind with a sizable rearguard to protect the departing troops and supply wagons. The day was brutally hot, and the temperature promised to exceed 100° Fahrenheit (38° Celsius) when Lee finally launched his attack. A properly coordinated attack might have been decisive in isolating Clinton's rearguard and subsequently smashing the slow-moving main column. However, Lee gave no specific orders, and instead he allowed his commanders to commit or deploy their troops as they saw fit. As the fighting expanded, Lee issued a confused series of orders that directed his troops to advance, withdraw, march and countermarch with no apparent objectives or purpose. The baffling maneuvers of Lee's army only alerted Clinton that the Americans had a sizable force, so he immediately recalled several regiments from the main column to reinforce his rearguard. With the added troops, Clinton advanced against Lee. Lee ordered Lafayette with three regiments to attack Clinton's flank, but Lafayette was forced to redeploy because of the strength of Clinton's newly augmented force. Some American commanders misconstrued Lafayette's redeployment as a retreat, and they also withdrew their regiments. When Lee saw several units apparently in retreat, he assumed the main British force was attacking in strength, so he began to withdraw his entire army. Within a short time, the withdrawal became a rout with Lee fleeing ahead of his troops in a wild disorderly rush to the rear.

Washington raced to the front where he found Lee and his army running in panic from the advancing redcoats. Washington rode up to Lee and confronted him, demanding to know the reason for the precipitous retreat. Lee stammered that contradictory intelligence had caused confusion, and he chose not to meet the enemy in that condition. General Lafayette, who was present, said that Washington called Lee a "damned poltroon,"[18] and General Charles Scott (1739–1813) said that Washington "swore that day till the leaves shook on the trees.[19] Charming! Delightful! Never have I enjoyed such a swearing before or since."[20] One witness stated that Washington angrily told Lee that regardless of Lee's opinion, the commander-in-chief expected his orders to be obeyed, and if Lee had not considered the operation viable, he should not have accepted command in the first place.

Washington summarily ordered Lee to the rear, and then personally reorganized the remnants of his army into a defensive line to halt Clinton's advancing redcoats. Clinton immediately hurled his force against Washington's patched-together defenses, and in spite of fierce fighting in the intolerable heat and a number of savage British frontal attacks, the American lines held. By five o'clock in the afternoon, the fighting began to abate more from heat exhaustion and thirst than for any other reason. When Washington noticed that the opposing British soldiers appeared to be stunned and disorganized from the heat and fatigue, he ordered a counterattack, but the weary American troops began to collapse on their arms as they tried to assemble for the assault. It was evident to the commanders that further attacks by either side were impossible, and Clinton took the opportunity to pull his troops back about a half-mile to the east. The exhausted Americans could only watch as the British staggered off. During the night, Clinton stealthily continued to withdraw his mauled army, and by daybreak they had painfully dragged themselves almost to the safety of Sandy Hook and out of reach of the Americans.

Tactically, the battle was a draw, but the Americans considered it a victory since the British had abandoned the field. In another sense it was a victory for the Americans, because for the first time they fought a veteran British force to a standstill. The training they received from General von Steuben had served them well. It was a turning point for the Americans, because now they believed in themselves and their ability to stand against Britain's finest troops, but of equal importance, they had faith and confidence in their commander-in-chief.

The American losses were 72 killed, 161 wounded, and 132 missing. Clinton's losses were 358 killed and wounded. Approximately 37 American troops and 62 British died from sunstroke. Washington's papers indicate that Americans buried at least 249 enemy dead. In addition, approximately 600 troops deserted from the British, including about 440 Germans who straggled into Philadelphia by the first week of July 1778.

II

Simcoe and
the Queen's Rangers

After the campaign season of 1778 ended, the people of Long Island once again steeled themselves for the prospect of British and Loyalist troops moving into the area for winter quarters. As had been the case in past winters, it was expected that the troops would demand quartering and would requisition food, forage and other materials, causing an already severe shortage to be critically strained. The Townsends were informed that they were required to provide accommodations for another British officer, and on Thursday, November 19, 1778, Lieutenant Colonel John Graves Simcoe (1752–1806) arrived at their residence.

Simcoe had a powerful appearing physique, a commanding presence and a rather supercilious and sullen demeanor that was initially intimidating to the Townsends. Although he was courteous and respectful toward the Townsends, Simcoe did not attempt to endear himself to the family or try to put them at ease as had the family's previous houseguest, Major Joseph Green. Simcoe told the family that he commanded the Queen's Rangers regiment[1] that would be deployed around Oyster Bay for the winter. The local population became very dismayed when they learned that the regiment was composed almost entirely of American Loyalists. Their terrible experiences at the hands of American Tory units like the brigands in DeLancey's and Fanning's regiments caused the citizenry to be distraught when yet another Loyalist regiment moved into the area. To the residents it meant they would once again be at the mercy of Loyalist troops who would pillage and loot unchecked during the long winter.

However, while Simcoe never really gained the affection of the population, the people grudgingly appreciated the fact that he tried to ensure that the citizenry were treated correctly if not politely. During drill and training formations, Simcoe was heard instructing his regiment that it was a soldier's responsibility to act as honorably with respect to the population as it was to act honorably and bravely during battle. The townspeople also heard Simcoe

Simcoe as a young man ca. 1770, attributed to William Pars (1742–1780) (Samuel E. Weir Collection, RiverBrink Art Museum, Queenston, Ontario).

tell his men that although general orders had previously been published by the high command prohibiting plunder or marauding by troops, he was satisfied that the general orders would not have been necessary if every other corps in the army behaved as correctly as the Queen's Rangers.

Almost immediately, Simcoe put his men to work improving fortifications on a conical hill across Main Road about 270 yards southwest of the
Townsend home.[2] DeLancey's 1st Battalion had designated the hill as a strongpoint for defense of Oyster Bay and had begun work in 1777; however, they
had not progressed much beyond clearing brush. Simcoe saw the merits of
DeLancey's initial choice for a strongpoint and decided that he would complete the fortification. Almost immediately, Simcoe's entire corps was
employed cutting fascines[3] and gabions[4] and digging earthworks on and
around the conical hill, which was only about 60 feet high. Even so, the small
hill commanded the town of Oyster Bay and the waterfront, and therefore
was of strategic value to the regiment. In his journal, Simcoe described the
fort: "There was a central hill, which totally commanded the village, and
seemed well adapted for a place of arms; the outer circuit of this hill, in the
most accessible places, was to be fortified by sunken fleches[5] joined by abatis,[6]
and would have contained the whole corps; the summit was covered by a
square redoubt, and was capable of holding seventy men; platforms were
erected, in each angle, for the field pieces, and the guard-house, in the centre,

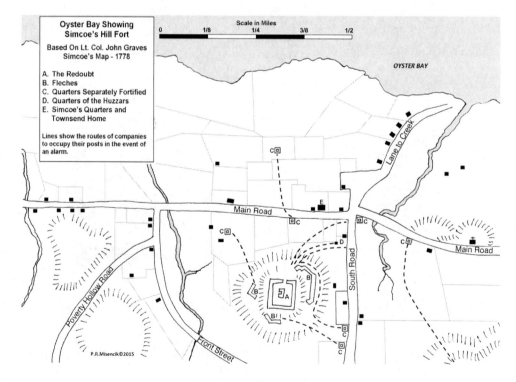

Oyster Bay and Simcoe's hill fort.

cased and filled with sand, was rendered musket-proof, and looped so as to command the platforms, and surface of the parapet; the ordinary guard, twenty men were sufficient for its defense."[7] The men worked almost continuously, and soon the shape of a redoubt surrounded by three fleches began to appear on the hill. At the same time, Simcoe had his men physically move a small house nearer to the beach where the Highland and Grenadier companies were quartered and from where they could quickly spot and respond to a waterborne attack.[8]

As the days passed the Townsends began to penetrate the somewhat frosty shell surrounding Simcoe. Around the dinner table, he told them of his life in England, his education, and about his father Captain John Simcoe, a Royal Navy captain of the HMS *Pembroke* who died at the age of 45 during the siege of Quebec in 1759. Young Simcoe was educated at Exeter, Eton, and Oxford, and in 1771 he entered the military as an ensign in the 35th Regiment of Foot. He saw action around Boston in 1775, and was promoted to captain of the 40th Regiment of Foot that year. After the Battle of Brandywine, he was promoted to major and named commander of the Queen's Rangers, a unit founded by the celebrated Robert Rogers, who was a hero of the French and Indian War. Simcoe related his involvement in several skirmishes and battles, including Monmouth Courthouse, after which he was promoted to lieutenant colonel. As they chatted, it also became apparent to the Townsends that the twenty-six-year-old lieutenant colonel was an ambitious officer. They heard Simcoe frequently repeat his belief that "nothing is more essential than to profess correct opinions unless it is to possess correct acquaintances."[9] He also mentioned that the reason he sought command of the Queen's Rangers was that command of an elite, light regiment was "generally esteemed the best mode of instruction for those who aim at higher stations."[10] Simcoe related how he had been wounded during the Battle of Brandywine on Thursday, September 11, 1777, but had completely recovered and took part in the campaigns of 1778, including the fierce battle at Monmouth Courthouse. He told the Townsends that he hoped that while in winter quarters, both he and his regiment would have the opportunity to recuperate from the previous year's vigorous campaign.

Even though he ambitiously sought recognition and advancement, Simcoe quickly demonstrated that he was an innovative and effective officer as well as a natural leader. He told the Townsends that when he first took command of the Queen's Rangers, they were exclusively light infantry. His first change was to form an associated mounted company called "The Queen's Rangers Hussars," but Simcoe simply referred to the unit as his "Huzzars." He also insisted that in addition to conventional military tactics, his troops be adept at more revolutionary methods of fighting. He believed they should learn hit-and-run tactics and be able to attack, advance and deploy stealthily or swiftly as the situation warranted. Simcoe related how, like many Loyalist regiments, the Queen's Rangers wore dark green uniforms. Their particular uniform consisted of a green coat with white facings, and leather breeches.[11] They originally wore cocked hats with white bands, but were transitioning to black light infantry style caps for rangers and black bearskin hats for the Hussars. Their hat device was a white metal horizontal crescent with the words "Queen's Rangers" engraved. He described how, at the end of the 1777 campaign, he successfully resisted an attempt by headquarters to have the rangers adopt red coats by arguing that rangers should be "accoutered for concealment" and that "green is without comparison the best color for light troops with dark accouterments; and if put on in the spring, by autumn it nearly fades with the leaves, preserving its characteristic of being scarcely discernable at a distance."[12]

The conversations with Simcoe were interesting and enlightening to Sally, who tried to memorize as many of the details as possible in order to relate them to her brother Robert. However, when Simcoe casually mentioned that one of his responsibilities was to seek out and apprehend any of the rebel spies and enemy intelligence gatherers who were known to be operating on Long Island, Sally experienced a feeling of dread. In short a British spy hunter was living under the same roof as she.

The Rangers numbered about 400 infantry and about 60 Hussars who were mostly American Loyalists with some "old country men"[13] from England, and a few deserters from Washington's army. Simcoe worked to keep his regiment up to strength as evidenced by his advertisement in Rivington's *Royal Gazette*:

ALL ASPIRING HEROES
Have now an opportunity of distinguishing themselves by joining
THE QUEEN'S RANGERS HUZZARS,
Commanded by
LIEUTENANT-COLONEL SIMCOE

Any spirited young man will receive every encouragement, be immediately mounted on an elegant horse, and furnished with clothing, accouterments, etc., to the amount of FORTY GUINEAS, by applying to Cornet Spencer, at his quarters, No. 1033 Water Street, or his rendezvous, Hewitt's Tavern, near the Coffee House, and the depot at Brandywine, on Golden Hill.
Whoever brings in a Recruit shall instantly receive TWO GUINEAS.
VIVANT REX ET REGINA ![14]

In spite of his stated desire for rest and recuperation, Simcoe put his men to work on the Oyster Bay hill fortifications. In between their work

Uniforms of the Queen's Rangers (© New-York Historical Society).

details, Simcoe also drilled his men incessantly. Whenever possible, Sally would stroll over to watch the work on the fort and also to observe the rangers during their training regimen. She remembered the satisfaction she felt when she told Robert about the British signal systems and now she wanted to be able to relate to him as many details as possible about the Queen's Rangers. One day, for example, instead of the usual drill formations, she witnessed a novel tactic in which the Hussars raced along at full gallop while the light infantrymen ran alongside grasping the horses' manes in order to be pulled along at a more rapid rate. Another time, she noticed that all ranks, including the cavalrymen, were being trained to infiltrate enemy positions by stealthily crawling forward on their stomachs. Simcoe took notice of Sally's frequent visits while his rangers were training, and how engrossed she seemed to be. He assumed that like many young ladies, she was impressed with the martial display, and he was somewhat flattered that she watched his training so seriously and intently. Sally, on the other hand, was somewhat surprised at the welcome she received from Simcoe and the evident pleasure he evinced when she came to observe his regiment's training. He seemed genuinely happy to see her and immediately walked over to direct the training from her side, during which time he explained to her the different training techniques as well as their military purposes.

He explained that the respective commanders were forbidden to teach their men to march in slow time, "and were to pay great attention to the instruction of their men in charging with their bayonets, in which case, the charge was never to be less than three hundred yards, gradually increasing in celerity from its first outset, taking great care that the grand division has its ranks perfectly close, and the pace adapted to the shortest men. The soldier is particularly, to be taught, to keep his head well up, and erect: it is graceful, on all occasions, but absolutely necessary if an enemy dare stand a charge; when the British soldier, who fixes with his eye the attention of his opponent, and, at the same instant, pushes with his bayonet without looking down on its point, is certain of conquest."[15] Simcoe also explained to her that the infantry and the hussars were to be trained together, so they could naturally operate in concert, particularly when attacking an enemy position. For crossing rivers or other bodies of water, the men were taught "how to make and navigate rafts, constructed on the simplest principles, and with the slightest materials."[16]

Sally often noticed that when she glanced at Simcoe, he appeared to be watching her. However, when she caught his eye he did not quickly look away like many of the other young men she was acquainted with, but Simcoe would continue to fix his eyes on hers and smile warmly. It also seemed that during family meals or other times when he and the Townsends were together, Simcoe made it a point to sit next to Sally and would direct most of his conversation toward her. This increased attention was not lost on Sally's sisters, who naturally teased her about Simcoe's obvious infatuation with her.

When he wasn't drilling his regiment, Simcoe frequently scouted the surrounding area to identify suitable locations for lookout posts, strong points, and fortifications to defend against possible rebel attacks from across the Devil's Belt. In the Oyster Bay area, rebel-held Connecticut was only separated from Long Island by about seven miles of water. Simcoe began to invite Sally to accompany him on survey tours, and he even procured a carriage in order that they could travel comfortably together. To avoid gossip or any sense of impropriety, Sally's sister Phebe normally accompanied them on those outings. Occasionally when Phebe wasn't able to go, Simcoe asked Audrey to join them, in order that Sally might still take the trip with him. During those outings, Simcoe pointed out possible landing places for rebel raiders, and he made notes to have patrols regularly check the area. In some instances, Simcoe posted permanent lookouts at what he considered a particularly suitable or vulnerable location, and then he arranged for a regular rotation of troops to man those positions. One ride took them twelve miles out on Lloyd's Neck to visit Fort Franklin,[17] which had been built in 1778 and was named after the Loyalist William Franklin,[18] Benjamin Franklin's estranged son and the last Royal Governor of New Jersey. Fort Franklin guarded the approach to Oyster Bay Harbor from the Devil's Belt and was strategic in the defense of that section of Long Island against American waterborne raiders from Connecticut. When they weren't visiting the surrounding military posts, Sally regularly accompanied Simcoe when he inspected the progress on his hill fort redoubt near her home.

When she returned from each of these visits, Sally retired to her room, where she wrote out and sketched everything she could remember about her visit. Then she carefully hid the documents deep down among the items in her dowry chest, or "hope chest," as some people called it. After her visit to Fort Franklin, she laboriously described the outpost including the number of troops in the small garrison and an estimation of the height and size of the earthworks. She also copied down any bits of information that Simcoe had imparted while he showed her around the Lloyd's Neck outpost.

Some sources infer that Sally may have taken the extraordinary risk of going through Simcoe's papers during his absences and copying whichever of his drawings and documents appeared important. That is a very unlikely scenario. Sally knew that Simcoe was extremely organized, and it would have been a grave risk indeed to rifle through Simcoe's papers and not return

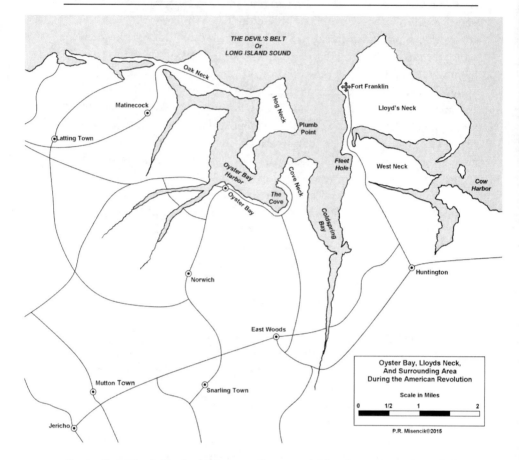

Oyster Bay, Lloyds Neck, and surrounding area during the American Revolution.

everything exactly as he had left them. She knew that Simcoe was security conscious and was no fool. He was in fact a spy hunter, and if he discovered that someone had examined his private documents, he would immediately suspect that it was someone in the Townsend family, perhaps even herself, and that would certainly place all of the Townsends in a very precarious situation.

The Beginning of
the Culper Ring

At the time, Robert was not involved with the Culper Ring for the simple reason that the espionage group had not yet been organized. Existing documentation indicates that the Culper Ring was formed some time during 1778, and the earliest reference of Robert Townsend communicating as Samuel Culper, Jr., is a message from him dated June 29, 1779. It's reasonable to assume that Robert joined the Culper Ring in late 1778 or early 1779. Prior to Townsend's recruitment into the Culper Ring, it's likely that any information gathered by Sally or Robert had not been forwarded to Washington's headquarters.

In New York, it turned out that Robert Townsend's residence at Underhill's boardinghouse on Queen Street was serendipitous. Certainly the establishment was convenient for Robert's business needs. However, his residency there put him in close proximity to members of the newly formed American spy network. In the spring or summer of 1778, George Washington directed his new chief of intelligence Major Benjamin Tallmadge (1754–1835) to establish an intelligence-gathering network to better anticipate British intentions and capabilities. Tallmadge was a close friend and Yale classmate of the ill-fated spy Nathan Hale, who was executed by the British in September of 1776. Tallmadge was aware of the operational shortcomings and mistakes that led to Nathan Hale's capture, and Tallmadge was determined that the espionage network he organized would not make the same mistakes.

Tallmadge was born and raised in Setauket on Long Island, where his father, the Reverend Benjamin Tallmadge, was the pastor of the Setauket Presbyterian church. When the Revolutionary War began, young Benjamin enlisted and was commissioned an officer in the 2nd Connecticut Light Dragoons, which later became the 2nd Continental Light Dragoons. In 1778 Tallmadge replaced General Charles Scott as Washington's chief of intelligence, and one of Tallmadge's first projects was the establishment of the Long Island

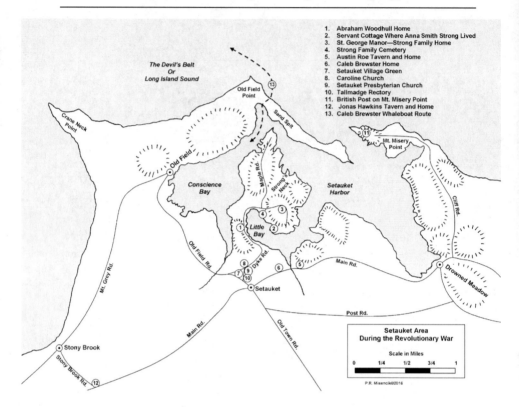

1. Abraham Woodhull Home
2. Servant Cottage Where Anna Smith Strong Lived
3. St. George Manor—Strong Family Home
4. Strong Family Cemetery
5. Austin Roe Tavern and Home
6. Caleb Brewster Home
7. Setauket Village Green
8. Caroline Church
9. Setauket Presbyterian Church
10. Tallmadge Rectory
11. British Post on Mt. Misery Point
12. Jonas Hawkins Tavern and Home
13. Caleb Brewster Whaleboat Route

Setauket area during the Revolutionary War.

spy network. Since the British headquarters and their main base of operations were located in New York and to some extent on Long Island, Tallmadge concentrated his espionage efforts there. As a native of Setauket, Tallmadge built a spy network that was centered in that town, and he recruited some of his most trusted friends and acquaintances from Setauket to serve in what became the Culper Ring.

Tallmadge's first recruit was the rough and tumble blacksmith and seafarer from Setauket, Caleb Brewster (1747–1827). He was described as being of great size with fine proportions, having a vigorous constitution, and possessing a devil-may-care attitude along with an unrivaled wit. Brewster had gone to sea at an early age to pursue the hearty life of a whaler out of Nantucket. Later he served as mate aboard a merchantman, where he learned the art of navigation, a skill that would serve him well while navigating the Devil's Belt in the dead of night. In December of 1775, after the bloodshed at Lexington and Concord, Brewster joined the Suffolk County, Long Island, Militia as a second lieutenant, and he was promoted to first lieutenant in the spring of 1776. Although he staunchly identified with the Whigs, Brewster wasn't affected by patriotism or political rhetoric as much as he loved action, and he was even happier if it involved hand-to-hand combat. He constantly looked for ways to engage the enemy. For example, during the autumn of 1776, Brewster led several whaleboats loaded with hand-picked commandos on raids across the Devil's Belt to Long Island. On one such raid, he and his men captured two enemy sloops near Setauket and killed or captured several British and Loyalist troops. Looking for more action, Brewster left the militia and joined the Continental Army, where the opportunities for combat were significantly greater. He served a short time with the 4th New York Regiment, and then in early 1777, he transferred to the 2nd Continental Artillery. Later, upon Tallmadge's recommendation, Washington arranged for Brewster to be detached from his artillery unit to work exclusively with Tallmadge on special operations. Brewster's main task was to maintain communications between Washington's headquarters in Connecticut and the growing network of patriot spies on Long Island. Brewster was in charge of a fleet of six lightly armed whaleboats that were used to ferry messages back and forth across the Devil's Belt in the dead of night, mostly between Fairfield, Connecticut, and Setauket on Long Island. However, Brewster occasionally used the whaleboats to carry out raids on enemy shore positions. The whaleboats were sharp at each end, made of cedar planking and were between thirty-two and thirty-five feet in length. They were equipped with up to twenty oars, carried two good sails, and were very fast and maneuverable. They were also light enough that they could be carried some distance, and easily hidden. The whaleboats were generally armed with at least one swivel gun or sometimes with a heavier cannon mounted in the bow.[1]

The Setauket farmer Abraham Woodhull (1750–1826) was selected to be the coordinator of the ring on Long Island and in New York City. Abraham Woodhull used the nom de guerre "Samuel Culper" and as a result, the name of the network became known as the "Culper Ring." Woodhull's role in the organization was to travel from Setauket to New York City, ostensibly for business, where he collected items of information pertaining to the British from an assortment of acquaintances and agents in the city. In New York, Woodhull stayed at the Underhills' boardinghouse, which was owned by his sister Mary and brother-in-law Amos. At the Underhills' Woodhull took the information he had gathered, supplemented by his own observations, and prepared the data for delivery to Washington's headquarters. To do this, Woodhull painstakingly wrote out the information using a two-part invisible ink formula called "sympathetic stain" or "white ink" that was invented by Sir James Jay, M.D. (1732–1815), brother of John Jay (1745–

1829). The ink would dry clear, and later wiping the paper with a chemical reagent wash would bring out the secret writing. The technique was to write out the secret message between the lines of a regular piece of correspondence, or to inscribe the message on blank pages or fly leaves of pamphlets, almanacs, or any other publication of small value. This procedure evolved into writing messages on a blank sheet or sheets of paper, which were inserted at a specific place in a larger packet of blank papers. At their destination, the pages were counted out, and the correct page or pages were removed and washed with a reagent to reveal the message. After he had gathered his information and transcribed his coded messages, Woodhull carried the documents back to Setauket where he rendezvoused with Caleb Brewster. Brewster then ferried the documents across the Devil's Belt to Fairfield, Connecticut, where express riders delivered them to Washington's headquarters.

The composition and manufacture of the Culper's sympathetic stain has been the subject of much discussion and research, and many different formulas have been tried over the years to match the description and approximate all of the qualities of the invisible ink the Culpers used. The most likely formula consisted of the following ingredients in similar proportions: combine 150 grains (0.343 oz.) of gallic acid, which is a trihydroxybenzoic acid, found in gallnuts, sumac, witch hazel, and some tea leaves, with 25 grains (0.06 oz.) of powdered acacia (gum Arabic). Then mix the compound with just enough water to achieve the color of pale straw. The reagent is made of 30 grains (0.069 oz.) of ferrous sulphate mixed with eight ounces of distilled water. To bring out the invisible ink, brush the reagent lightly over the coded message with a fine brush. Too much reagent or too vigorous a brushing will smear and blur the hidden text. The message should appear in a pale green or light blue-black color that will ultimately turn coal black. The ferrous sulphate in the reagent will oxidize over time and eventually turn the paper a brownish color.[2]

As it turned out, Abraham Woodhull, who coordinated the Culper Ring activities, was almost too timid to face the mental stress involved with espionage work. The British eventually came to suspect that Americans were engaged in espionage activities in New York and somewhere on Long Island. As a result, British troops and even Loyalist civilians were constantly on the lookout for any suspicious activity that might uncover a spy. Cavalry units patrolled the Long Island roads, and naval patrols on the Devil's Belt were increased in an effort to interdict clandestine activities between New York, Long Island and Connecticut. One of the more feared British naval patrol ships was the six-gun schooner *Halifax* under the command of Captain

William Quarme (?–1802). The *Halifax* was regularly stationed offshore in the vicinity of the channel leading into Oyster Bay between Lloyd's Neck and Plumb Point. From there the *Halifax* could quickly intercept rebel waterborne traffic from Connecticut to Long Island.[3] Not only was the *Halifax* armed with cannon, but it also carried a complement of tough rangers for hand-to-hand combat.

All of the British activities aimed at thwarting American espionage added to Abraham Woodhull's worries. He soon developed a pervasive fear of exposure and capture, and after only a few trips, he became terrified at the prospect of taking another trip to New York. The thought of being in the midst of the enemy where he would be the most vulnerable was almost unbearable. To be sure, he had a few negative experiences that added to his angst, and these heightened the inescapable dread he constantly felt. Before long Woodhull's fears bordered on pathological, and he was unable to shake them. On one trip he was robbed by highwaymen near Huntington, and as bad as that was, Woodhull was convinced that the thieves were Loyalists, and it was only a matter of time before they searched through his belongings and discovered something incriminating. He was also terrified of the guards at the Brooklyn ferry who cursorily checked all passengers in and out of the city. Woodhull was worried that they were becoming increasingly suspicious of his frequent comings and goings. This increased anxiety began to affect his work. Once when Woodhull was in his room at the Underhills' boardinghouse laboriously transcribing a message, his sister Mary Underhill walked into his room unannounced. Her unexpected entry startled Woodhull, and he spilled all of his precious supply of sympathetic stain. This required obtaining a fresh batch from Connecticut by way of Caleb Brewster. These events along with his constant worries had a cumulative effect on Woodhull, and after each occasion, he would take to his bed for several days where he lay sick with worry. Woodhull became so terrified of his trips to New York that he considered quitting the Culper spy network.

Fortunately about that time, Robert Townsend was brought in as the Culper agent in New York. Whatever the reason Robert chose to live at the Underhills', it's altogether likely that sometime after he took up residence at the boardinghouse, he was recruited into the Culper Ring. It's not known exactly how Robert became affiliated with the spy network, but it's very probable that Amos and Mary played some part in his recruitment. Robert Townsend knew Abraham and Mary because of their kinship with the late General Nathaniel Woodhull, a friend of the Townsend family, and the general for whom Robert had been appointed to serve as quartermaster prior to the Battle of Long Island. Abraham Woodhull, alias "Samuel Culper," was the head of the ring and Amos and Mary Underhill were involved to some degree in the patriot espionage network. At times, they all were at the Underhills' boardinghouse, and somehow Woodhull and the Underhills brought Townsend into the network. Perhaps recalling the stress and abuse his father and indeed his entire family had suffered at the hands of the occupying British, and also remembering his and Sally's wish to aid the American cause, Robert agreed to join the Culper Ring using the nom de guerre "Samuel Culper Jr."

With Robert Townsend joining the network and taking over operations in New York, Abraham Woodhull continued to work with the Culper Ring, but for the most part he remained in Setauket, where he coordinated the transfer of messages with Caleb Brewster. However, it was necessary to find a more expedient method of delivering the messages between New York and Setauket. Having Robert Townsend travel between New York and Setauket on a regular basis was for the most part unworkable. It not only took him away from his mercantile business for extended periods, but also limited his intelligence-gathering opportunities in the city. To facilitate the delivery of messages between New York and Setauket, Austin Roe (1748–1830) became the Culper Ring's courier. Roe owned a tavern in Setauket, and once every week or so, he made the fifty-five-mile ride to New York to purchase supplies for his tavern and to bring back personal items for his family and friends. Under the cover of being a businessman-tavern-keeper, it was thought that Roe's regular trips to New York for supplies would not be considered a suspicious activity.

Around Christmas of 1778, a storekeeper and tavern owner named Jonas Hawkins was recruited by Woodhull to serve as an additional courier for the Culpers. Hawkins owned a store and an ordinary[4] near Stony Brook, close to the present intersection of Stony Brook Road and Route 25A. However, Hawkins's addition to the group did not work out as satisfactorily as Woodhull had hoped. Apparently Hawkins was not as committed to the cause as Austin Roe or the rest of the Culper group. By April of 1779, Hawkins was increasingly unavailable for courier duties, and even then his performance was questionable. Townsend in particular was quickly losing patience with Hawkins. In August of 1779, Hawkins for some reason destroyed two coded messages he was carrying from New York for Townsend. As a reference, the messages between the Culpers and Tallmadge were numbered sequentially, and Hawkins destroyed Townsend's messages #5 and #6. Townsend referred to the destruction of the messages in a letter dated September 11, 1779. "No. 7 ... Long Island, Sept. 11th, 1779. Sir, Your No. 11 & 12 have come to hand, the contents I duly note. I am very sorry that N. 5 was destroyed, tho' I can't say that it contained any intelligence that wou'd have been of material consequence—The bearer [Hawkins] thought himself in danger. I believe it was merely imaginary. From timidity and the situation of affairs at the time, he did not choose to come to N. Yk; I [Townsend] therefore met him at a place quite out of danger on Long-Island. I then made an appointment for No. 6, at wch. Time he came, I wrote it, and took it over the Ferry that he [Hawkins] might run no hazard from the Inspector of Letters there. However he was so much intimidated that it shared the same fate as No. 5."[5] That was the final straw. Having lost confidence in Hawkins's reliability, the Culper Ring did not call on him for courier duties after September 1779.

Tallmadge's primary concern was that an agent would be captured through some mistake or because of bad luck. Once captured, a spy's chances of survival were virtually nonexistent, and he or she would likely be hanged from the nearest tree. Worse yet, there was the likelihood that the enemy would learn of the invisible ink and find a way to make the Culpers' messages visible. Tallmadge knew firsthand how mistakes or bad luck could pose a serious threat to the spy network. On Friday, July 2 1779, at about five o'clock in the morning, a force of two hundred dragoons under the command of Lieutenant Colonel Banastre Tarleton (1754–1833) made a surprise attack on Tallmadge's bivouac. Tallmadge was able to fight his way clear, but he lost a sum of money that was intended for the Culpers along with some secret correspondence. Unfortunately that correspondence mentioned one George Higday (1750–?), who was considered as a potential recruit for the Culper Ring. Predictably, Higday's home was raided, but Higday was able to escape the noose only because the British could not find anything incriminating. However, now that he was suspect, Higday was no longer of use to the Culpers.

What Tallmadge did not know is that the British had previously captured some papers that were written in plain ink, mentioning "C___r" and a "liquid," which the British concluded referred to some sort of invisible ink. Tarleton's July 2nd raid on Tallmadge's camp was a result of that earlier discovery, and was an attempt to catch Tallmadge himself. In anticipation of the possibility that the British might learn how to develop a reagent for the sympathetic stain, Tallmadge devised a code as an additional security measure. While the messages would continue to be written with the sympathetic stain, they would also be transcribed in what Tallmadge hoped was an unbreakable code. It's fortunate that Tallmadge did so, because there are some indications that the British did indeed learn the process of developing the messages written with sympathetic stain, but they were thwarted by Tallmadge's code.

Tallmadge's code was based on what he called a numerical dictionary. He chose 763 words, phrases, places, and names that he reckoned would be commonly used in coded messages, and assigned them numeric designators. The following are some of the coded designations from Tallmadge's numerical dictionary.

above	9	agent	23	arrest	31	attack	38
alarm	39	abatis	43	artillery	46	ammunition	47
bay	49	battle	59	beacon	61	boat	55
brigade	68	battery	70	battalion	71	British	72
camp	73	Congress	85	captain	86	clothier	109
date	120	day	121	dragoon	135	deceive	144
delay	145	enemy	178	evacuate	183	fort	192
fleet	193	grenadier	228	general	235	glacis	234
horse	255	horseman	261	hunger	267	it	284
ink	286	impress	290	inforce	295	infantry	309
introduce	328	kill	344	lady	355	infection	323
longitude	365	latitude	365	map	372	messenger	396
navy	423	occupy	451	peace	470	pilot	481
passenger	509	sail	586	sea	588	scheme	589
safe	593	soldier	613	surrender	619	troops	635
tory	639	traitor	642	victory	659	vigilant	660
wind	679	war	680	warlike	69	woman	701

Proper Names:

Washington	711	Clinton	712	Tryon	713
John Bolton	721	Culper Sr.	722	Culper Jr.	723
Austin Roe	724	C. Brewster	725	Rivington	726

Place Names:

New York	727	Long Island	728	Setauket	729
Kingsbridge	730	Staten Island	732	Boston	733
Connecticut	735	Head Quarters	763		

Note, the Clinton that was referenced in Tallmadge's numerical dictionary referred to British General Henry Clinton. Tryon was Royal Governor William Tryon, John Bolton was Benjamin Tallmadge's nom de guerre, and of course Culper Sr., and Culper Jr., referred to Abraham Woodhull and Robert Townsend, respectively

Tallmadge then wrote out a mono-alphabetic substitution code where one letter was simply substituted for another. His mono-alphabetic substitution code was as follows:

For the Letter	Write		For the Letter	Write
a	e		n	p
b	f		o	q
c	g		p	r
d	h		q	k
e	i		r	l
f	j		s	u
g	a		t	v
h	b		u	w
i	c		v	x
j	d		w	y
k	o		x	z
l	m		y	s
m	n		z	t

Numbers

1	e
2	f
3	g
4	i
5	k
6	m
7	n
8	o
9	q
10	u

He included detailed instructions on the use of the codes.

N.B. the use of this alphabet is when you wish to express some words not mentioned in the numerical Dictionary. For instance the word <u>heart</u>, would be expressed thus <u>bielv</u>. Look [at] the letters of the real word in the first column of the alphabet and then opposite to them. Let those letters in the second column represent them; in this case always observe to draw a line under the word, as <u>fwv</u>, stands for but.

Numbers are represented by their opposite letters which must have a double line under them as <u>fikm</u> is 2456. & <u>nqu</u> is 790…

Directions for the numerical Dictionary.

In the numerical Dictionary it is sufficient to express a part of a sentence only in figures, to make the rest perfectly unintelligible, as all words cannot be mentioned those of synonimous meaning must be sought for. & if not to be found, & the word not proper to be wrote, then the alphabet must be used—When numbers are used always observe to put a period after the number thus 284. stands for "it" & 295. "inforce." It will often happen that the same word may need to be changed thro the different moods, tenses, numbers. Thus if you would express the word introduce the number would be 328. if you would express the word introduced make a small flourish over the same 3̃2̃8̃. Horse is repress. by 255. Horses by 2̃5̃5̃. Kill by 344. Killed by 3̃4̃4̃. impress by 290. impressed by 2̃9̃0̃. In such cases the fore going & subsequent parts must determine the word.[6]

But, even in Setauket, Woodhull continued to worry, and he took pains to keep as low a profile as possible. Woodhull was afraid that it would be suspicious if he and Austin Roe were noticed exchanging documents, so a surreptitious delivery system was devised. Roe had arranged to pasture some of his cattle on Woodhull's farm, and when Roe returned from New York, he would check on his cattle in Woodhull's pasture. While there, Roe left the messages in a box that was secreted in the pasture, and from the box, he also collected any messages for Townsend in New York. Later that night, Woodhull retrieved the messages from the hidden box, but he was still too fearful to have Brewster come to his farm for the messages. As a solution, Anna Smith Strong (1740–1812), a wealthy Setauket matron who was also referred to as "Nancy"[7] in some accounts, was brought into the group.[8] Anna Strong was married to Judge Selah Strong (1737–1815), an outspoken Whig and Revolutionary War officer who fought on the American side at the battle of Long Island. He was arrested in December 1777, on suspicion of "Surreptitious correspondence with the enemy."[9] The Saturday, January 3, 1778, edition of Riv-

View from the vicinity of Abraham Woodhull's farm, looking across Little Bay toward the vicinity of Anna Smith Strong's cottage (author's photograph).

ington's *Gazette* reported that Selah Strong was confined in the Sugar House Prison in New York, but family tradition indicates that he was later imprisoned on the *Jersey*, the most notorious of the Wallabout Bay prison hulks.[10] To make matters worse, his wife, Anna, had been summarily evicted from St. George's Manor, their family home on Strong's Neck. The manor itself had been taken over by local British troops, and Anna was forced to live alone in a tiny servant's cabin at the edge of their property on the shore of Little Bay.[11] While life in the servant's cabin posed somewhat of a hardship for Anna, it proved beneficial to Washington's spy network. Anna's cabin was visible from Abraham Woodhull's home across Little Bay, and the two developed a signal system by which Anna informed Woodhull when Caleb Brewster had arrived in Conscience Bay from Connecticut, and also exactly in which of the several little coves Brewster and his whaleboat were hidden.

Anna regularly hung out her wash to dry on a line outside her cabin. When Brewster arrived, he got word to Anna where his boat and men were hidden. The following morning when Anna hung her wash to dry she placed a black petticoat on the line to signal that Brewster was in Conscience Bay. The number of white handkerchiefs following the black petticoat indicated in which of the little coves Brewster was concealed. Knowing exactly where Brewster was hidden gave Woodhull a measure of confidence, and he would sneak there in the middle of the night to exchange documents with Brewster. With the messages placed in a weighted bag that could be tossed overboard in case they were intercepted by British patrol ships, Brewster and his crew dragged their boat across the sand spit and made their way back across the Devil's Belt to Fairfield, Connecticut.

The Destruction
of the Apple Orchard

During the time he stayed with the Townsends, it was becoming increasingly evident to Sally that Simcoe was indeed infatuated with her. In addition to his almost constant attentiveness, he now bought her gifts whenever they traveled together, and he also brought her presents when he returned from trips he had taken alone to New York, Jericho or some parts of Long Island. When Simcoe entered the house after one of his trips he would always bring her luxuries like chocolate, fancy tea or silk material. Sally began to realize that the feelings were mutual, in that she genuinely liked the British officer and enjoyed his company. She found herself looking forward to the times they could be together, but she was uncertain of the level of her affection toward the ranger. Worse, she was beginning to feel conflicted about encouraging his courtship; after all he was a member of the occupying enemy army. Sally also felt conflicted about enjoying and encouraging Simcoe's affection as she was trying to gather military information for her brother.

Any sense of guilt at her duplicity was subdued by disbelief and anger when Simcoe callously ordered his men to cut down every tree in the Townsends' prized and valuable apple orchard. That event occurred toward the end of December 1778, and ironically it coincided with a planned neighborhood holiday party at the Townsend home to which Lt. Colonel Simcoe and several of his officers were invited as guests of honor. The day before the party, Lieutenant-General Sir William "Wooly" Erskine (1728–1795), commander of British forces on Long Island, visited Simcoe at the Townsends' home. Erskine declined an invitation to stay for the Townsends' party, but he got to the point of his visit when he informed Simcoe that it was his intention to relocate the Queen's Rangers to Jericho. Simcoe argued that a garrison at Oyster Bay was better situated to react to an enemy assault from Connecticut, and that Jericho was too great a distance to provide a timely and effective response in the event of an enemy landing. He added that maintaining a garrison at Oyster Bay would provide the British with "a more watchful eye over the landing places, and to acquire a knowledge of the principles of the inhabitants in these important situations; and that provisions from New York might be received by water."[1] Simcoe was effectively persuasive, and after an inspection tour of the almost completed Oyster Bay hill fortification, General Erskine told Simcoe that he was pleased with the efforts taken to ensure defense of eastern Long Island, and he approved Simcoe's request to maintain the regiment's present winter quarters at Oyster Bay. Not wanting to jeopardize Erskine's confidence in his ability to defend Oyster Bay against attack, Simcoe accelerated work on the hill redoubt.

The next morning, which was the day of the Townsends' holiday party, Sally's brother David rushed into the house and gasped that the soldiers were cutting down the apple orchard. Sally couldn't believe her ears and rushed out to see for herself. Sure enough Simcoe's soldiers were cutting the trees at their bases and hauling them off toward the hill fort. Sally's parents watched from an upstairs window as the rangers cut down their precious fruit trees, and the devastation to their prized orchard affected Samuel to the point where he dejectedly retired to his room and took to his bed. Sally frantically looked for Simcoe to appeal to him to save the rest of the orchard, but he was nowhere to be seen. She rushed to a soldier who appeared to be in charge of the tree cutting and boldly ordered him to stop immediately while there were some trees left standing. The soldier knew that Lt. Col. Simcoe had a high regard for the Townsend lass, so he told her as politely as he could that Simcoe himself had given the orders to take every tree from the orchard for the abatis around the hill fort, and that Simcoe was at that moment supervising the placement and construction of the abatis. With a sinking feeling that her efforts to stop the destruction of their family's orchard were in vain, Sally nevertheless hurried over to the hill fort, where she found Simcoe. He was directing the placement of the trees around the redoubt and fleches, bunching them together into a thick impenetrable barrier. She saw that after the trees were anchored on the hill with the branches facing outward, a score or more of soldiers were trimming the branches and sharpening their tips into wicked points.

Simcoe noticed Sally's arrival and cheerfully greeted her, apparently not noticing the anger that she barely contained. Without any preamble, Sally hotly demanded to know why he ordered the pillage of her family's property, especially after they had welcomed him into their home and had treated him as one of the family. Simcoe was taken aback by Sally's verbal attack and even more so by the venomous look she directed at him. He was surprised at her tirade, as she loudly denounced his lack of honor and his pretended chivalry toward civilians. Simcoe's men overheard the exchange and stopped to watch as their commander tried to placate the girl. However, when she stridently equated him and his rangers with the other thugs and brigands that preyed on the Long Island citizenry, his face turned a deep red in anger and embarrassment. Unwilling to endure any more abuse, he angrily shouted at her to be silent, after which he sternly told her that the requisition of the Townsends' trees was a military necessity, and it was well within his authority to order their appropriation. He added that all citizens under the protection of the British army were contributing to ensure the continued defense of their homes and families, and the Townsends were not contributing any more than other Long Island families. With that, he icily bid her good morning, turned on his heel and strode away to continue his work on the hill fort's defenses. Interestingly, some anecdotal accounts indicate that Simcoe at his own expense later replaced the trees with saplings ordered from England. However, no definitive documentation or other supporting evidence has been found to corroborate that supposition.

In spite of the day's events, the holiday party was held that evening as planned. Samuel Townsend, however, was so distraught over the wanton destruction of his orchard that he did not attend the party held in his home, nor did he even leave his room. His wife Sarah made polite excuses for her husband's absence, but everyone was aware of what had occurred. Even though they were affected by the dreadful events of the day, Sarah and her daughters bravely carried on with the festivities and managed an outward cheerfulness. Fortunately, all of the attendees were in a festive holiday mood and everyone seemed to enjoy the party. It was up to Sally and her sisters, Audrey and Phebe, to introduce their guests of honor, Lt. Colonel John Graves Simcoe and his officers to the other attendees. With a forced smile and feigned cheerfulness, Sally greeted everyone and somehow made the appropriate introductions, even though she found it difficult to be civil, much less welcoming, to the British and Loyalist officers, whom now more than ever, she regarded as arrogant enemy oppressors.

During Robert's next visit, he knew that his family was very distraught at the destruction of their apple orchard. It was just one more of a series of injustices they had suffered at the hands of the occupying British and Loyalist troops. Certainly Simcoe, as Major Green had before him, treated the family politely, and for the most part neither had been an unpleasant occupant in the Townsends' home. Even so, there was no escaping the fact that the officers had been peremptorily imposed on them in a manner meant to convey the fact that the Townsends, like the other families of Oyster Bay, were totally at the mercy of the British and Loyalist forces. There could be no doubt that the troops could take what they wanted and use the personal possessions and indeed the homes of the local citizenry in any manner they chose. While Robert seethed inwardly at the imperious attitude of the occupying army, he knew it was important to try to rationalize the destruction of the orchard in hopes of calming Sally. He knew his sister had a fiery temper and that she was barely keeping it under control. He told her that Simcoe likely took the trees as a matter of military expedience, since they were the handiest to the fort. Robert surmised that another possible reason for the destruction of the orchard could have been that the politically astute Simcoe, who was known to be fond of Sally, may have wanted to appear impartial concerning requisitions in case some influential Tories complained to headquarters about favoritism toward the Townsend family. This was especially important, since Samuel Townsend's loyalty to the crown was still somewhat questionable in the minds of many. Robert warned Sally that any friction between the Townsends and the Loyalists could be detrimental to the family.

Robert knew that it wasn't just the Townsends who felt the weight of the oppressor's boot; almost everyone, whether Whig or Loyalist, suffered abuse from the occupying force. Many of the officers treated the citizens with contempt and demeaned them in many different ways. If a person objected, he was called a "damned rebel" and was liable to be punished severely. Some officers required that any civilian whose route passed in front of an officer's quarters, dismount and doff his hat prior to passing. Farmers were told when to harvest their crops and when and which animals to slaughter. The farmers were required to sell whatever the British demanded, including crops, seed grain, livestock, produce, and even their tools, furniture, equipment, and clothing. The inhabitants were also powerless when British or Loyalist troops tore down fences, barns, and almost any other thing they desired for firewood or to construct shelters, or when the military turned their horses and livestock loose in farmers' meadows and gardens to graze and trample the crops.

Sally listened patiently as Robert explained that as difficult as it was, they would have to bear indignities like the destruction of their orchard in silence. Otherwise, the occupying troops would become vindictive toward the entire family. Sally agreed to keep her anger in check, and later she secretly gave him the bundle of papers containing information she had laboriously gathered over the past several weeks. Robert scanned the documents and saw that she had included descriptions of ranger training along with drawings of the outpost at Lloyd's Neck and a very precise sketch of the hill fort. Her description of the hill fort included features of the defenses as Simcoe had explained them to her.

Robert clearly didn't expect this. He looked at Sally very seriously and told her that what she was doing was very dangerous not only to herself, but to the entire family. If she insisted on continuing ferreting out information, she should be very careful, otherwise it could result in dire consequences for the Townsend family. Sally nodded in agreement, and wondered what Robert would do with those documents, and whether he had some way of passing them on to the American army. She hoped that if they did somehow reach the Americans, they would be of some value to the cause.

14

Etched Windows and
a Valentine

During her brother's visit, Sally noticed a change in Robert's demeanor. Not only had he abandoned his rather drab Quaker clothing and was now dressed more colorfully and fashionably, but he also had a careful and almost furtive wariness about him. She assumed the change in clothing was probably the way a businessman had to dress in cosmopolitan New York, and his caution was a result of the incriminating documents she had thrust upon him. Sally was also surprised to learn that her brother had invested in a New York coffeehouse as a silent partner with the notorious Tory printer James Rivington. The coffeehouse on Wall Street and Hanover Square was located across from James Rivington's print shop. It was a very fancy and somewhat exclusive establishment that catered to British officers, government personnel and higher caste Loyalists. The coffeehouse was very popular with British and German officers who found that they could easily get a favorable mention in Rivington's newspaper. Rivington made it a point to provide the officers who were mentioned in the paper with sufficient copies to send home to family, wives, and sweethearts. The printer also customarily allowed his patrons wide latitude with credit, and many of the British and German officers ran up excessive debts. It was customary that officers would clear their obligations on payday, but often they were embarrassed when they owed more than their pay would cover. Henry Wansey, an acquaintance of Rivington, wrote in his journal: "During the time the British kept possession of New York, he [Rivington] printed a newspaper for them, and opened a kind of coffee-house for the officers; his house was a great place of resort; he made a great deal of money during that period, though many of the officers quitted it considerably in arrears to him."[1] The entrepreneurial Rivington developed a unique way to capitalize on those debts. He would often forgive a portion or sometimes all of an officer's debt if the officer provided the publisher with a particularly newsworthy item that Rivington could publish in his newspaper. Of course Robert Townsend was also very interested in those tidbits of information.

The coffeehouse was an immediate success with British and Hessian officers, and Rivington worked to develop it into a lucrative source of information for the *Royal Gazette*. Townsend of course used it as a source of information that might benefit the American cause. The coffeehouse was usually crowded with redcoat officers who sought to converse with Rivington or Townsend in hopes of a flattering mention in the *Royal Gazette*. The printer did not disappoint them. He and Townsend spent a good deal of time circulating among the patrons' tables, chatting with them about their activities. The casual conversations in the coffeehouse often included details of troop deployments, planned maneuvers and other military matters that Townsend forwarded to Washington via the Culper Ring network.

Sally was most surprised to learn that Robert was also writing articles for Rivington's newspaper, the *Royal Gazette*. At first she couldn't believe it, because most of the Whigs and even many Loyalists referred to the paper as "the Lying Gazette." She couldn't understand why her brother, whom she admired so much, decided to associate with the likes of the despicable Rivington, much less cater to the British and Loyalists who read his Tory newspaper. What Sally did not know at the time was that the stridently Loyalist Rivington was not what he appeared to be. His Culper Ring code designation was "726," and he was another of Washington's spies in New York. Rivington was secretly working with Sally's brother to forward military intelligence to General Washington. Rivington played his role as a Tory to perfection, which caused him to be reviled by American patriots and earned him the enmity of the Americans, and that hostility followed him for the rest of his life. However, Rivington was never once suspected of working against the British, even though he was responsible for obtaining and passing on to Washington some of the British military's most sensitive secrets.

Sally was even more perplexed when Robert told her that if she needed to get information or a message to him quickly, she should ask Daniel Youngs if he could arrange to have her message packet delivered to Robert the next time he sent a courier to British headquarters in New York. Sally was shocked at that suggestion. Certainly Daniel and Susannah Youngs had always been friends of the Townsends, but they were Loyalists, and worse, Daniel was a captain in the Loyalist militia. It did not make any sense to trust that Daniel would not examine any message that Sally sent to her brother. Robert instructed her how she should hide her message in a packet of orders requesting merchandise from the Townsend warehouse at Peck's Slip in New York.

Robert explained that the Townsend business in New York catered to the British military and many influential Loyalists, and he was considered by most to be a neutral Quaker merchant who might even be somewhat loyal to the crown. He said that it was good for the Townsend business to maintain that outward neutrality, regardless of where his loyalties really lay. Additionally, because of his partnership in Rivington's coffeehouse and his writing for the blatantly Tory *Royal Gazette*, Robert's New York acquaintances would never consider him to be a rebel Whig.

Less than two months later, in early February 1779, the Townsends once again gave an evening entertainment, and like the previous party, the guest list included several British officers, including John Simcoe. During the parties, young officers, as they have throughout history, sought out attractive females and engaged them in flirtatious conversations. Sally, who was one of the most beautiful girls in Oyster Bay, was always beset with suitors. It was no different at that night's party. However, Sally was surprised when a number of officers requested that she intercede with her brother Robert to interview and feature them in one of his *Royal Gazette* articles. It amused Sally that her brother was not only known, but was as popular or perhaps even more so than she among the British officer corps. That was certainly preferable to being considered one of the Whiggish Townsends. Among the guests was a young officer, Captain John McGill (1752–1834),[2] who apparently took the opportunity to amuse and perhaps impress several of the young ladies by using a diamond ring to scratch tributes to them in the Townsends' parlor windows. The glass panes survive to this day in the Raynham Hall Museum at Oyster Bay. In the first pane John McGill takes credit for his tribute to Sally Townsend by including his name. McGill originally etched, "The Adorable Miss Sally Townsend J. McGill;" however, for some unknown reason, he then drew lines through the words "Sally Townsend" and then added the word "Sarah" above the crossed out "Sally." The second pane contains an obvious reference to Audrey Townsend and reads, "Miss A. T. The most accompl Young lady in Oyster Bay." In the third pane, McGill wrote "Sally Coles" without any other reference to that particular young lady.

The specific circumstances of what caused the words "Sally Townsend" to be struck through and replaced with "Sarah" are not known. One family account states that Sally called the young officer to account for his presumption of familiarity and ordered him to make the changes. Another variation of the same account states that the young officer made the changes after realizing his rashness, because "he feared the scorn of Sally's hazel eyes."[3] Yet a third account states that Lt. Colonel Simcoe himself ordered McGill to make the alterations after rebuking the young captain for vandalizing the Townsend family's windows in return for their hospitality. However, this same source also infers that Simcoe's primary motive was to warn the young captain away from the object of Simcoe's affection, and less in defense of the Townsend's windows.

The account of Simcoe's intervention is especially plausible in light of the ardently romantic message Simcoe gave to Sally on Valentine's Day in 1779. On the Valentine he included a sketch[4] of two hearts, one bearing the initials "J. G. S." and the other "S. T." Simcoe wrote a passionate poem in which he asked Sally, "O choose me for your Valentine!"

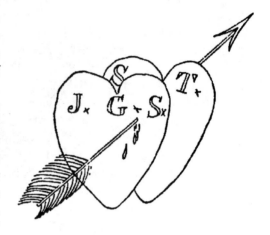

Simcoe's 1779 Valentine Sketch.

From Lieutenant-Colonel J. G. Simcoe to Miss Sarah Townsend;
Written and delivered at Oyster Bay, L. I. St. Valentine's Day 1779:-

> Fairest Maid where all are fair,
> Beauty's pride and Nature's care;
> To you my heart I must resign;
> O choose me for your Valentine!
> Love, Mighty God! thou know'st full well,
> Where all they Mother's graces dwell,
> Where they inhabit and combine
> To fix thy power with spells divine;
> Though know'st what powerful magick lies
> Within the round of Sarah's eyes,
> Or darted thence like lightning fires,
> And Heaven's own joys around inspires;
> Thou know'st my heart will always prove
> The shrine of pure unchanging love!
> Say; awful God! since to thy throne
> Two ways that lead are only known—
> Here gay Variety presides,
> And many a youthful circle guides
> Through paths where lilies, roses sweet,
> Bloom and decay beneath their feet;
> Here constancy with sober mien
> Regardless of the flowery Scene

With Myrtle crowned that never fades,
In silence seeks the Cypress Shades,
Or fixed near Contemplation's cell,
Chief with the Muses loves to dwell,
Leads those who inward feel and burn
And often clasp the abandon'd urn,—
Say, awful God! did'st thou not prove
My heart was formed for Constant love?
Thou saw'st me once on every plain
To Delia pour the heartless strain—
Thou wept'sd her death and bad'st me
change
My happier days no more to range
O'er hill, o'er dale, in sweet Employ,
Of singing Delia, Nature's joy;
Thou bad'st me change the pastoral scene
Forget my Crook; with haughty mien
To raise the iron Spear of War,
Victim of Grief and deep Despair:
Say, must I all my joys forego
And still maintain this outward show?
Say, shall this breast that's pained to feel
Be ever clad in horrid steel?
Nor swell with other joys than those
Of conquest o'er unworthy foes?
Shall no fair maid with equal fire
Awake the flames of soft desire;
My bosom born, for transport, burn
And raise my thoughts from Delia's urn?
"Fond Youth," the God of Love replies,
"Your answer take from Sarah's eyes."[5]

Major John André
Visits Oyster Bay

That spring, the Townsends entertained yet another prominent British houseguest. They were surprised one day when a handsome young British officer knocked at their door, introduced himself as Major John André,[1] and asked to be announced to his friend Lieutenant Colonel John Graves Simcoe.

André, who was General Clinton's aide in New York, had become ill with what he described as a "treacherous complaint"[2] brought on by his Sisyphean labors[3] at headquarters. Simcoe was delighted to see his friend André, with whom he had previously formed a close association in Philadelphia. André explained that he had been ordered by Clinton to go into the country to recuperate from what was likely stress from overwork, and he decided to come to Oyster Bay for the fresh air and to visit his friend Simcoe. Simcoe prevailed upon the Townsends to provide temporary lodging for André, and the two most likely shared Robert's room in the lower level of the house.

During the weeks[4] that André stayed at the Townsend home, he and Simcoe engaged in many "sober and various occupations and conversations."[5] André enjoyed the company and interaction with his hosts the Townsends, but he was especially attracted to the Townsend daughters, particularly Audrey and Sally, who were closer to his age. Even though André's flirtations extended to Sally, the good-natured competition to impress the young women never resulted in any animosity between him and Simcoe. The dashing Simcoe could almost rival the elegant André as a poet, but André was able to captivate Sally with his skill as an artist and silhouette cutter. During his visit, André cut a silhouette of Sally[6] and also sketched her in various poses, including one drawing he made of her when she was going riding. When it was completed, he titled it, "A beautiful girl in a riding habit,"[7] and he surreptitiously placed it under her dinner plate where she would find it when the family gathered for their main meal.

During André's visit, the Townsends held a tea party in honor of the two

British officers, and the day before the party, Sally made a large plate of a popular 18th-century pastry known as "olykoeks." Olykoeks, which were also known as oly koeks, oliebollen, and oliebol, were a traditional treat that originated with the early Dutch settlers of New Amsterdam. Olykoeks were sweet dough balls fried in pork fat. In Flanders and parts of Belgium they were called "Smoutenbollen," literally "balls of lard." Often they contained currents, raisins, apples or other tidbits, and were the predecessors of today's donuts. They were a favorite indulgence during winter parties and holiday events among Long Islanders during the colonial period.

Sally mixed the dough concoction and then hand-formed the dough into little balls, which she deep-fried in a large iron pot of hot lard. It took only a few minutes to fry them to a nice golden brown color. After she fished them out, she

Major John André, from an engraving by J.K. Sherwin (Emmet Collection, Miriam and Ira D. Wallach Division of Art, Prints and Photographs, The New York Public Library, Astor, Lenox and Tilden Foundations).

rolled them in sugar, and piled them on a large tray to cool. Since the olykoeks were going to be served the very next day, Sally covered the pastry tray with a cloth and placed it on the table to cool.

The following afternoon during the party, when Sally went to serve the olykoeks, she couldn't find them on the table where she had left them. She assumed that her mother or one of her sisters had moved the tray, but though she looked everywhere she could think of, she couldn't find it. Worse yet, her mother and sisters said that they had not moved the olykoeks. The tray had mysteriously vanished, and now Sally was in a quandary about what she would serve their guests with tea. During her frantic search for the missing treats, she noticed that John André watched as she searched high and low for the missing pastries, and he seemed to be amused by her "state of frantic excitement and perplexity."[8] The more she searched and the more frantic she became, the more he seemed to enjoy her discomfort, until finally André offered to help Sally find the missing olykoeks. André went through the motions of looking here and there in feigned earnestness, and just in time for them to be served with tea, André "found" them in the corner cupboard in the parlor where he had hidden them in the first place. The joke that André had played on Sally was related much to the amusement of all the guests, Sally included.

André left Oyster Bay and returned to New York, but he apparently was not fully recovered from the illness that sent him to Oyster Bay in the first place. His pervasive fatigue and bouts of fever frequently kept him bedridden. General Clinton again ordered him to rest and recuperate, but although André would have preferred to return to Oyster Bay, Clinton found him a retreat in New York that was nearer to headquarters.

16

Simcoe—Dashing But Ruthless

During that winter and spring of 1778–1779, while John Simcoe lived with the Townsends, his affection for Sally continued to grow. He began to direct a fervid courtship toward Sally, and in return he looked for any signs of reciprocal feelings or affection on her part. The truth was that Sally was very fond of Simcoe, but she could not subdue the feeling that he was a member of an enemy occupying force, who was living uninvited in her home. Yet, she frequently found that when Simcoe traveled to New York or one of the Long Island posts, she looked forward to his return and was happy when he walked through the door of her home. Sally also realized that she rather enjoyed the little poems he wrote in praise of her and even looked forward to the gifts he brought her when he returned from his trips. She began to worry that in spite of her resolve, she might be falling in love with Simcoe.

Even so, there were several incidents that reinforced the feeling that Simcoe was one of the enemy who were imposing martial law on her community. He had taken up residence in the Townsend home uninvited and then repaid her family's hospitality by destroying her father's apple orchard. In addition, some months previously, the Townsends found themselves with a dwindling ink supply, which might have been a minor inconvenience to most people, but was an important factor in Samuel Townsend's business. Simcoe was aware that the Townsends were very short of ink, and though he procured a supply for his own use, he did not share any of his ink with the Townsends. Sally couldn't understand whether he was merely thoughtless or wanted to demonstrate his authority. Simcoe had often mentioned in passing that as a British officer, he wasn't there to make friends, but rather to serve the king. In spite of those somewhat questionable events on Simcoe's part, Sally realized that she was attracted to the dashing ranger officer. Even her family had somehow put the destruction of the orchard and Simcoe's stinginess with his ink supply behind them. Once again, the family seemed to be on very congenial terms with the lieutenant colonel, and they treated him almost as one of the family. However, that spring, any romantic inclinations Sally might have had toward Simcoe were shaken when she saw a darker side of him that demonstrated a personality that could for the most part be gallant and charming but suddenly transition into something utterly callous and ruthless.

Sally had heard that earlier in 1778, Simcoe commandeered the Huntington home of the Reverend Ebenezer Prime (1700–1779) as quarters for his troops. The Reverend Prime had come to Huntington in 1719 after graduating from Yale College. He was ordained in 1723, and was a very avant-garde type of minister, unusual for his time. Among his nonstandard religious practices, Prime wished to baptize every child within three days of its birth, and he even allowed non–Christians to receive the sacraments. In 1759 Prime started one of the first lending libraries on Long Island. He amassed a large literary collection and allowed the townspeople to borrow books for a specified period of time. If the books were not returned on time, the borrowers were fined for their tardiness. The library was of great importance to him and indeed to the town of Huntington. When Simcoe and his rangers commandeered Prime's home, the 78-year-old minister objected, so Simcoe decided to teach Prime proper deference to the British by having his troops break up the furniture in Prime's home and also destroy his library. They even went so far as to ransack and desecrate his church. Heartbroken, Prime never returned to his house, and he died the following year in 1779.

Sally had heard about Simcoe's cruel treatment of the Reverend Prime, but in April 1779, she saw Simcoe's cruel streak first-hand. On the night of Sunday, April 18, 1779, shortly after the new moon, and on one of the darkest nights of the month, Simcoe sent a party of nine Queen's Rangers across the Devil's Belt to Fairfield, Connecticut, where they hoped to capture two American generals,[1] Samuel Holden Parsons (1737–1789) and Gold Selleck Silliman (1732–1790).[2] For some reason, the party decided not to risk an attack on Parsons, but went after Silliman. After beaching their longboats, the rangers stealthily crept up on Silliman's home. They knew the layout, because one of Simcoe's rangers had once worked as a carpenter for Silliman, and he described in detail where Silliman would likely be found and how best to approach the house unseen. At midnight, the party forced their way into the house, seized General Silliman and his son and brought them back to Oyster Bay. The next morning, the captives were paraded before Simcoe, and Sally who was present, was surprised at Simcoe's manner when he met the returning rangers and their captives. Simcoe asked the ensign in charge of the raid if they had suffered any casualties, and after being assured that all his men had returned unharmed, Simcoe strode up to the captive general and taunted him by proclaiming that all of the Sillimans were not worth one of Simcoe's rangers. Sally was disappointed at Simcoe's lack of chivalry, kindness or even basic civility toward his prisoners. She was further dismayed when Simcoe ordered that Silliman and his son be taken to New York and delivered to the Provost Marshal William Cunningham, where they would likely be confined in the worst prison camps or possibly the prison hulks in Wallabout Bay.[3]

Another event that distressed Sally occurred the following week, after a paroled Long Island sailor named John Wolsey (1737–1819) returned from British captivity. Wolsey, a Long Islander, had been operating as a crewmember on an American privateer when the British captured him. A privateer was essentially a ship whose captain was issued a letter of marque by a government, which authorized attacks on enemy shipping during wartime. Privateering was the most expeditious way for a government to mobilize armed ships and sailors to supplement their national navy. In spite of the authorization to act for their respective governments, the distinction between a privateer and a pirate was vague, and the crew of a captured privateer stood every chance of being treated as pirates. Wolsey found himself in that precarious predicament and was no doubt anxious to bargain for more lenient treatment. To ingratiate himself with his captors, Wolsey informed the British authorities of a rumor that Abraham Woodhull of Setauket was involved in illegal communication and interaction with the rebels in Connecticut. It's not known where or how Wolsey got that information, but it was spot on. Perhaps he heard someone talking while he was ashore in Setauket, or he may have spotted Brewster's whaleboats entering or leaving the area. Although Wolsey's accusation was hearsay and circumstantial at best, Simcoe acted on the information as if it were true, which ironically it was. Fortunately, Simcoe was not aware of the depth of Woodhull's involvement in the patriot espionage network, or even of the existence of the Culper Ring at that time.

On Saturday, April 24, 1779, Simcoe mustered his mounted Hussars and prepared for the twenty-five-mile ride to Setauket to arrest Abraham Woodhull and bring him back to Oyster Bay for interrogation. Sally heard the activity and rushed outside to see what was happening, and she was shocked to hear that Simcoe and the patrol were going after Abraham Woodhull. Sally was acquainted with Woodhull and was concerned for him. Woodhull's sister Mary had wed Amos Underhill, and the two operated the boardinghouse where Sally's brother Robert lived in New York. Abraham was the son of Judge Richard Woodhull,[4] the first cousin of General Nathaniel Woodhull,[5] who was murdered by Oliver DeLancey Junior in 1776 after Woodhull surrendered during the Battle of Long Island. She recalled that Robert had been appointed commissary for General Woodhull and could possibly have suffered the same fate if he had been captured with him. What Sally did not know was that her brother Robert was involved with Abraham Woodhull, and she certainly was not aware that the two were the principal members of the Culper Ring spy network. Woodhull was Samuel Culper Senior and her brother Robert was Samuel Culper, Jr. If she had known that the capture of Abraham might have resulted in her brother Robert being implicated as a spy, her worries certainly would have been far greater than they were.

Later Sally learned that as soon as Simcoe and his Hussars reached Woodhull's home on Dyke Road on Little Bay in Setauket, they burst through the door and spread throughout the house looking for their quarry. Fortunately for Abraham, he was in New York City at the time, but his sixty-seven-year-old father, Judge Richard Woodhull, was in the house, and he angrily denounced Simcoe and his men for invading his family's home. Simcoe's men roughly pushed the elderly man aside and ransacked the house from top to bottom as they searched for Abraham as well as any other incriminating evidence. Judge Woodhull attempted to intervene several times, and he sustained significant and painful injuries from the troopers, who roughly manhandled and knocked him about. In spite of their thorough search, Simcoe and his patrol were unable to find anything that implicated Abraham Woodhull or his family. The patrol finally departed without an apology or any attempt to pay recompense or restore the damage they did to the Woodhull home. They simply mounted up and rode back to Oyster Bay.

Their ruthless vandalism was meant as a clear warning to Woodhull that he and his family would suffer if there were any suspicion of treasonous activities on his part. Sally learned that Simcoe and his troop of Hussars had left the Woodhull home in a shambles, and worse, they made no attempt to treat the injured Judge Woodhull, but simply left the old man to fend for himself. What bothered her most about the affair was that Simcoe did not exhibit the slightest remorse for the abuse and injuries to Abraham Woodhull's father or for the vandalism and damage they caused the Woodhull family home. Simcoe's only apparent regret was that he had to return to Oyster Bay empty-handed.

Abraham Woodhull returned to find his father injured and his home in a shambles, and it took him several months to learn the full circumstances that led to Simcoe's raid. Woodhull was concerned that Simcoe's interest in him could jeopardize the activities of the Culper Ring network, so on Saturday, June 5, 1779, he wrote to his contact, "John Bolton," which was the nom de guerre of Major Benjamin Tallmadge, Washington's spymaster.

"On the 24 of April John Wolsey returned from Connecticut, being

Paroled ... and lodged information against me before Coll. Simcoe of the Queen's Rangers, who thinking of finding me at Setauket came down, but happily I set out for N. York the day before his arrival, and to make some compensation for his voige he fell upon my father and plundered him in a most shocking manner."[6]

Ironically, Woodhull was saved from further harassment by British or Loyalist troops through the intercession of Woodhull's friend Colonel Benjamin Floyd, who was a Loyalist militia officer stationed at Setauket. Woodhull was able to convince Floyd of his loyalty to the crown, and Floyd personally guaranteed Woodhull's British allegiance to Simcoe's superior officers. By this time Simcoe and his regiment had departed Oyster Bay for the summer campaign, but Floyd's intervention helped prevent follow-up raids on Woodhull by Loyalist troops. Floyd was a good choice to vouch for Woodhull. He was the younger brother of Colonel Richard Floyd, a militant Loyalist, whose property was regularly raided by rebel whaleboat men from Connecticut. For some reason, Captain Caleb Brewster, the seafaring member of the Culper Ring, had an intense dislike for the Floyds and for Richard Floyd in particular. Interestingly, the two Floyds were cousins of William Floyd, the Long Island patriot who was a member of the Continental Congress and signer of the Declaration of Independence. In addition, the Floyds were in a roundabout way related by marriage to Abraham Woodhull. General Nathaniel Woodhull, who was killed during the Battle of Long Island, was married to Ruth Floyd, sister of William Floyd and cousin of the Loyalists Benjamin and Richard Floyd. Regardless of Benjamin Floyd's intercession, Simcoe's raid terrified the timid and fearful Abraham Woodhull. Those increased fears, along with the pressures of his clandestine activities and the ever-present threat of discovery, caused Woodhull great distress and worry throughout the war.

After watching Simcoe and his rangers aggressively attack Americans, Sally could not understand why the Americans had not retaliated with raids of their own against the British outposts on Long Island. She wondered if the information she had given her brother about the British defenses around Oyster Bay and the Long Island signal system had found their way to Washington's army. Whatever the reason, she was somewhat discouraged that the Americans did not strike back at the British and Loyalist outposts on Long Island. Even so, she determinedly continued her intelligence-gathering efforts.

During the spring of 1779, Simcoe frequently mustered the Rangers for combined training and patrol activities in preparation for the coming campaign season. Now more than ever, Sally would rush to the assembly points to count the men, list their equipment and take note of anything she saw or heard that could be of value to the American army. Simcoe always noticed her presence and in fact seemed to look forward to her arrival. He loved having her near him and was flattered by her apparent interest in his regimental activities. It was apparent that Sally was genuinely impressed with the way Simcoe drilled and trained his men, and he believed that the way her large, beautiful eyes keenly studied everything he and his regiment did reflected her adoring interest in the way he commanded his troops.

The truth was that Simcoe was very smitten with Sally Townsend, and he was somewhat sad that warm weather was approaching, because it signaled the beginning of the campaign season. He realized that it wouldn't be long before he had to leave the pleasure of Sally's company and march his regiment out of Oyster Bay to join the main army for the summer campaign. Simcoe told Sally that he would likely be leaving soon, and he was flattered that she seemed distressed at the news. Her apparent unhappiness at his departure emboldened him to ask her if she would consider being his wife when he returned in the fall. If she would, he would immediately ask her father for her hand, and they could announce their engagement. Simcoe also consoled her on her sadness at their impending separation by telling her that he would surely return as soon as possible. Sally was not at all surprised by his proposal of marriage as she had expected it for some time. Though she found herself pleased and flattered by his offer, she also felt somewhat guilty and sad that she had been exploiting Simcoe's feelings to gather information for her brother. Sally was genuinely conflicted regarding her feelings for Simcoe, and it showed in her unhappy expression. Simcoe, on the other hand, interpreted Sally's melancholy as sadness that he was leaving her, and he believed that her interest in his regiment's deployment was because of her fear for his safety in facing the perils of war. Sally was torn. She did feel considerable affection for Simcoe and concern for his safety, but she was surprised that she also was somewhat miffed that she was losing a possible means of obtaining information to pass on to her brother.

It had been apparent to Sally's sisters, Audrey and Phebe, that Simcoe was actively courting their sister, and they couldn't understand her reticence to marry the handsome and dashing officer. Now that Sally was forced to give Simcoe an answer, she told him that the dangers he was constantly exposed to, the battles he had been engaged in, and the wounds he had suffered, caused her much dismay. She knew that he and his regiment would surely face many more perils before the war was over, and if she was his wife she knew her fears for his safety would be intolerable. For that reason, she told Simcoe that it was best to wait and that she would look forward to considering his proposal when the war was over. Simcoe begged her to reconsider, but Sally was adamant, and the disappointed officer could only glumly accept her decision.

As anticipated, Simcoe and his rangers marched out of Oyster Bay in May of 1779 to join the main army for the summer campaign. With the departure of Simcoe's regiment, Oyster Bay became an intelligence vacuum, in that there was little if any news regarding the war. Sally would read every copy that she could find of the *Royal Gazette, Packet, Mercury,* or *Register* newspapers, or she would visit Captain Daniel Youngs's headquarters hoping to get some news of the war. It was from Youngs that Sally learned that Simcoe and the Queen's Rangers had been sent to Westchester County, but there wasn't much more information regarding the regiment's activities.

Spring stretched languidly on into summer, and unexpectedly on Tuesday, August 17, 1779, Simcoe returned. Sally was working in the house when she heard her sister Phebe shout excitedly that the Queen's Rangers were returning, so she rushed outside to see for herself. Sure enough, she looked west down Main Road, and through the haze and dust, she could see Simcoe proudly leading his regiment back into Oyster Bay. Sally was surprised when tears began to flow down her cheeks and also that she couldn't stop waving wildly at Simcoe, who rode at the head of the approaching rangers. When Simcoe spied her, he beamed broadly, spurred his horse forward, and soon was dismounted by her side, where he took her hands in his and told her how much he had missed her during the preceding three months. Sally was thrilled to see her handsome ranger again, and in truth, all of the Townsends were happy to see that Simcoe had returned unharmed; they had come to regard him almost as one of their family.

During the time that Simcoe and his regiment had been gone from Oyster Bay, Sally often wondered why the Americans had not launched an attack against British strongpoints on the northern shore of Long Island. She couldn't think of a more opportune time for an American attack, because during the summer campaign season, only smaller Loyalist militia forces garrisoned the majority of the Long Island posts. They were more vulnerable to attack than when regular units like the Queen's Rangers were in the area. She had given detailed information about the outposts and the signals network to her brother, and she had hoped that her efforts would have resulted in an American expedition across the Devil's Belt. Now that the Queen's Rangers had returned to Oyster Bay, she assumed the opportunity was lost, and she no longer considered that an American attack would occur. As it turned out, neither did the British and Loyalist troops on Long Island.

At eight o'clock on the night of Sunday, September 5, 1779, Major Benjamin Tallmadge, with 50 dismounted dragoons, 28 continental infantrymen, and 50 whaleboat men launched their long-boats from Shippan Point near Stamford, Connecticut. They swiftly crossed the eight miles of Devil's Belt and landed on Lloyd's Neck, Long Island, in the vicinity of Fort Franklin. Their objective was to destroy the British outpost in retaliation for Loyalist depredations, including General Silliman's kidnapping and the assault on Abraham Woodhull's home in May. The American force landed at about ten o'clock at night and completely surprised the 500 Tories manning Fort Franklin. Some of the Loyalists escaped into the woods at the first sound of musket fire, but most were captured and brought back to Connecticut. The American raiders did not lose a single man in the attack. Before they departed Lloyd's Neck, Tallmadge ordered the destruction of the Loyalists' whaleboats and other watercraft, which halted Tory waterborne raids for some time.

The following morning Sally learned of the American raid when Tory survivors from Lloyd's Neck reached Oyster Bay to report to Simcoe. Judging from Simcoe's response, Sally could see that the raid had not only caught him by surprise, but it stung his ego that the rebels had the audacity to launch an attack against an area he was defending. Worse yet, they were successful. Sally was impressed at how quickly Simcoe reacted, when he immediately sent reinforcements to Fort Franklin and to other nearby outposts in case the rebels were brazen enough to launch a second attack. It was when Simcoe dictated a message to headquarters informing them of the rebel attack that Sally felt most sorry for him. She could tell that it mortified him to admit that the rebels carried out their surprise attack and escaped before the Queen's Rangers were able to respond. Yet, in spite of her sympathy for Simcoe, Sally was thrilled by the Americans' success and secretly hoped that the raid was a result of the information that she had given to her brother. The thought that she might have contributed to the American victory energized her, and she was now more than ever determined to continue her intelligence-gathering efforts.

17

Simcoe Is Captured
by the Americans

After the raid on Lloyd's Neck, the summer passed rather uneventfully. Most of the troops on Long Island were preparing to end the campaign season and go into winter quarters. It was no different with the Queen's Rangers. However, on Tuesday, October 19, 1779, Simcoe received orders to march his rangers to New Jersey to subdue rebel militia units that were operating in the vicinity of the Amboys.[1] Simcoe knew that by leaving Long Island this late in the season, it was almost certain that he and his regiment would find themselves in winter quarters somewhere other than Oyster Bay. When Sally heard the news, she pestered Simcoe with questions about his orders, where was he going and how long he would be gone. She suspected that the British were about to conduct some sort of late season, surprise campaign. Touched by her apparent concern at his impending departure, Simcoe tried to console Sally by promising that he would return to her as soon as possible. He held her hands and once again begged that she allow him to ask her father for permission to marry her so they could announce their engagement before he marched off with his regiment. In truth, Sally was sad to see her handsome lieutenant colonel leave. She realized that she was strongly attracted to him, but she steadfastly insisted that she would not consider discussion of marriage until the war was over. However, she softened her insistence by coyly hinting that she was looking forward to the time when he would have that conversation with her father. Dismayed by her continued refusal to consider his proposal until the war ended, Simcoe placed his hand over his heart and tore one of the bright silver buttons from his tunic. He placed the button in Sally's hand and softly asked if she would always keep the button in her possession, and always keep the giver of the button in her memory.

A week later Simcoe and the Queen's Rangers were in New Jersey, and on Tuesday, October 26, 1779, they were in pursuit of a band of rebel militia in the vicinity of New Brunswick. American scouts spotted the Queen's Rangers, and New Jersey Governor Livingston ordered a squad of troops to follow in Simcoe's wake. They were ordered to periodically fire alarm guns to pinpoint the location of the Queen's Rangers to make it easier for American militia units to locate and converge on Simcoe's force. Simcoe's men destroyed rebel equipment and materiel along their route of march and freed three Loyalist prisoners from the Somerset Court-House, where they had been chained to the floor. The prisoners had been unfed and nearly starved to death, so in retaliation, Simcoe's men burned the courthouse to the ground.

The alarm guns continued to follow Simcoe's regiment, alerting the countryside to their location and direction of march. At one point Simcoe ordered a group of women to inform the party that was trailing his rangers that if another alarm gun sounded he would burn every home he passed.

As his regiment neared New Brunswick, Simcoe spotted a group of men deploying across his planned route. Realizing that he was being ambushed, Simcoe immediately led his Hussars in a charge to split the rebel party before they could get established and fully close the gap in the road. As he raced forward, he saw that a group of men concealed in some bushes were taking aim at him. Simcoe heard one of them shout "Now! Now!" and they fired a volley that struck and killed Simcoe's horse. Simcoe was not hit by any of the bullets, but he was stunned by the impact as his horse tumbled and threw him. When he recovered his senses, he found he was a prisoner of war. However, because of Simcoe's precipitous charge into the midst of the rebels, the rest of his Queen's Rangers were able to avoid the ambush with few if any casualties.

Regrouping nearby, the Queen's Rangers discovered that Simcoe was not among them, and some of the troopers, who saw Simcoe fall, believed that their commander had been killed in the charge. The regimental surgeon said he would ride toward the rebels with a flag of truce to parley and inquire about Simcoe's fate. However, when the surgeon advanced under his white flag, he was fired upon, and a skirmish ensued, during which a Captain Voorhees of the rebel militia was killed. Members of Voorhees's militia unit were enraged at the death of their commander, and they wanted to kill Simcoe in revenge. For a while, it appeared very grim for Simcoe, but fortunately cooler heads prevailed, and New Jersey Governor Livingston was asked to intervene. Livingston immediately issued an order directing that Simcoe not be harmed or mistreated.

> The Governor being informed that some people have a desire to abuse and insult Lieut. Col. Simcoe, a British captive, and wounded in a skirmish that happened this day between our militia and the British horse: though the Governor

is not inclined to believe a report so great a disgrace upon the people of this State as that of the least inclination of revenge against a wounded enemy in our power; yet, to prevent the execution of any such attempt, it is his express order to treat the said officer according to the rules of war known and practiced among all civilized nations; and it is his desire to be carried to Brunswick, it is his further orders that no molestation be given to him in his being carried hither, and that while there he be treated with humanity which the United States of America have always observed toward their prisoners.

William Livingston

Brunswick Landing
2nd October, 1779 [sic][2]

Two days later, on Thursday, October 28, 1779, Simcoe was taken to Bordentown, New Jersey, and kept in a tavern owned by a Colonel Hoogland of the New Jersey militia. He was treated kindly and was even offered expense money by an American officer, Lt. Colonel Henry "Light Horse Harry" Lee.[3] Although they were technically enemies, Lee and Simcoe held each other in high regard and struck up a lasting friendship. Simcoe requested that he be paroled, but instead in November 1779 he was transferred to the jail in Burlington, New Jersey, where he was held in close confinement and not treated as well as he had been in Bordentown. When Simcoe arrived in the Burlington jail, he found that another British officer, Colonel Christopher Billop, was being held there. Billop was being terribly mistreated in retaliation for Americans who were suffering in British captivity. When Billop was brought to the prison, his jailer was given a written order from the American Commissary of Prisoners that directed:

To the Keeper of the Common Jail for the County of Burlington—Greeting:
    You are hereby commanded to receive into your custody the body of Col. Christopher Billop, prisoner of war, herewith delivered to you, and having put irons on his hands and feet, you are to chain him down to the floor in a close room in the said jail; and there so detain him, giving him bread and water only for his food, until you receive further orders from me, or the Commissary of Prisoners for the State of New Jersey for the time being.
    Given under my hand at Elizabethtown this 6th day of November, 1779.
    ELISHA BOUDINOT, Com. Pris. New Jersey.[4]

Simcoe constantly complained without result about the conditions that he and Billop were forced to endure. Finally he wrote directly to General Washington pleading for assistance. In the letter he even offered to take Billop's punishment in order to secure Billop's release.

Sir—I am induced to lay myself before you from what I conceive to be a principle of duty, and that not merely personal. You may perhaps have heard, sir, of the uncommon fortune that threw me into the hands of the Jersey Militia. Governor Livingston told me I was a prisoner of state, a distinction I never till then was acquainted with, and observed that it was probable I should be soon exchanged as such, naming to me officers of similar rank as the likely persons.

I was not allowed my parole, was taken from it on the 9th, and have ever since been confined a close prisoner in Burlington, with Col. Billop, who is in irons and chained to the floor, to retaliate for F. Randolph and Leshier, the latter of whom is said to be confined in the same manner in New York. My mittimus[5] hath not expressed what I am imprisoned for, but by the tenor of Governor Livingston's letters I suppose it is to retaliate for the former of those citizens, whom he allows to be a private soldier, and who is simply confined as such.

I apply to you sir, either as a prisoner of war or as appealing to you from an unjustifiable stretch of power, without precedent or generosity. I am led to consider myself as a prisoner of war under your authority, from Governor Livingston's doubts expressed to me of his having the disposal of me; from his correspondence with General Robertson, published in the newspapers, where he submits Gen. Dickinson's prisoners to your disposal, and from Col. Billop, my fellow-prisoner, being taken by a party of Continental troops, receiving his parole from Mr. Beaty, and living under it till he was taken from it by a party of militia, and by Mr. Boudinot's orders confined in Burlington jail.

He claims the protection that was first extended to him by the first Continental Commissary of prisoners.

I hope, sir, you will make use of the power that I conceive enabled you to transfer Col. Billop to the State of New Jersey, in extending to me the rights allowed by civilized nations, and which, without a given reason, I have been deprived of.

If, by any law I am acquainted with, I am in the power and disposal of Governor Livingston, I think myself entitled to appeal to you, sir, from the injustice used toward me, as I cannot suppose there is no application for redress in a case which, if drawn into a precedent, must confound every distinction of rank, and will operate in a wider circle than that of the State of New Jersey.

Governor Livingston has offered, as he has written to me, to exchange me for Lieut.-Col. Reynolds and Col. Billop for as many privates as made up his rank, naming among them the people for whom Col. Billop is avowedly retaliating. This proposition, I conceive, it never was supposed General Sir Henry Clinton could comply with.

I hope, sir, you will do me the favour of early attending to this letter; if Col. Billop only should be claimed by those whose prisoner he unquestionably appears to be, I should look upon it as a fortunate event, though I should be doomed to wear his ignominious chains.

I am your obedient and humble servant.

J. G. Simcoe[6]

Washington did not answer Simcoe's letter directly, but both Simcoe and Billop were informed that on Friday, December 31, 1779, they would be exchanged. As promised, the two men were released at the end of the year, and as soon as Simcoe crossed the lines and reached Staten Island, he was given a message from his old friend Major John André, who was now General Clinton's Adjutant General. Simcoe had hoped to return to Oyster Bay to see Sally, but now he was directed to rejoin his regiment at Richmond, on Staten Island, where the Queen's Rangers were in winter quarters.

The Winter of 1779–1780

No sooner did Simcoe rejoin his regiment on Staten Island than the weather conditions turned brutal. By Monday, January 10, 1780, the winter cold and winds became so fierce that it was impossible to travel between Staten Island and Manhattan Island. Massive ice floes and very strong winds made any sort of water crossing between the two islands too dangerous to attempt. On the other hand, the strait that separated Staten Island from New Jersey froze over and the ice was thick enough to support cannons. This put the troops on Staten Island in a precarious position. The rebels could attack from New Jersey, but assistance or reinforcements could not be sent from New York to Staten Island. Ominously, Simcoe's outposts reported that the rebels were measuring the thickness of the ice in the strait, which inferred that the Americans in New Jersey were contemplating an attack on Staten Island.

The attack came during the early morning hours of Saturday, January 15, 1780, when three thousand American Continentals and militia under General Alexander[1] swarmed over the ice from New Jersey. The British on Staten Island were outnumbered, so Simcoe did his best to fortify the high ground and strengthen his defensive positions. American units scouted Simcoe's works, but surprisingly they didn't attack. A few American deserters crossed the lines and told Simcoe that the Americans were reluctant to attack the Queen's Rangers, because they were certain Simcoe's regiment would put up "obstinate resistance."

Instead, the American militia units contented themselves by indiscriminately looting and plundering the Loyalist farms on Staten Island, before they withdrew to New Jersey with about seventeen prisoners. Ten days later, in retaliation for pillaging the Loyalist farms, the British launched a raid across the ice, and burned the academy at Newark along with the courthouse and meetinghouse at Elizabethtown. General Washington learned of the New Jersey militia's wanton plundering of Loyalist Staten Island farms, and he immediately issued explicit orders that the loot that was taken from the Loyalist homesteads should be recovered. All of the booty that was regained was subsequently turned over to the British under a flag of truce.

To prevent another surprise attack by the rebels, Simcoe ordered regular around-the-clock patrols to provide an early warning. In addition, he ordered that his men should sleep in their clothes with weapons handy, so that an immediate response could be made if the rebels appeared. On Tuesday, January 25, 1780, the cold had not abated and thick ice still connected Staten Island with New Jersey, prompting Simcoe to reissue his earlier orders to the Queen's Rangers:

> That he expects the order relative to officers and soldiers sleeping in their clothes be strictly complied with, such recruits excepted whom the officers commanding companies may judge as yet unequal to the duties of the regiment; if any half-bred soldier disobeys this order, the first officer, or non-commissioned officer, who meets with him will deliver him to the officer of the guard, to be put on some internal duty. The Lieut.-Col. Has particular satisfaction in seeing the General's approbation of that good countenance which enabled him, on the late inroad of the enemy, to rest perfectly at ease without augmenting the duty of the regiment; he knows its universal spirit, and, certain of the fidelity of those on guard, that the garrison cannot be snatched away by surprise, is confident that Richmond redoubts will be too dear for the whole rebel army to purchase.[2]

Simcoe's men were not allowed to undress for the night until Tuesday, February 22, 1780, when the ice connecting Staten Island and New Jersey finally broke up, lessening the risk of an attack.

Since Simcoe left Oyster Bay the previous October, Sally had not received any news concerning him and she was not aware that he had been taken prisoner and subsequently exchanged. She merely assumed that his regiment was ordered into winter quarters somewhere far from Oyster Bay. The fierce winter weather that kept Simcoe occupied on Staten Island also kept the Oyster Bay residents mostly indoors and gathered around their fires. The winter passed with only some occasional skirmishing between the outposts of the major armies.

When winter finally broke and before Simcoe could return to Oyster Bay, he and his regiment were ordered to board transports that would take them south to join in the siege of Charleston, South Carolina. The Queen's Rangers took part in the battle, and they were present on Friday, May 12, 1780, when about 5,500 American troops surrendered Charleston in the most stunning defeat suffered by the Americans to that point in the war.

A Hint of Treason

Meanwhile, in Oyster Bay, Sally Townsend continued to keep an eye on the British and Loyalist troops who were stationed there. During the middle of July 1780, she was aware of an abnormal amount of activity among the detachments that were manning the outposts overlooking the Devil's Belt and among the soldiers who were operating the British signals network. It seemed that hardly an hour passed without a dispatch rider racing through town. Sally tried to find the reason for this activity by visiting Captain Daniel Youngs's home and also by conversing with soldiers and officers she encountered on the streets of Oyster Bay. She picked up some conflicting snippets of information that indicated a major British operation, but there were also rumors of an imminent American attack against New York.

What Sally didn't know was that the French General Rochambeau had arrived at Newport, Rhode Island, with 6,000 French troops, and General Washington had sent General Lafayette to Newport to help coordinate the Franco-American alliance. In New York, Sally's brother Robert learned that the British commander, General Clinton, intended to send a powerful force to smash the French at Newport before they could organize themselves and effectively establish a cooperative effort with the Americans. Robert's coded message reached Washington's headquarters on Friday, July 21, 1780. It informed Washington that Clinton was embarking 8,000 British troops on transports at Whitestone, and they would sail that day or the next. A powerful fleet under Admiral Graves escorted the British transports, which would engage the French Navy and support a British assault on Newport with a naval bombardment.

Washington realized that the French army was extremely vulnerable while their troops and materiel were being disembarked. He knew that a devastating attack on the French would prevent their army and navy from taking part in major operations for some time to come. However, Washington also knew from Culper Ring intelligence that General Clinton was fearful of an all-out American assault on New York. In fact, since 1776, Clinton had continuously strengthened and improved the defenses of New York in anticipation of an American attack. In actuality, Washington did not have sufficient strength to attack the city, but he reasoned that if Clinton were convinced an attack on New York was imminent, Clinton would be reluctant to send 8,000 troops and the bulk of his navy to Rhode Island. To convince the British commander that an American attack on the city was imminent, Washington wrote out fictitious orders with detailed attack plans, and placed them in an official leather dispatch pouch. A man posing as a Tory farmer gave the pouch to a British patrol, telling them that he had found it. While the pouch was being delivered to Clinton in New York, Washington ordered an increase in army activity across the Hudson. That increased American troop activity was duly reported to Clinton at just about the time he was reviewing the contents of Washington's dispatch pouch. That was enough to convince Clinton of an impending American attack on New York. He immediately issued orders to recall the fleet that had already sailed.

The British ships were abeam Huntington Bay when the signal fires all along the Long Island coast were ignited, ordering the fleet to return to Whitestone. That night Sally saw the beacon ablaze at the summit of Norwich Hill, and she hoped that the intelligence she had given her brother regarding the signals system helped the Americans interpret the meaning of the signal fires. In fact they had. American watchers on the Connecticut shore spotted the signal beacons that confirmed the success of Washington's ruse. A short time later, the watchers were rewarded with the sight of the fleet reversing course and sailing back toward New York. The British attack on Newport was cancelled.

In the meantime, Simcoe had returned to New York. After taking part in the capture of Charleston, South Carolina, the Queen's Rangers boarded transports, and they reached Staten Island on Wednesday, June 21, 1780. The day they landed, Simcoe and his regiment were ordered to support operations in New Jersey, but upon reaching Springfield, New Jersey, Simcoe fell so ill that he could not command his regiment. He went to New York, where it took him almost a full month before he began to regain his health. By Wednesday, July 19, 1780, he thought that he had recovered sufficiently to rejoin the Queen's Rangers, but no sooner had he taken command of his regiment in New Jersey when he received orders to march them to Long Island. This was fortuitous for Simcoe, because the combined effects of captivity, arduous campaigning, and two unhealthy ocean voyages had taken a toll on his once powerful physique. While leading his regiment back to Long Island, his health relapsed, and he found that it was often difficult to remain in the saddle.

On Wednesday, August 23, 1780, as she had a year previously, Sally was roused by the cries of her siblings that the Queen's Rangers had returned to Oyster Bay. Sally rushed outside and peered down Main Road toward the west. Sure enough, ten months after they had left, the Queen's Rangers marched smartly into town with their commander riding at their head. Sally wildly waved her greeting and was at first surprised and then concerned that Simcoe didn't gallop forward when he spotted her. He was only able to wave weakly in reply. This was certainly not the energy Simcoe regularly displayed, and it was nothing like his normal reaction when he saw Sally, especially after such a long absence. When Simcoe finally reached Sally, she saw that he was very pale and gaunt, and she wondered if he had again been wounded in battle.

Simcoe had to be helped from his horse and into the house, and in spite of his obvious illness and fatigue he managed to smile broadly and tell Sally how happy he was to see her again. Sally was happy to see Simcoe, but was worried about his health and well-being. She and her sisters reacted by making every effort to make him comfortable, and they continually brought him food to help him regain his health and rebuild his gaunt body. Simcoe responded quickly to the care from the Townsend girls and within a short time was on the mend. He didn't seem as reticent to talk as in the past, and while he recuperated, he spent many evenings telling the Townsends of his activities since he left Oyster Bay. It wasn't long before Simcoe began to look, feel and act like his old self.

A short time after Simcoe returned to Oyster Bay, his friend Major John André arrived at the Townsend residence. Of surprise to all, André was returning to New York from the eastern end of Long Island. He had accompanied General Clinton to an abortive meeting with Admiral Arbuthnot at Gardiner's Bay. The two had endured a long carriage ride the entire length of Long Island in the stifling August heat, and there they spent several days waiting for Arbuthnot to show up for the meeting. However, the admiral never arrived, and Clinton and André had no choice but to return to New York. On the return trip, André took the opportunity to stop off at Oyster Bay to enlist Simcoe and his regiment in a very secret development that could hasten a British victory. For the previous fifteen months, André had been engaged in clandestine correspondence with Major General Benedict Arnold, perhaps the most brilliant and able officer in the American high command. Arnold had been a thorn in the side of the British since the very beginning of the war and was almost single-handedly responsible for several American victories. Now, Arnold was offering to defect to the British and surrender the strategic fortifications at West Point on the Hudson in the process.

It is thought that Arnold's wife, Peggy Shippen Arnold of the Philadelphia Shippen family, who were known to be lukewarm Loyalists, may have influenced her husband to defect to the British. Peggy had kept up a correspondence with André since the romantic and heady days of the British occupation of Philadelphia. At that time, she had been the belle of the ball at the frequent parties, dances, and soirées that were given by the dashing and virile young officers of Howe's staff. It was a time that Peggy referred to as those "halcyon days, forever dear."[1] Arnold exchanged messages with André, in which Arnold interestingly signed his messages with the name "Monk"[2] after George Monck, 1st Duke of Albemarle (1608–1670), who, after supporting Oliver Cromwell's Commonwealth and Protectorate, turned against his former cause and helped bring about the restoration of Charles II, for which Monck was handsomely rewarded by the grateful king. Also of interest is the method by which André and Arnold exchanged coded messages. The two men each had a copy of *Bailey's Dictionary*, 21st edition, which was used as the key. The messages would be in the guise of normal business communications with certain sensitive sections written in code. André's instructions were that "three numbers make a word, the first is the page, the second the line, the third the word."[3] Later in the plot, Arnold gave up the name "Monk" and took one with more grandiose overtones: "Gustavus,"[4] after Gustav Vasa (c. 1496–1560), who was instrumental in gaining Swedish independence from the Danes and was rewarded by being elected King Gustav I Vasa in 1523.

André stayed with the Townsends a few days, and during that time he and Simcoe took long, private walks and also carried on quiet conversations in Simcoe's room. Sally was the first to notice the apparent seriousness and intensity of the meetings, in sharp contrast to André's previous visits when the men had been active and energetic in generating fun and recreational activities, which always included Sally and her sisters. Sally was certain that something significant was in the offing, but there didn't seem to be any way for her to find out what it was. She tried to join in on André and Simcoe's conversations, but other than some polite, banal responses from the officers, they seemed too engrossed to include her. Sally was discouraged by her attempts to learn what they were up to, and in frustration she stamped her foot and scolded the two for being very ungallant in ignoring her. She purposefully strode away in an obvious fit of pique, but before she was able to get too far, Simcoe caught up with her and grabbed her arm. He apologized for their ungentlemanly behavior and said that they were discussing some mundane military matters for which André had asked Simcoe's opinion. Simcoe told her that he was very flattered that General Clinton's Adjutant General valued his opinion even on such insignificant matters. Sally was no fool. She knew Simcoe well enough to know that his discussions with André were not about trivial issues. She sarcastically asked if he rudely ignored her because he considered her less important than those minor military matters. Simcoe simply answered that they were mostly administrative issues that were too routine and dull for her pretty ears, and he promised not to ignore her in the future. He also told her that André was planning a return to New York in a few days, and after that time, Simcoe assured her that he would certainly devote more attention to her as he had in the past. Then Simcoe got very serious and taking her hands in his, he softly asked if she still promised to consider his proposal of marriage when the war was over. Not knowing why the question was brought up at this time, Sally could only answer that she would happily keep her promise. Simcoe smiled broadly, and kissing her hand he enigmatically said, "Maybe I will speak again this year."[5] Sally was so shocked she could hardly react. Simcoe's comment indicated that he believed the war would end soon, perhaps before the end of the year. Moreover his demeanor implied that he was confident that Britain would emerge victorious.

Later that day, Sally told André that she learned he would soon be returning to New York. She asked if he could delay his departure so that she and her sisters could host a tea party in his honor. André said he was flattered and would be happy to stay a little longer, especially since he hadn't sufficient opportunity to spend time with Sally or her sisters. He said he hoped that during the additional few days, he could rectify that sad circumstance. He added that he looked forward to a convivial gathering with the Townsends and their neighbors and offered that he and Simcoe would provide some of the entertainment. André said it would be like times past in Philadelphia during 1777–1778, when Simcoe frequently took part in André's theatrical productions that were staged to help pass time more pleasantly. Simcoe and André became close friends at that time, and they acted and painted scenery together. Sally said she was pleased that he would stay, and she, along with her mother and sisters, would plan a party for the coming Saturday, September 2, 1780.[6] She added that they would invite many of the friends and neighbors whom André had met on his previous visit.

Sally's family agreed that an afternoon tea party in André's honor would be great fun, and they all involved themselves in planning and preparing for the event. A guest list was drawn up and the Townsend girls delivered the invitations that afternoon. That same evening, while in her room, Sally wrote out an account of the two officers' secretive conversations and Simcoe's curious intimation that the war would soon end with a British victory. As she was writing, she heard André and Simcoe chatting as they entered the house.

She hurriedly hid her notes and silently crept out into the upstairs hall in time to hear the men enter Simcoe's room, closing the door behind them.

Sally stood listening for a few minutes, then softly tiptoed downstairs, her slippers not making a sound. She wasn't sure why she was sneaking around in her own house, but she certainly didn't want either of the two officers to suspect she was writing notes about them in her room. As she reached the bottom of the narrow staircase, she came up to the door to Simcoe's room and heard the sounds of a muted conversation inside. Not fully realizing the chance she was taking if one of the two men should suddenly open the door and discover her, Sally got as close to the door as she dared and listened intently to the sounds from within. Simcoe and André were indeed speaking very softly, and try as she might, Sally couldn't hear what they were saying. Just as she was about to give up, she distinctly heard one of the men say, "… settled then." She couldn't tell which of the men had said it, because it was in a hoarse whisper, but it was enough to keep her in place listening at the door. As she concentrated on the whispered conversation, Sally was rewarded with a few other incomplete phrases. She heard one of the men refer to the shores of the Hudson River, and then she heard them refer to "West Point" several times[7]: "…a simple operation … fall like a stone …" and finally, "… West Point … will fulfill … long desired…."[8] The words "West Point" certainly piqued her interest. Sally was well aware from her conversations with Simcoe that the American stronghold was a strategic fortification on the Hudson, and in addition it contained vast quantities of supplies, equipment, and materiel for the American army.[9] Why were two British officers discussing West Point in such a clandestine manner?

As Sally listened intently, she suddenly heard a chair slide back in the room. The harsh sound alerted her that someone stood up and perhaps was preparing to leave the room. She realized that if they opened the door, they would discover her eavesdropping. No, she thought, they would consider it more than just eavesdropping; she would be accused of spying on them. Sally felt a momentary panic as she silently raced to the parlor in the front of the house where she grabbed a book at random from her father's small collection. She opened the book as she sat in one of the chairs in the far corner, staring at the pages as she tried to calm her nerves. It seemed she waited an eternity for something to happen, all the while fearfully expecting them to burst from their room and accuse her of spying. She had no idea how she would respond to a charge like that, and she feared that she would not be able to successfully hide her guilt if they confronted her. Eventually, she heard the men casually exit Simcoe's room into the hall and leave the house through the back door, closing it after they exited. She breathed a sigh of relief as she realized that they hadn't seen her and had not a hint that she had listened in on their conversation. While the snippets of the overheard conversation were still fresh in her memory, Sally raced upstairs to her room where she hurriedly added them to her notes. A short time later, Sally heard her mother and sisters enter the house, and after carefully hiding her papers, she went downstairs to join her family.

In addition to overhearing Simcoe and André discussing West Point and the Hudson, Sally accidentally learned additional information regarding Major André that would prove to be immensely important to the Americans. It's not known exactly how Sally learned this information, but according to popular legend, it happened on or about Thursday, August 31, 1780,[10] while Sally was working in preparation for Saturday's party. During the time that she was baking pastries, Sally couldn't help but think of her conversation with Simcoe or the whispered comments she had overheard from the two officers. Most of all she wondered how she could get that information to her brother in New York. All that morning Sally noted that several military dispatch riders had stopped at the house to drop off or pick up sealed documents from both Simcoe and André. In addition several officers from the Queen's Rangers were seen entering and leaving the house by the rear door to meet with the two officers. This was more military activity than she had previously seen. Later that morning, both André and Simcoe rode off with a small group of officers, and Sally was alone in the house. About an hour after André and Simcoe departed, Sally went upstairs to her room to replace her mobcap,[11] which had become somewhat damp from perspiration in the heat of the kitchen. As she descended the stairs, she heard the front door slowly creak open. At first she assumed the officers had returned, but when she realized that whoever entered was trying to be quiet, she froze and crouched back into the dark shadows of the narrow staircase. Concerned that the person was trying to pilfer some of the Townsends' silver or other valuables, Sally peered from the stairs and watched as a stranger dressed in civilian clothing furtively crept into the parlor. As soon as he passed out of her line of sight, Sally silently rushed down the stairs and crept into the back room behind the door to the parlor. The door was slightly ajar, and Sally slid alongside the wall to where she could look through the crack between the door and the jamb. She watched as the stranger stealthily crossed to the corner cupboard and stooped to open the lower door to the compartment where André had playfully hidden her olykoeks during his last visit. She wondered what the man was doing and why he was looking in the cupboard, but something about his furtiveness compelled Sally to remain unseen and observe his moves rather than to challenge him. She watched as the man removed a sealed document from his pocket, which he placed deep in the back of the cabinet where it would not readily be seen if someone opened the cupboard door.[12] After he deposited the message, he closed the door, fastened the latch, then glanced around to see if anyone had noticed him. Sally saw him start to turn and she quickly ducked behind the door and pressed herself against the wall, hoping he would not come into the back room. It was only after she heard the man walk out the front door and softly close it behind him that Sally realized she had been holding her breath the entire time.

After waiting several minutes to see if the stranger or anyone else would enter the house, Sally finally mustered enough courage to go over to the corner cupboard. As she bent to open the lower door, she told herself that if someone came in the room, she would merely say that she was getting a platter on which to place her pastries. She paused at the cabinet and listened to hear if anyone was approaching. When she was satisfied that no one was coming she opened the cupboard door and located the document deep inside the compartment. Sally examined the message, and saw that it was tightly sealed and addressed to "James Anderson."[13] Sally had no idea who James Anderson[14] was or why a letter addressed to him had been placed in her family's cupboard. She briefly considered breaking the seal and reading the message or taking it to examine later; however, she dismissed that idea as impractical. Whoever the letter was meant for would quickly deduce that she had taken or read the message. She chose the safest course of action, which was to place the letter back where the stranger hid it. Then she could try to determine for whom the letter was meant and what it might be about.

Around midday, Major André returned just as Sally had finished her baking. She chatted with André for a while and learned that some regimental affairs detained Simcoe, and he had not returned to the house with André. Sally placed her platter of pastries on the table in the back room to cool, during which time André complimented her on her baking skill. He also expressed his appreciation for the Townsends' hospitality. Sally enjoyed talking with André, who seemed to be remarkably knowledgeable about poetry, art, fashion and all the things that Sally was interested in. Sally was hot and sweaty from her baking, so she said that she was going outside where the air was cooler, and she invited André to accompany her. André said he first wanted to put his accouterments and his dispatch case in his room, and then he would join her. After several minutes André joined Sally in the yard, and sat with her in the shade. They chatted for quite some time, and André told her a little about his life. His father was a Swiss merchant living in London with his French-born wife. André was sent to Geneva, Switzerland, to be edu-

Townsend parlor showing the corner cupboard (photograph courtesy Raynham Hall Museum).

cated, and in the process he became fluent in French, Italian, and German, as well as English. He told Sally that to pass the time and entertain himself, he liked to play the flute, draw and paint pictures, and write lyrics and comic verse.

Sally told André that a handsome and talented young officer like himself must have a sweetheart who was anxiously waiting for him to come home from the war, but André only smiled wistfully and said that no one waited for his return. He admitted that he had once lost his heart to a young maiden named Honora Sneyd, but she had refused his offer of marriage and wed another. Sadly, she had died of consumption during the previous year of 1779.

Shaking off his melancholia, André began to talk about the present and how he and Simcoe were planning a short production of excerpts from *Macbeth* as entertainment at the Townsends' tea party. "Of course," he added, "you and your sisters will be cast in leading roles to ensure the success of my theatrical production." "And which role will I have, Major André?" she asked. "If you're thinking of casting me as one of Macbeth's witches, you'd better look elsewhere for members of your troupe." For the first time, Sally saw André at a loss for words. It appeared that he didn't know what to say. Sally laughed aloud when she realized that it was indeed André's intent to cast her and her sisters as the three witches. She continued to stare at him with her feigned glower, until he realized that she was teasing him. "Be assured, lass that you'll not be portraying a broomstick riding crone in this production, but rather a beautiful and captivating siren. In short, you'll only have to play yourself in body and in spirit."

The two continued their banter and laughed about the ideas André had in adapting Shakespeare's *Macbeth*, until Sally realized that she had to clean up from her baking before her family returned. André joined her as she walked into the house, but upon entering the back room Sally immediately saw that something was amiss; the plate of pastries she had worked on all morning had disappeared. At first, Sally couldn't believe they were missing, but when she heard André's soft chuckling, she realized that before he joined her in the yard, he had repeated his prank of the previous year and had hidden her pastries. Sally turned and scolded the young major for teasing her, and she admonished him that if he continued to play tricks on her, he would discover that she could play the role of a witch full well. She added that if he persisted in interfering with her preparations, she would not be able to adequately prepare for "his" party. André could hardly keep from laughing, but he steadfastly proclaimed his innocence and sanctimoniously declared that since her fame as a pastry cook was known far and wide, it was not surprising that some unscrupulous fellow would sneak in and steal them. André said that if they rushed outside, they might still be able to catch the naughty fellow. Sally replied that she didn't have to rush outside to nab the naughty fellow and to reclaim her pastries; both were much nearer at hand. Turning abruptly, she smugly and confidently walked through the connecting door into the parlor and over to the corner cupboard. She bent and opened the very cabinet door where André had previously hidden her olykoeks and where the stranger had clandestinely placed the mysterious letter that very morning. Sure enough, there were the pastries. "Bravo! Lass," shouted André as he clapped his hands, "you've solved the great mystery." Sally leaned forward to retrieve the platter and in so doing peered deep into the interior, where she saw that the message was no longer in the cupboard. She smilingly told André, "I think the culprit has returned to the scene of his crime once too often," but she also thought to herself, "Yes, I have indeed solved the great mystery."

20

The Message
Is Sent to Tallmadge

Sally replaced the platter of pastries in the back room, then began to clean up after her baking. André remained in the room, and the two continued to chat. When she was finished, Sally said that she needed to go upstairs to her room to freshen up and change clothes. André walked with her to the staircase, and the two parted as André entered the room he shared with Simcoe. Once in her room, Sally added to her notes, writing about the stranger who had snuck into the house and left a message for someone named "James Anderson." She added that Major John André retrieved the message, and she suspected that André was the mysterious "James Anderson."[1]

Now her dilemma was how to get this information to her brother. Sally sensed that the material she had gathered during André's visit was very important and should be forwarded to Robert as quickly as possible. She only hoped that he had some means of getting the information to the right people. She decided that it might be important enough to use the method that Robert had told her about a couple years earlier. She hastily wrote out a note addressed to her brother requesting that he send some items from the Townsend store in New York. Sally was aware that Simcoe's favorite brand of tea was Bohea, and that the family's supply in Oyster Bay was running a little low. In the letter, she asked Robert to send three pounds of Bohea tea to Oyster Bay and added that she hoped it would arrive in time for the party on Saturday. She also included a couple of hastily written pages of personal notes about events in Oyster Bay and details of other family matters that had occurred since his last visit. Sally buried her notes at the end of her request for tea and her mundane, personal letter to Robert. Her notes included a synopsis of Simcoe and André's conversations, as well as the strange events surrounding the mysterious letter. She also added her suspicion that André was the equally mysterious "James Anderson." Sally hoped that if anyone examined the papers they would be satisfied the documents were no more than a shopping list and a personal letter to her brother. Hopefully, the examiner would stop before discovering her notes regarding André and Simcoe at the bottom of the stack. When she was finished, she wrapped and sealed the packet of papers and addressed it to Robert Townsend at the Underhills' boardinghouse in New York.

As soon as she finished preparing her packet, Sally went to the barn, saddled her horse and immediately set off for the Youngs's home on Cove Road, about two miles away. During the ride, Sally worried that Daniel might be suspicious of her message and examine it. There was no way that she could explain away her notes about André and Simcoe if they were discovered. She couldn't for the life of her figure out why Robert had been so insistent that the best way to get a message to him would be through Daniel Youngs. Daniel was a Tory officer! Why should she or her brother believe that he would deliver a message without being curious as to its content? Robert had assured her that it was the best way to get a message quickly to him in New York, but he had been most insistent that she not give the message to anyone other than Daniel Youngs. Robert also cautioned her that this method of passing information to him in New York was very dangerous and should not be attempted more than once or twice at the most. Sally believed that her information was important enough to risk it. She only hoped that the message would be delivered quickly to Robert and that he could somehow get it to someone who would be able to make sense out of it. In all truth, she had no idea what André and Simcoe were up to.

Sally's horse galloped down Cove Road, and as she neared the Youngs's home she could see that several horses were tied outside, and some militiamen were standing in small groups in the shady yard chatting with one other. The men turned at the sound of her approach, and Daniel Youngs waved as he walked to meet her. Sally stopped in front of the house, glad that she was able to talk to Daniel without being too near the other Loyalist soldiers. Daniel helped her down and tied her horse to the hitching post in front of his house. He asked Sally why she had ridden at a gallop, and inquired if there was something wrong at the Townsend home. Sally told him that there was no emergency, but she only wanted to ask if the next time he sent a messenger to New York, she could include a message to Robert for some supplies from the Townsend store. She added that she hoped that an express rider would be making the trip within the next day or so to bring back some tea in time for the party. Sally knew that Daniel and Susannah were coming to the tea party on Saturday, and she told Daniel that, because the party was being held in Major André's honor, she especially wanted it to be a success, since he was General Clinton's adjutant general. She told Daniel that the Townsends' tea supply was running low, which could be an embarrassment, and she hoped Robert could send a few pounds of Bohea tea in time for the party. She blushed slightly as she added that Bohea also happened to be Lieutenant Colonel Simcoe's favorite tea. As she explained her request to Daniel, Susannah came out and beckoned Sally and Daniel to come inside for some refreshments and a cool drink. She said that Sally must be thirsty after such a sprightly gallop in the heat. Daniel led Sally into the house, and once inside, he told her that he would be happy to deliver her message to Robert. He added that, because it was for such a good cause, honoring the adjutant general of the British Army, he would send an express rider immediately to New York to deliver her message to Robert along with some other mail that had to go to headquarters.

Sally handed the packet to Daniel and when he looked at it, she quickly blurted out that it wasn't only a request for supplies, but it also contained some personal letters relating news of the family. Sally immediately regretted her comment as sounding suspicious, because Daniel turned the packet over in his hands and appeared to look it over more closely. However, he just smiled at her and said that she need not worry; it would be delivered unopened to Robert. While Sally sat with Susannah and sipped a cool glass of cider, Daniel placed Sally's message in his dispatch case and walked outside. A few minutes later Sally heard the sound of hoofbeats, and glancing through the window, she could see the express rider racing down the road toward New York.[2] When Daniel came back inside, he said that he told the messenger to be sure to wait and bring the Bohea tea back in time for Saturday's party, because it was not only Colonel Simcoe's favorite but also his and Susannah's. With that he gave Sally a wink and went outside to join his men.

Sally was not aware that in spite of their Loyalist appearance and affiliations, Susannah and Daniel Youngs were in fact patriots who aided the American cause through Daniel's position as a captain of the Loyalist militia. Their true allegiance was known only to the Youngs's lifelong friend Robert Townsend and one or two others, including Major Benjamin Tallmadge. On two occasions near the end of the war, April 1, 1783, and July 16, 1783, Washington arranged for £400 to be paid to Daniel Youngs in compensation for his expenses and for his service to the American cause. As a further indication of the Youngs's loyalty, Daniel and his family were not molested in any way, nor were they forced to leave Long Island, as most Loyalists were after the war ended. In fact during his tour of Long Island in April 1790, President Washington visited Daniel and Susannah Youngs and spent the night in their home.[3]

Sally thanked Susannah for the refreshments and said that she had to return home to help her mother and sisters with dinner and to prepare for the party. She said that she was glad the Youngses were coming and appreciated Daniel's help in making the party a success. When Sally walked toward her horse, Daniel came over and helped her mount. She thanked him again for his help and said she looked forward to seeing him on Saturday. Daniel said that when the express rider returned with the tea, he would send it right over to the Townsends' home. He added that he wished Robert could be at the party, because it was quite a while since he had last talked with Sally's brother. Sally pulled her horse around, and as she cantered off she waved back at Susannah, who joined Daniel in the yard.

When Sally arrived home she returned her horse to the barn and was walking toward the house when Simcoe and André met her in the yard. The men casually enquired where she had ridden. Sally hadn't prepared for the question from the two officers and it flustered her. Realizing that she did not want to tell the two officers that she had sent a message to her brother in New York, she hesitated a little and stammered that she had just gone for a ride. The two men seemed surprised at her somewhat guarded response, and she saw that her evasiveness caused Simcoe's eyebrows to arch in a manner that she had previously seen when he became inquisitive or examined a puzzle. Not wanting to arouse his suspicions any further, Sally told Simcoe that she knew Bohea tea was his favorite, but they were almost out of it and she wanted to see if she could get some more in time for the party on Saturday. Simcoe was stopped from further questions when André clapped him on the back and told him that he was a lucky fellow indeed that a comely lass like Sally would make such an effort to get him his favorite tea. Sally's explanation and André's praise of her efforts completely disarmed Simcoe, and he was visibly touched that Sally had taken such measures on his behalf. He clasped her hands and thanked her for thinking of him, and then he softly added that he soon hoped that it would be opportune to have a chat with her father to obtain his permission to marry Sally.

Daniel Youngs's express rider reached New York in the early evening and found Robert at the Underhills' boardinghouse, where he handed him the message packet from Sally. He added that Captain Youngs had told him to wait and return with the tea that Sally had ordered. Robert gave the trooper some money for his troubles and asked him to return in the morning to pick up the tea. After the rider left, Robert opened the packet and read Sally's notes. He let out a soft whistle as he read about the references to West Point, the Hudson River, and the inference that West Point would fall like a stone. What also caught Townsend's attention was Sally's belief that Simcoe hinted that the war would shortly end in a British victory. To Robert, it seemed that those issues might somehow be related. He was also intrigued by Sally's account of the secretive letter addressed to "James Anderson" and her suspicion that André was using that alias. Robert recopied Sally's notes in code on a blank sheet of paper using "sympathetic stain" or invisible ink. As Robert laboriously wrote out the message, he considered how fortunate it was that Austin Roe happened to be at the Underhills, that very night. Roe had recently arrived on his regular run from Setauket and was preparing to return the following morning with writing paper, ink and other light commodities for his own use and for some of his Setauket friends. Now Townsend was hurrying to prepare yet another parcel for Austin Roe to carry to Setauket. Roe's Culper Ring designation was number "724." In Setauket Roe would pass the dispatches on to number "722," Abraham Woodhull, who in turn would give them to Captain Caleb Brewster, number "725." Brewster would then ferry the messages across the Devil's Belt to Tallmadge's waiting couriers, who would rush them to Washington's headquarters.

When he finished coding the message in invisible ink, Robert walked out of the building, crossed King Street and walked a block or so to Rivington's print shop on the corner of Queen and Wall Streets. There he purchased a quire[4] of fine writing paper, which was exactly the same paper on which he had written his message in sympathetic stain. When Robert returned to his room at the Underhills, he carefully unwrapped the quire of paper and removed the number of sheets that he was going to add. Those sheets would be used for future messages, and with the message papers added to replace them, the quire in Roe's saddlebags would have the appropriate number of papers. Robert then counted a predetermined number of sheets in the quire and carefully added the apparently blank pages on which he had written his message in invisible ink. After he had carefully rewrapped the quire, he walked down the hall to Austin Roe's door and gave him the packet of writing paper. He told Roe that delivery of the message was urgent, and it must arrive in Setauket for delivery as quickly as possible. To leave New York, Austin had to take the Brooklyn Ferry to Long Island, but because of the curfew he would not be able to cross until morning. Roe promised Robert that he would be on the first ferry that left New York, and he should arrive in Setauket by tomorrow afternoon. Of course, getting the message across the Devil's Belt would depend on when Caleb Brewster's whaleboat would next visit Setauket. That could take anywhere up to several days, sometimes due to adverse weather, but often because Brewster had to take care to avoid British patrol boats. The British were diligently trying to prevent the flow of intelligence information to Washington's army, and vessels like the *Halifax* and several other British and Loyalist gunboats constantly patrolled the Devil's Belt.

Unfortunately, there wasn't a more expeditious way of getting the message to Washington. They could only hope that Brewster would be available to deliver it to Tallmadge sooner rather than later.

The pages on which Robert had written his message would appear blank and unused to any stranger who might examine them. Hidden among the pages of a quire of writing paper, the coded pages would be completely indistinguishable from the other papers in the stack. It would require a wash of chemical reagent to bring out the coded message. On every trip, Roe carried several quires of writing paper for various friends in Setauket. The papers were all purchased from the Tory printer James Rivington, and were always exactly the same type that Robert used for his messages. That way, the papers with the hidden messages would not stand out in any way if they were examined. After they had finished chatting, Austin returned to bed to try to get as much sleep as possible before he started his long fifty-five-mile ride to Setauket.

Robert did not return to his room but rather exited the boardinghouse and walked the block or so to the Oakman & Townsend store on the corner of Prince's and William Streets. Once inside, he measured out and securely wrapped three pounds of his finest Bohea tea. He also wrapped and labeled two more packages of fine tea, one for the express rider and another for Susannah and Daniel Youngs. When he was finished he locked the shop and returned to Underhill's, where he spent a sleepless night wondering what Sally's message might portend. A little before dawn, Robert was still awake when he heard Austin Roe exit his room. Robert hurriedly dressed and walked outside in time to help Roe saddle up and stow his supplies, including the quires of paper in the saddlebags. Without any further comment, Roe swung into the saddle, gave a small salute and rode off in the direction of Water Street and the Brooklyn Ferry.

On Friday, September 1, 1780, the Townsend women spent most of the day preparing for the next day's party, while André and Simcoe occupied themselves by putting the finishing touches on their short adaptation of *Macbeth*. Simcoe was fond of Shakespeare and kept a well-read copy of *Macbeth* along with two books on military tactics in his portmanteau,[5] which he even took with him on campaigns. During the course of the day, the two officers held several short rehearsals, in which Sally and her sisters playfully emoted their roles much to the amusement of everyone present. By the end of the day, all the preparations for the party had been completed, and most of the Townsend family, along with the two officers, sat together in the yard chatting. As dusk settled in, they heard the sound of hoofbeats drumming down Main Road from the west, and when they heard the horse slow in front of the

Townsend house, both André and Simcoe stood, believing that a message or orders had arrived for one or both of them. After the rider tied his horse at the drinking trough, he walked around the side of the house, slapping his dusty hat against his thigh with one hand and brushing dust from the front and shoulders of his frock with the other. The large bulging haversack the trooper wore slung over his shoulder bounced in time with his step. When he saw André and Simcoe approaching, the messenger hastily slapped his dusty hat back onto his head and smartly saluted the two officers. "Well, man, what is it," Simcoe asked as he held out his hand. "Do you have dispatches for one of us?" "No, sir. I don't," the trooper answered. "I have a parcel here for Miss Sarah Townsend from New York. Captain Youngs told me to deliver it to her on the way back to the Cove." With that he dug into his haversack and pulled out a wrapped package and walked toward Sally who had stood at the mention of her name. The trooper handed her the parcel and said, "Captain Youngs's compliments ma'am," then he turned to the two officers and saluted them saying, "I'd best be returning to the Cove now, sirs, unless you have other orders for me." Simcoe and André only shook their heads and turned to reclaim their seats; however, Sally took hold of the trooper's arm and said, "Before you go sir, would you please have a mug of cool cider? You must be hot and thirsty after such a long, hard ride." The trooper was at a loss for words. He was dry and thirsty, but he was uncomfortable in the presence of the two high-ranking officers. Sally immediately sensed his discomfort and led him by his arm toward the house. She said, "Please come with me to the kitchen for a mug of cider and some other refreshments." The trooper smiled in gratitude and said earnestly, "Thank you, ma'am, I would be much obliged. In truth it was a hot and dusty ride from New York." "You have done me a great favor," she answered. "Giving you some refreshment is the very least I can do." As they walked toward the kitchen, Sally glanced at the parcel. On the wrapping in Robert's neat and distinctive handwriting, was, "3 lbs. Bohea—Samuel Townsend Dr."[6] Sally knew that Robert had received her information.

Saturday, September 2, 1780, was a beautiful day in Oyster Bay, and everyone at the Townsends' afternoon tea party had an exceptionally good time. Both Simcoe and André were in fine form, relating anecdotes of their experiences and how they collaborated on theatrical productions during the winter months in Philadelphia, painting scenery, creating costumes and then acting in the plays. They told the guests how they had presented an adaptation of Shakespeare's *Macbeth* for the leading families and officers of Philadelphia early in 1778, and that they would reprise that production today for the Townsends and their guests. A small stage had been constructed on the Townsends' lawn, and the play was presented much to the amusement of everyone, who especially whooped it up when the three Townsend daughters cackled theatrically, "Double, double, toil and trouble; Fire burn and cauldron bubble...."

When the short play ended, and after the troupe took their bows, André was asked by many of the Loyalists present about his satirical poem, "The Cow Chace." The poem was being serialized in Rivington's *Royal Gazette*, and André was queried about when the final cantos would appear in the paper. André remained on the stage and gave a short background of his poem, which had become very popular among the Loyalists. He reminded them that it was written to commemorate an abortive raid by an American force under the command of Major General "Mad" Anthony Wayne (1745–1796).

On Wednesday, July 21, 1779, three regiments of Americans with light artillery had attacked a small British blockhouse on Bergen Neck that was built primarily to protect woodcutters and a herd of cattle that were grazing on the meadows there. André described how the cannonballs from the American light fieldpieces would not penetrate the blockhouse walls and how Wayne broke off the action after firing several ineffectual volleys in frustration at the tiny fortified British garrison. The young major laughingly mentioned that before the war, General Wayne had been a cattle drover and tanner of hides and that Wayne apparently used his drover skills to capture the grazing cows and thereby gain some measure of success from the venture. André said that he had indeed completed the final cantos of the poem, and they were in the hands of James Rivington, who promised they would be published in the Saturday, September 23, 1780, edition of the *Royal Gazette*. Some of the Loyalist spectators pressed André for a recitation of "The Cow Chace," and he readily acquiesced, telling them that they would be the first to hear the complete satire.

André was in his element and his dark eyes sparkled as he began to recite his poem in a sing-song manner that was very amusing to the Loyalists in his audience:

> To drive the Kine one summer's morn,
> The Tanner took his way,
> The Calf shall rue that is unborn
> The jumbling of that day.

> And Wayne descending Steers shall know,
> And tauntingly deride,
> And call to mind in ev'ry Low
> The tanning of his hide.

> Yet Bergen Cows still ruminate
> Unconscious in the stall,
> What mighty means were used to get
> And lose them after all.

As André recited stanza after stanza, the Whigs among the guests maintained a stony-faced silence, while the Loyalist members of the audience laughed aloud at his satirical references. André referred to the shoeless rebels as "Nathan Pumpkin" who got courage from casks of rum, but ran away when tanner Wayne, who pretended to be a general, shouted "Charge!" In closing, André recited the final cantos that had not yet been published, and he ended the poem with the final verse

> And now, I've clos'd my epic strain,
> I tremble as I shew it,
> Lest this same warrior-drover Wayne,
> Should ever catch the poet.
> FINIS.[7]

André departed Oyster Bay for New York on Sunday, September 3, 1780, the day after the gathering. The Townsend family history states, "Major André spent the last week before he started for West Point at the old house."[8] Before he left, André thanked the Townsends for their generosity, hospitality and for honoring him with a splendid tea party. Earlier that day, Sally noticed that André and Simcoe had several lengthy conversations together and that the two men would occasionally glance at each other, and their eyes flashed and their lips formed half smiles as if they were sharing some sort of a secret. As André rode off, he gaily waved his farewell and promised to return soon.

On Monday, September 4, 1780, Simcoe mustered his regiment for drill, and as usual Sally was present. Almost immediately she sensed a heightened level of energy in Simcoe as he addressed his men. She became especially interested when he ordered that all officers and men should have their weapons and accouterments in absolutely first-rate order and that their kits be organized and prepared for an extended march at a moment's notice. After the drill, Sally asked Simcoe the reason for his orders, and Simcoe laughingly told her that he was not going to be surprised by a rebel attack as he had been by the attack on Lloyd's Neck the previous September. Sally had become familiar enough with military matters and Simcoe's style of command to know that he was not telling her the truth. His men were always expected to have their weapons in first-rate order and there had been no dereliction on their part. It simply wasn't like Simcoe to reiterate an order for no apparent reason other than perhaps he was excited about some sort of imminent operation. His excuse about ordering his men to pack for an extended march did not make much sense in the context of his answer. If the Americans launched one of their raids against Long Island, the Queen's Rangers would have to respond swiftly, traveling as lightly as possible and not be encumbered with baggage for an extended march. In truth, anywhere the Americans might attack between Flushing and Setauket could be reached by the Hussars in a matter of hours, and they certainly would not need their full kit. Sally dutifully recorded this new information and hid it away, waiting for the opportunity to pass it along to Robert.

In the meantime, Austin Roe had taken the coded messages that contained Sally's information to Setauket.[9] The night he arrived, he stealthily rode out to Strong's Neck and secretly placed the papers in a strongbox that was buried in a corner of Abraham Woodhull's farm. On Sunday afternoon, September 3, 1780, Roe encountered Abraham Woodhull in the Presbyterian Church[10] yard and privately signaled that a message had been placed at the pickup point. That afternoon, after taking great pains to ensure that he was not observed, Woodhull recovered the packet of coded messages and took them to his house, where he hid them away. Next, Woodhull took his spyglass and turned it east across Little Bay toward a cottage on the shore of Strong's Neck, the servant's quarters for St. George's Manor, where Anna Strong was living. She had taken residence there, because British troops had taken over her manor house after her husband had been imprisoned.

The cottage where Anna Strong lived was plainly visible across Little Bay from Woodhull's yard, but Woodhull focused his glass on the clothesline that stretched between two nearby trees. Anna washed clothes almost daily and several articles of clothing were almost always drying on the line. However, Woodhull specifically looked for a black petticoat, which would have told him that Caleb Brewster was on Long Island. If the black petticoat had been visible, the number of white handkerchiefs, up to six, would have told him in which of the six coves Brewster's whaleboats were hiding. However, Woodhull was disappointed to see there was no black petticoat. Brewster had not yet crossed over to the Long Island side of the Devil's Belt. For the next several days Woodhull periodically scanned the clothesline, hoping that Anna Strong would soon signal Brewster's arrival.

André had returned to New York, and without spending much time at headquarters, he continued up the Hudson River to meet with Benedict Arnold at Dobb's Ferry. The meeting was planned for Monday, September 11, 1780. Arnold was also on his way to meet André at the preplanned location, but the meeting was aborted when a British gunboat opened fire on Arnold's barge as he came down the Hudson toward the rendezvous point. Arnold returned to his headquarters at Beverly House[11] across the river from West Point, and André had no choice but to return to New York and try to establish another rendezvous time. After a clandestine exchange of messages, the two decided to meet again on September 20, 1780. Arnold would send a boat to bring André from the Royal Navy brig *Vulture* that would be anchored somewhere between Dobb's Ferry and Haverstraw Bay.

In Oyster Bay on Thursday, September 14, 1780, Simcoe acted on the orders he had previously received through André regarding the Queen's Rangers participation in the capture of West Point as a result of Arnold's defection. In Oyster Bay, Sally was visiting Daniel and Susannah Youngs, where Daniel mentioned that he had just received orders from Simcoe to requisition wagons and teams for the Queen's Rangers. Realizing that Sally was not aware of Simcoe's order, Daniel let Sally read the copy.

Oyster Bay 14th September, 1780
Sir:

    By order of Colo. Simcoe am directed to desire you to furnish seven waggons or ox teams upon the next advice sent of the Regt. Moving. These waggons will be discharged the first Post the Regt. halts at. This is only to intimate to you to have the teams in readiness upon the first notice that the baggage, stores &c. of the Regt. may not suffer by delay when the march is ordered.

                            Robert Gardner, Sergt. (endorsed) Complied with,
                            Quart. Master, Q. R.[12]

When Sally returned home, she asked Simcoe about the teams. In answer, Simcoe told her he received orders that indicated a possible extended march. He told her that he was not aware of the reason or the possible destination; he was simply ordered to be prepared to march at a moment's notice, and if the Queen's Rangers would have to go into winter quarters away from Oyster Bay, the wagon teams would have their tents, equipment and baggage. Listening to Simcoe's somewhat glib reply, Sally was more than ever convinced that something was up, and she was determined to keep an eye on everything Simcoe and his regiment did, hoping to find out what it might be.

Monday morning, September 18, 1780 in Setauket, the weather was cloudy with strong gusty winds blowing from across the Devil's Belt. Abraham Woodhull walked out into the cold blustery weather and focused his spyglass on Anna Strong's clothesline just as he had regularly done for the past two weeks. This time Woodhull saw that in spite of the weather, Anna was hanging wash on her clothesline. He scanned the line and his heart raced when he saw the telltale black petticoat signaling that Brewster had finally crossed the Devil's Belt and was in Conscience Bay. He also counted the four white handkerchiefs, which pinpointed the cove in which Brewster would be waiting. Woodhull waited until nightfall, then made his way through the darkness along a series of back paths to the cove, where he found Brewster and his crew waiting. The whaleboat commander greeted Woodhull in the hearty manner of a mariner and handed over a dispatch pouch from Tallmadge. In return Woodhull handed Brewster a packet and watched as the whaleboat commander stuffed Woodhull's packet into an oilcloth case that was attached to a three-pound cannonball, in case it had to be hurriedly discarded over the side. Woodhull mentioned that there was urgency attached to the message for Washington and that he hoped it would still be of benefit to Washington. Brewster replied that it couldn't be helped, because not only were storms and high winds buffeting the Devil's Belt for the past week, but British patrol boats were lying thick along the Connecticut shore. Better late than never, they hoped, as Brewster ordered his crew to launch the whaleboat and make ready to take it up to the Narrows, where they would haul it across the sand spit into the Sound. They had to go across the sand spit, because the British fortification on Mount Misery Point across from Old Field Point guarded the narrow channel into Setauket Harbor. Woodhull shook hands with Caleb Brewster and wished him luck. Then he watched as Brewster nimbly leapt aboard his whaleboat, and the crew swiftly rowed away from the shore. The cloud cover indeed made it a dark night, and Woodhull watched as the whaleboat quickly disappeared into the inky darkness.

The Capture of André

Brewster's whaleboat crossed the Devil's Belt unopposed and reached Fairfield around midnight. The dispatches from Woodhull were immediately sent by a series of express riders to Major Benjamin Tallmadge, who was at Lower Salem, New York.[1] By dawn of Tuesday, September 19, 1780, Tallmadge had applied the developing wash to the "blank" pages and had decoded the now visible message. He was intrigued by Sally's references to the letter addressed to "James Anderson" and her suspicion that André was using that name as a nom de guerre. However, Tallmadge was even more curious about the clandestine discussions in Oyster Bay between André and Simcoe in which West Point and the Hudson River were mentioned. Tallmadge hurriedly bundled his decoded messages together to forward on to Washington and enclosed a cover letter that read:

Greenfield, Tuesday morning, 6 o'clock
19th Septr. 1780

Sir.

I have been impatiently waiting at this place for some time for the arrival of C's [Culper's] Dispatches, which have this instant come to hand. A very heavy gale of wind prevented the boat from crossing at the time appointed. I hope the enclosed may be satisfactory.[2]

On Wednesday, September 13, 1780, after his first attempt to meet with André two days earlier, Benedict Arnold was taking measures to protect André from any American patrols he might encounter. On Wednesday evening, September 20, 1780, Benjamin Tallmadge received a letter from Benedict Arnold dated September 13. One paragraph in Arnold's message immediately caught Tallmadge's attention.

If Mr. James Anderson, a person I expect from New York should come to your quarters, I have to request that you will give him an escort of two Horse to bring him on his way to this place, and send an express to me that I may meet him. If your business will permit I wish you to come with him.

B. Arnold[3]

Benedict Arnold was certainly familiar with Benjamin Tallmadge as the leader of a troop of continental dragoons, but he had no idea that Tallmadge's real duties were to coordinate Washington's spy networks. Arnold had unknowingly ordered Washington's head of intelligence operations to escort André to Arnold's headquarters. Ironically, André was Tallmadge's counterpart in the British espionage system.

Tallmadge recalled that just the day before, he had read the name "James Anderson" in Townsend's coded message from Long Island. The pragmatic intelligence officer was not readily inclined to accept this as mere coincidence, and he determined to dig deeper into the matter. Tallmadge responded to Arnold the following day in a letter that contained no hint of his unease at Arnold's reference to "James Anderson."

> Lower Salem, Septr. 21, 1780.
>
> Sir.
>
> I had the Honor last evening to receive your favor of the 13th inst.[4] I arrived here in due season, and as I was absent on Command by special Directions of His Excellency Genl. Washington, the letter was opened and the instructions therein contained I trust have been duly attended to. I expect to join Col. Jameson immediately, and should Mr. Anderson come to my Qrs. I will do the needful, and shall be very happy to wait on him to Hd.Qrs.... I have also just received an accurate return of the Enemy, so far as respects their Corps and the Posts they occupy. If you have not the present distribution of the Enemies forces, I can give it to you from the best authority, and taken on the spot. The Express is now waiting. I have no time to add, save that I am with Every Sentiment of Esteem, Sir, your most Obedt. Servt.
>
> Benj. Tallmadge[5]

On the night of Thursday, September 21, 1780, Benedict Arnold sent an acquaintance, Joshua Hett Smith of Haverstraw, and the brothers Samuel and Joseph Cahoon to go by boat to pick up André from the *Vulture*, which lay about twelve miles from Haverstraw. If it were necessary for Smith and the Cahoon brothers to row as far as Dobb's Ferry to meet the *Vulture*, Arnold gave Smith the password for the day, which was "Congress." In the meantime, Arnold waited for André at Smith's house in Haverstraw. Arnold had also given Smith a pass dated September 22, 1780, in case he and André should encounter American patrols enroute.

> Head Quarters, Robinson House,
> Sep'r 22d, 1780 ___
>
> Joshua Smith has permission to pass with a boat and three hands and a flag to Dobb's Ferry, on public business, and to return immediately.
>
> B. Arnold, M. Gen.[6]

Joshua Hett Smith returned with André in the early hours of Friday, September 22, 1780, and Arnold and André conversed in the woods until about four o'clock in the morning. Realizing that it was too late for André to return to the *Vulture* under cover of darkness, the two conspirators went to Joshua Smith's home to wait until the following night to row André back to the *Vulture*. Arnold and André reached Smith's house about dawn, and no sooner had they entered than they heard cannon fire. Colonel James Livingston, who commanded an American four-pounder battery at Teller's Point on the east side of the Hudson River, discovered the *Vulture* just offshore and immediately opened fire. Both André and Arnold watched in horror from an upstairs window as the *Vulture*, which had sustained several hits, got under way and sailed out of sight down the Hudson River. The departure of the *Vulture* effectively stranded André behind American lines. André sensed that the operation was deteriorating rapidly, and the odds of success were getting longer. The two men tried to think of some way of getting André to the *Vulture*, but no plan seemed feasible. Arnold finally decided that they had no choice but to improvise a new escape route to New York; André would have to return by a longer and more dangerous overland route.

Smith was ordered to guide André through the American positions, and in order that André would remain inconspicuous, Smith was told to provide André with a coat. André reluctantly removed his bright red uniform tunic and made the fatal mistake of traveling in disguise. Now, if he were captured, he would without question be considered a spy. In addition, Arnold gave André several incriminating documents describing the fortifications, defenses and personnel at West Point, which André hid in his stockings. One was a chart titled "Return of ordnance in the different forts batteries, etc. at West Point and its dependencies." There were also documents that described the construction of the various fortifications, the size of their garrisons, and the disposition of artillery protecting them.

In the event that André and Smith were stopped by American patrols, Arnold furnished them with passes.[7] The first pass was for both Smith and Mr. "John" Anderson, which for some reason Arnold used as André's alias instead of the "James" Anderson he mentioned in his message to Tallmadge.

Head-Quarters, Robinson's[8]
House Sep[t] 20th, 1780 .

Permission is given to Joshua Smith Esquire, a gentleman, Mr. John Anderson, who is with him and his two servants, to pass and repass the guards near King's Ferry at all times.

B. Arnold, M. Genl..

Arnold also gave André a second pass to protect him from American patrols after he left the company of Joshua Hett Smith.

> Head-Quarters Robinson's
> House Sep.ᵗ 22nd. 1780
>
>   Permit Mʳ. John Anderson to pass the guards to the White Plains, or below, if he Chuses. He being on Public Business by my Direction.
>
> B. Arnold M. Genˡ.[9]

Smith and André, along with Smith's Negro servant set out on Friday afternoon and crossed the river at King's Ferry, just below Stony Point, while Arnold returned to his headquarters at Beverly House. André and Smith spent the night at Crompond, New York, about three and a half miles east of the Hudson River. They started out again before dawn on Saturday, September 23, 1780, and when they reached Pine's Bridge over the Croton River, Joshua Hett Smith left André to complete the remaining fifteen to twenty miles alone. The area south of their present location all the way to the British lines was not under the control of either side, and because of the possibility of encountering a British patrol Smith was reluctant to travel any further. In the unlikely event that André should encounter an American patrol, he would have to depend on Arnold's pass to provide him safe conduct.

The previous morning, Friday, September 22, 1780, in Oyster Bay, Sally watched as the Queen's Rangers formed up with equipment for what appeared to be an extended deployment. She asked Simcoe where he was going and how long he would be gone, to which he answered tersely that they were marching to headquarters at Jamaica where the regiment would receive further orders. Unable to get any additional information regarding the purpose of their deployment, Sally could only watch and wonder as the Queen's Rangers marched out of town. Unknown to Sally, Simcoe was fully aware of his regiment's destination. Once the Queen's Rangers reached Jamaica, Simcoe turned west and continued to Staten Island, where he and his regiment waited for word from André. The Queen's Rangers were part of the force that would take West Point, and now Simcoe was in position to move the regiment swiftly up the Hudson as soon as he received word that Arnold was ready to surrender the fort.

Somewhere north of White Plains, André was making his way alone through the neutral area toward New York. The neutral area was the region between the British and American lines that was not completely controlled by either army. Early Saturday morning, September 23, 1780, André met some northbound travelers who told him they had seen American patrols ahead on André's planned route. Hoping to avoid the Americans, André turned southwest toward Tarrytown, from where he planned to make his way along the Hudson, thinking that area more likely to be patrolled by the British. The area of no-man's land between the Croton River and Tarrytown was notorious for "cowboys" and "skinners" who preyed on anyone they encountered, regardless of their political allegiance. "Cowboys" and "skinners" were essentially marauders or brigands who operated in the neutral areas of New York. Their main occupation was stealing cattle, which they sold in New York City. The names were loosely applied to all thieves, but the cowboys were generally considered to be Loyalists while the skinners were thought of as favoring the Whig faction. André apparently considered encountering them to be less of a threat than meeting an American patrol.

Just before ten o'clock in the morning near the bridge to Tarrytown, André was stopped and challenged by John Paulding (1758–1818), Isaac Van Wart[10] (1762–1828) and David Williams (1754–1831), who emerged from the underbrush and pointed their muskets at his chest. Paulding had been a prisoner of the British for a short time and escaped only a few days before, taking a Hessian uniform coat with him. André noticed Paulding's Hessian coat and made the fatal mistake of assuming the three were Loyalists. Instead of presenting Arnold's pass, André greeted them gaily, "My lads, I hope you belong to our party." Paulding kept his musket aimed at André's heart and replied, "Which party is that?" André, thinking they were Loyalists, answered that he belonged to "the lower party," meaning the Loyalist faction. Paulding nodded and answered, "We do," which caused André to blurt out, "Thank God, I am once more among friends. I am glad to see you, I am a British officer; I have been up in the country on particular business, and I hope you won't detain me a minute."[11] To illustrate the fact that he was a British officer, André then showed them his gold watch. He hoped to convince them that an expensive item like a gold watch was beyond the means of a provincial rebel. The gold watch certainly caught the three men's attention, but not in the manner André anticipated. Paulding stepped closer and thrust his musket barrel menacingly toward André's breast and ordered him to dismount. Paulding then told André that they were Americans, and André realized his mistake in assuming the three were Loyalists, and he tried to change his story. He produced the pass signed by Benedict Arnold and attempted to make light of it. "God bless my soul, a body must do anything to get along now-a-days." Then he told the men, "My, lads, you had best let me go or you will bring yourselves into trouble, for your stopping me you will detain General Arnold's business; I am going to Dobb's Ferry to meet a person there and get information for him."[12] Paulding appeared to be cowed by André's reference to Benedict Arnold and was unsure what to do, but one of the men stepped forward and said, "Damn Arnold's pass. You said you was a British officer. Where is your money? Let's search him!"[13] André was ordered to strip and his captors found two watches, the gold one he had exhibited to them and a silver watch engraved with André's name. They pocketed both watches along with some money André was carrying. It was André's polished white-topped boots that had first attracted the men's attention, and now they ordered him to remove them. André pulled off his boots and the men noticed that papers were hidden in his stockings. The documents were removed and examined, and the incriminating documents pertaining to West Point were found. John Paulding was the only one of the three who could read, and when he examined the papers, he exclaimed, "He's a spy!"[14]

André's final effort to gain his release was his suggestion that he would write a letter to General Clinton requesting a payment of one hundred guineas for his release. He proposed that while two of the men remain guarding him, the third would deliver the message and return with the money. In addition they could have his watches, his horse, bridle and "any quantity of dry goods"[15] they would want. When he saw the men hesitate, André quickly added that they would be rewarded with ten thousand guineas. The last sum was so exorbitant that it likely caused more suspicion than greed. The three men thought it over, but one of them suggested that whoever delivered the letter would likely be arrested and interrogated and the British would send an armed party to capture the other two. Instead, the three decided they would play it safe and deliver their captive to the American post at North Castle.

They arrived at North Castle at about five o'clock in the afternoon, and Paulding and his confederates turned over their prisoner "John Anderson" to Lieutenant Colonel John Jameson (1751–1810), the commander of the post. Jameson was somewhat puzzled why Anderson, who had a pass signed by Benedict Arnold was apprehended in the first place, but when Jameson examined the documents found on the prisoner, he saw they appeared to be "of a very dangerous tendency."[16] Jameson was in a quandary, because Arnold was his superior officer and regardless of the suspicious circumstances, "John Anderson" had a pass signed by Major General Benedict Arnold. Jameson decided to play it safe by sending an express rider to General Washington with a letter describing the apprehension of "John Anderson" along with the captured documents. Since the prisoner carried a pass signed by Benedict Arnold, Jameson decided to send a patrol commanded by Lieutenant Solomon Allen (1751–1821) to escort "John Anderson" to Arnold's headquarters. Jameson included a message describing the events of the capture of Anderson and a description of the documents that had been found hidden in Anderson's stockings. The message also explained that the original documents and a similar letter had been dispatched to General Washington.

Lieutenant Allen had already set out with his prisoner when Major Benjamin Tallmadge returned to North Castle. When Tallmadge heard of the capture of "John Anderson," he remembered the message he had received three days earlier in which Sally Townsend referred to a "James Anderson" and her suspicion that Major John André was using that alias. The quick-witted Tallmadge immediately suspected that the prisoner was André, who was on some type of covert operation. Furthermore, since André was carrying a pass signed by Benedict Arnold, the association of those two individuals required further investigation. Tallmadge insisted that Jameson recall Lieutenant Allen and keep the prisoner in custody at North Castle. He also advised Jameson that Benedict Arnold should not be informed of the matter until it could be sorted out. Jameson argued that it would be insubordination not to inform Arnold, who was his superior officer, and he indignantly stated that it was unthinkable to suspect a commanding general, especially one as distinguished as Arnold, of anything bordering on treason. Since Jameson outranked Tallmadge, he initially refused to recall the prisoner until he remembered Tallmadge's well-known influence with General Washington. That caused Jameson to give in. Even so, Jameson would only agree to retrieve the prisoner, but he insisted that Allen continue to Arnold's headquarters and deliver Jameson's message regarding the apprehension of "John Anderson." The necessary orders were issued, and Lieutenant Joshua King (1758–1839) and a party of swift-riding dragoons caught up with Lieutenant Allen around Peekskill and retrieved the prisoner. In an ironic twist of fate, the final canto to André's satirical poem "The Cow Chace" was published in the Saturday, September 23, 1780, edition of the *Royal Gazette*; the very day of John André's capture. The final verse contained the somewhat prophetic stanza:

> And now, I've clos'd my epic strain,
> I tremble as I shew it,
> Lest this same warrior-drover Wayne,
> Should ever catch the poet.[17]

On Sunday, September 24, 1780, after having been questioned by Major Benjamin Tallmadge, the prisoner "John Anderson" admitted that he was in fact Major John André, adjutant general of the British army.

On Staten Island, John Simcoe was nervous and edgy. He queried every express rider he saw whether there were any messages for the Queen's Rangers. He sent several of his own express riders to New York and anxiously waited for their return. He continually paced his bivouac area, nervously waiting for orders. No one in the British command was yet aware that André had been captured and that their plan to take West Point had unraveled.

On Monday morning, September 25, 1780, Jameson's express rider brought Benedict Arnold two messages. The first contained word of André's capture, and it read in part, "Sir; I have sent Lieutenant Allen with a certain John Anderson, taken going into New York. He had a passport signed in your name. He had a parcel of papers taken from under his stockings, which I think of a very dangerous tendency. The papers I have sent to General Washington."[18] The second message however, informed Arnold that Jameson had in fact rescinded his order to deliver "Anderson" to Arnold at West Point. However, while André was solidly a prisoner of the Americans, the incredibly imprudent Colonel Jameson had alerted Arnold in sufficient time to escape.

Arnold now realized that Washington likely had the incriminating documents that were found in André's possession. He also knew that Washington was approaching the Beverly House with a strong detachment of his mounted Life Guards, and at most they were only a few miles away. Arnold knew that once Washington read Jameson's letter and examined the captured documents, he would understand their significance and quickly realize that Arnold was involved in a treasonous plot with André. Arnold's only alternative was to flee before Washington arrived at the Beverly House. Once Washington and his elite guards arrived, any hope of escape for Arnold would be gone. Arnold ran to his bedroom to tell his wife, Peggy, that he had no choice but to flee. He then told his staff he was going to make a quick trip across the river to West Point, but instead he fled to his barge on the river and ordered the crew to ferry him down the Hudson to the *Vulture*.

At first Arnold's barge crew was somewhat reticent to approach the British warship, but Arnold told them they were proceeding "as a flag,"[19] and he promised them two gallons of rum when they returned. Captain Andrew Sutherland (?–1795), commander of the *Vulture*, and Colonel Beverly Robinson (1721–1792) were anxiously awaiting the return of John André, and they both breathed a sigh of relief when they saw Arnold's barge approaching. Beverly Robinson was born in Virginia and served with Wolfe at Quebec during the French and Indian War. He married the wealthy Susanna Phillipse (1727–1822) and settled in New York. When the Revolutionary War started, Robinson sided with the Loyalist cause and was colonel of the regiment that he raised. His country mansion, "Beverly House," located across the river from West Point, was taken over by the Whigs, and the house became Benedict Arnold's headquarters.

As Arnold's barge neared the *Vulture*, it quickly became apparent that André was not on board, and Sutherland and Robinson became very concerned. Arnold climbed aboard the *Vulture* and brought his barge crew on board, where they loitered, gossiping with the British sailors. In Sutherland's cabin Arnold explained that the plan to surrender West Point had been undone by André's capture. The two men admonished Arnold for sending André overland rather than returning him to the *Vulture* by water, and both Robinson and Sutherland were fearful of General Clinton's reaction when he learned of André's capture.

Arnold apparently tried to demonstrate that the example of his defection would cause other Americans to follow suit. He went on deck and told his astonished barge crew that he had abandoned the American cause and had gone over to the side of the British, grandly announcing that he was now a British general and was empowered to raise a Loyalist brigade. He promised his barge crew that if they would join him, he would make them all noncommissioned officers, and he told his coxswain, Corporal James Larvey (some accounts use the name Lurvey), that he would even do something more for him if he joined Arnold. "No sir!" Larvey indignantly replied. "One coat is enough for me to wear at one time."[20]

There are differing accounts as to what happened next. The popular version is that Arnold became enraged at Larvey's response, and he ordered the British seamen to place the American bargemen in irons and take them below. Larvey stood his ground and said that he and his crew had come on board "under sanction of a flag," but Arnold was adamant and ordered Sutherland to confine the bargemen in the hold as prisoners of war. When the prisoners were taken to New York, General Clinton considered their capture while under a flag of truce as dishonorable, and he ordered that they be immediately paroled. However, the American General William Heath (1736–1814), who took over command of the Highland Division after Arnold's defection, wrote in his memoirs, "When Arnold got under the guns of the *Vulture*, he told Corporal Larvey, who was cockswain of the barge, that he was going on board the ship, not to return, and if he, Larvey, would stay with him, he should have a commission in the British service. To this Larvey, who was a very smart fellow, replied, that he would be d__d if he fought on both sides. The General [Arnold] replied that he would send him on shore. Arnold then told the barge crew that if any of them would stay with him they should be treated well, but if they declined staying, they should be sent on shore. One or two stayed, the rest with the cockswain, were sent on shore in the ships' boat; the barge was kept. Larvey, for his fidelity, was made a sergeant. He thought he deserved more, and that he ought to have as much as Arnold promised him.

He continued uneasy until, at his repeated request, he was allowed to leave the army."[21]

By Tuesday, September 26, 1780, news of the capture of Major John André by the Americans had spread like wildfire through the city. The adjutant general of the British army was now a prisoner of the Americans. It was during this time that Simcoe learned of André's capture and that the plan to capture West Point had collapsed. He immediately dispatched an express rider to headquarters with a message that his regiment was ready to travel at a moment's notice. In his message he appealed to Clinton "that if there was any possibility of rescuing him [André], he and the Queen's Rangers were ready to attempt it, not doubting to succeed in whatever a similar force would effect."[22]

No sooner did the express rider race off toward Clinton's headquarters than Simcoe summoned his officers and told them that because of André's stature in the army, it was likely that he would be sent to Philadelphia to be examined by the American Congress. In hopes of intercepting and rescuing André, Simcoe ordered his Hussars to patrol the roads between Washington's headquarters at Tappan and Philadelphia.

Desperate to help his friend, Simcoe also wrote a letter to the American Colonel Henry "Light Horse Harry" Lee, whom he had met while he was a prisoner of the Americans in 1779. Simcoe asked Lee to try to arrange a meeting to discuss an exchange of prisoners, but Simcoe's real motive was to get information regarding André's whereabouts in order to devise a plan to secure André's release. Simcoe's letter traveled through the lines under a flag of truce, but it did not reach Lee for several days.

Now that the Americans were aware of the plot, the British abandoned the operation to take West Point. Dejected, Simcoe led his rangers back to Long Island, and on Wednesday, September 27, 1780, Sally watched as Simcoe and his regiment somberly marched into Oyster Bay. When he saw Sally waiting in her front yard, Simcoe spurred his horse forward and dismounted by her side, blurting out that André had been captured by the Americans. He looked so sad and dejected that Sally was moved to console him, and in truth she was sorry that the genial André had been taken prisoner. "At least," she reasoned, "he was not harmed and would likely soon be exchanged." However, it was apparent from Simcoe's expression that he was not as certain as Sally of André's safety.

Simcoe's intuition proved correct. The next day, Thursday, September 28, 1780, he received another dispatch from headquarters informing him that André was captured behind American lines, using a false identity, wearing civilian clothing and carrying several incriminating documents. The message went on to state that the Americans planned to try André as a spy. When she heard Simcoe's pained gasp, Sally rushed to his side, and she felt her own chest tighten as Simcoe explained that their friend André could be hanged as a spy. She tried to reassure herself as well as Simcoe that the adjutant general of the British army would never be a spy or even be considered as one, but Simcoe replied that unfortunately, the truth was otherwise. Sally could hardly believe her ears when Simcoe explained that André was on a secret mission to arrange for the defection of Major General Benedict Arnold, the rebel's most accomplished fighting general. As Simcoe talked, everything Sally had seen and heard during André's last visit began to make sense. Simcoe stammered on how André was captured using the alias of either John or James Anderson and that he was finalizing the defection of Arnold and the surrender of West Point on the Hudson. He said that if successful, the capture of the vital stronghold could have quickly ended the war with a British victory. Simcoe added that he had been privy to the plan, and he and his Rangers were to be among the first troops involved in taking West Point and its garrison. They had waited at Staten Island for the signal to dash up the Hudson, but the plan had been undone by André's capture. Sally became fully aware that a guilty verdict to a charge of spying would likely result in André's execution, and she was terribly saddened that the elegant, artistic and fun-loving prankster André, whom she considered a dear friend, was in grave jeopardy. The fact that André was caught using the alias "Anderson" certainly caught her attention, and she realized that her message must have played a part in André's capture. That realization caused her great turmoil. On one hand she was excited that she may have been instrumental in preventing the loss of the vital fort on the Hudson, but on the other she was concerned about her action's dreadful cost to a dear friend.

Simcoe finally received a response from Colonel Henry "Light Horse Harry" Lee on Monday, October 2, 1780. Lee's message bluntly stated that Major John André had been tried and sentenced to death for spying, and that the date and time of the execution was set for five o'clock in the afternoon of October 1, 1780. When Simcoe read Lee's letter, he believed that André had been executed the day before. However André had been given a short reprieve.

As a courtesy, Washington wrote to the British commander-in-chief, General Clinton, informing him of the verdict.

To his Excellency Sir Henry Clinton,
Headquarters, Sept. 30, 1780.

Sir,

In answer to your Excellency's letter of the 26th instant, which I had the honor to receive, I am to inform you that Major André was taken under such circumstances as would have justified the most summary proceedings against him. I determined, however, to refer his case to the examination of a Board of General Officers, who have reported on his free and voluntary confession and letters, "That he came on shore from the *Vulture* sloop of war, in the night of the 21st of September instant," &c. &c, as in the report of the Board of General Officers.

From these proceedings, it is evident Major André was employed in the execution of measures very foreign to the objects of flags of truce, and as such they were never meant to authorize or countenance in the most distant degree; and this gentleman confessed, with the greatest candor, in the course of his examination, "That it was impossible for him to suppose he came on shore under the sanction of a flag."

> I have the honor to be your Excellency's
> Most obedient and most humble servant,
> G. Washington[23]

Washington's letter to Clinton was delivered to a British officer at Paulus Hook by Captain Aaron Ogden (1756–1839), an American light infantry officer in General Lafayette's brigade. Ogden carried four messages, including Washington's letter. One letter was from Peggy Arnold to her husband[24]; another was a personal letter from André to Clinton. The fourth letter, addressed to Clinton, was surreptitiously slipped into the packet and is believed to be a clandestine message from Lieutenant Colonel Alexander Hamilton (1757–1804), who was Washington's secretary and aide-de-camp. In it Hamilton wrote:

> It has so happened in the course of events that Major André, adjutant general to your army, has fallen into our hands. He was captured in such a way as will, according to the laws of war, justly affect his life. Though an enemy, his virtues and his accomplishments are admired. Perhaps he might be released for General Arnold, delivered up without restriction or condition, which is the prevailing wish. Major André's character and situation seem to demand this of your justice and friendship. Arnold appears to have been the guilty author of the mischief and ought more properly to be the victim, as there is great reason to believe he meditated a double treachery and had arranged the interview in such a manner that if discovered in the first instance, he might have it in his power to sacrifice Major André to his own safety.

The letter had an added postscript that urged, "no time was to be lost."[25]

Without a doubt, André's life could have been saved in an exchange for Benedict Arnold, and Clinton was unquestionably tempted by the offer for the return of his favorite adjutant general. Other than having an officer of Arnold's stature switch sides, none of the other plot's dividends were forthcoming. In fact, Clinton soon realized that Arnold was of dubious value to the British high command. Most British officers considered Arnold's actions dishonorable and publicly voiced the opinion that a turncoat could not be trusted, no matter which coat he was wearing at the time. Regardless, Clinton knew that trading Arnold to the Americans for André was completely out of the question, because military policy prohibited such a trade. If Arnold were given up, it would deter any future defections from the Americans. Arnold was certainly aware that overtures were made to have him given up in return for André. Legend has it that Arnold queried an American officer who was a prisoner of the British, asking what the Americans would do if they ever captured him. The officer knew that Arnold had been one of the most heroic of America's fighting generals, having been seriously wounded twice in his left leg, which was now two inches shorter than the other and which caused him constant pain. The officer sarcastically replied that the Americans would cut off his shortened leg for a Christian burial, and hang the rest of him from the nearest tree.

General Clinton rushed a response to Washington requesting a delay, so that the British could provide new information that would mitigate André's situation. Clinton proposed to send emissaries to parley at Dobb's Ferry with either Washington or his representatives, inferring that his deputies would present "a true state of the facts."[26] Washington acquiesced, and André's execution was postponed for one day. Clinton sent as his emissaries General James C. Robertson (1717–1788), Lieutenant Governor Andrew Elliot (1728–1797), and Chief Justice William Smith (1728–1793), who incidentally was Joshua Hett Smith's brother. Washington appointed General Nathaniel Greene to represent him at the parley. André was informed of the postponement, which coincided with a letter he received from Clinton. The letter and postponement must have given André some encouragement. Clinton wrote, "God knows how much I feel for you in your present situation, but I dare hope you will soon be returned from it—believe me, dear André."[27]

At the same time, Benedict Arnold also sent a letter to Washington that was given to Greene. In it Arnold expressed his gratitude and thanks for the kindness and care Washington had shown to Peggy Arnold, and he also made a plea for André's life. "Suffer me to entreat your excellency for your own and the honor of humanity, and the love you have of justice, that you suffer not an unjust sentence to touch the life of Major André." But then Arnold unwisely chose to add a threat to Washington. "But, if this warning should be disregarded, and he suffer, I shall call heaven and earth to witness, that your excellency will be justly answerable for the torrent of blood that may be spilt in consequence."[28]

At Dobb's Ferry, Nathaniel Greene would only meet with General Robertson, who was the sole military person of the three. All that Elliot and Smith could do was watch from a distance. Instead of presenting anything new or even a "true state of the facts," Robertson reiterated that André was under the protection of a flag of truce. He also made the surprising argument that "whether a flag was flying or not was of no moment,"[29] because André had landed and acted under Arnold's direction. Greene cited André's own admission that he did not travel under protection of a flag and that André was no less involved in the enterprise than Arnold. Robertson attempted to further delay the execution by requesting another inquiry in which Generals Knyphausen and Rochambeau be included, because "both are distinguished gentlemen with knowledge of war and nations; and since they are neither British nor American, they will undoubtedly be more objective."[30] General Greene flatly stated that André would be released on one condition, the surrender of Benedict Arnold to the Americans. When Robertson answered only with "a look," the parley ended. After Washington listened to Greene's report that nothing new was presented to change the verdict of the court martial, he rescheduled the execution for Monday, October 2, 1780, at twelve noon.

On Long Island, John Graves Simcoe continued to receive updates regarding the status of the discussions with the American emissaries in hope of some progress in obtaining André's release. When the negotiations appeared to be faltering, Simcoe became desperate. He again appealed to Clinton to allow his Queen's Rangers to attempt a rescue operation. Simcoe also had hopes that through Colonel Henry "Light Horse Harry" Lee, he could somehow arrange an exchange of Arnold for André. Unfortunately, it all came to naught, because at twelve noon on Monday, October 2, 1780, thirty-year-old Major John André was hanged at Tappan, New York, as a spy.

22

Cries for Vengeance

Simcoe learned the details of the death of his friend through André's servant, Peter Laune, who brought clean clothing and regimentals for André from New York and stayed to attend to the major. André was reconciled to his death but hoped that he would be able to die a "soldier's death" by firing squad rather than suffer an ignominious end on the gibbet. Tears filled both Simcoe's and Sally's eyes when they learned that when André's request to be shot rather than hanged was denied, André sadly commented, "It will be but a momentary pang."[1] Sally sobbed openly when Simcoe read aloud André's last words, "I request you, gentlemen, that you will bear me witness to the world that I die like a brave man."[2] Sally knew that on some level she had helped save West Point from falling to the British, but at the same time she was guilt-ridden that her actions may have led to the death of the dear, artistic, and fun-loving John André. She was even more saddened by the grief it caused John Simcoe. She wished with all her heart that Arnold had been taken instead of André, and she secretly questioned herself whether she could play the same role again.

Sally noticed a change in Simcoe after the death of his close friend André. He was frequently absent from the Townsend home, and when he was present, he said little and rarely smiled. In the past, Simcoe considered American Whigs as misguided Englishmen at worst, who sooner or later would realize the error of their ways and return to the warm embrace of the British Empire. Now, it appeared that Simcoe regarded her countrymen as little more than murderous barbarians, and when he spoke of the André affair, Simcoe refused to speak of it as a military execution, but instead he referred to it as an outright murder. He denounced Washington for his "barbarous and ungenerous act"[3] and blamed General Lafayette, who was part of the court-martial board for using his influence to urge Washington to order André's execution. Simcoe read that after André's death, the great lexicographer Dr. Samuel Johnson[4] denounced Americans with, "I am willing to love all mankind, except an American,"[5] and Simcoe echoed Dr. Johnson's sentiment at every opportunity.

167

Sally chided Simcoe by asking whether he felt the same about her family and whether he also considered her unworthy of love. Simcoe softened his tone somewhat in response, but Sally felt that on some level the bereaved lieutenant colonel was indeed including her with all Americans. As the days passed it became very apparent to Sally that Simcoe's bitterness toward Americans was not abating and that his feelings toward her were changing for the worse. She sadly sensed an ever-widening gap separating what Simcoe considered his world from hers. She saw that he no longer looked at her in the same manner as when he handed her his Valentine poem or when he proposed to her. He seemed indifferent when she appeared, and he no longer walked over to stand by her side while he drilled and trained his men. She noticed that when he did look at her, he sometimes arched his eyebrows as if he was analyzing her loyalty. Sally came to realize that her ranger officer somehow considered all Americans, including her, complicit and responsible for the death of his dear friend André. When she thought of the messages she had sent to her brother that described André's activities in Oyster Bay, she sadly thought to herself that Simcoe was more justified than he realized in her complicity.

As a sign of mourning for André, Simcoe issued orders that his regiment be provided with black and white feathers with which to decorate their caps. As usual, Sally was present when Simcoe had his orders read to the assembled regiment. "He had given directions that the regiment should immediately be provided with black and white feathers as mourning, for the late Major André, an officer whose superior integrity and uncommon ability did honour to his country, and to human nature. The Queen's Rangers will never sully their glory in the field by any undue severity: they will, as they have ever done, consider those to be under their protection who shall be in their power, and will strike with reluctance at their unhappy fellow subjects, who, by a system of the basest artifices, have been seduced from their allegiance, and disciplined to revolt: but it is the Lt. Colonel's most ardent hope, that on the close of some decisive victory, it will be the regiment's fortune to secure the murderers of Major André, for the vengeance due to an injured nation, and an insulted army."[6]

André's death came as a shock to everyone associated with him, including the Townsends. Though André's death caused a great sense of anger and dismay among the British troops and Loyalists, it was nothing compared to the consternation and worry it caused Robert Townsend. Culper Junior was more than aware of the cries for vengeance after André's execution, but he was more concerned that Benedict Arnold might be able to reveal some of the names of the Culper Ring operatives. If that happened, it would be only a matter of time before he and the rest of the group were implicated. If that happened, the British would certainly extract maximum vengeance from the Townsend family as being complicit in André's death. Most of his immediate family would either be summarily hanged or sent to rot in the prison hulks. Robert closed his New York store for almost three weeks, and his accounts show expenditures of over £500 in cash that had been given out to various people, presumably to prepare an escape plan for himself and his family should the need arise.

When Arnold reached New York, he did indeed begin to name some of the citizenry as probable spies and Whig sympathizers. Arnold had previously pressed Washington for names of American agents in the city, but Washington wisely demurred, believing that only those with a need to know should have that information. In fact even Washington did not know the names of many of his most important agents in New York. To ingratiate himself with his new masters, Arnold also volunteered six names of people in Canada who he believed were not loyal to the Crown, and that list included the Jesuit Superior in Québec. During the time Arnold was naming names, Robert Townsend was very concerned, but apparently his clandestine activities had failed to arouse any suspicion. He wrote to Tallmadge on October 20, 1780, saying, "I am happy to think that Arnold does not know my name. However, no person has been taken up on his information. I was not much surprised at his conduct, for it was no more than I expected of him. Genl. Clinton has introduced him to the General officers on parade as General Arnold of the British service, and he is much caressed by General Robinson. This will tend to gloss his character with the venal part of the enemy, but the independent part must hold him in contempt; and his name will stink to eternity with the generous of all parties."[7] However, not all of the agents associated with the Culpers escaped the frenzied witchhunt. In November of 1780, Hercules Mulligan, one of Townsend's contacts in the city, was arrested on the basis of Arnold's allegations that the affable tailor and clothier was a probable spy. Townsend wrote to Tallmadge on November 12, 1780, that "several of our dear friends were imprisoned, in particular one that hath been ever serviceable to this correspondence."[8] In fact Mulligan had been spying for Washington for several years and had some close calls with the British authorities, but fortunately Arnold was unable to furnish any proof. As a result, and much to the chagrin of the British provost marshal William Cunningham, Mulligan was released the following February.[9]

23

A Sad Farewell

A week or so later at dinner, Simcoe informed the Townsends that he and his regiment would be departing the following day and would be gone for an extended period. Sally was profoundly saddened that Simcoe was leaving. She admitted to herself that she did care for him and deep down inside she had hoped that when the war finally ended, he would ask for her hand. Simcoe noticed the sadness in Sally's beautiful eyes, and some of the hardness he acquired after André's death seemed to melt away. He told her how much he appreciated the Townsends' hospitality and how much he enjoyed his time with her. He told her that he might be gone for a year or more, but that he would return again someday. Her sadness increased and tears filled Sally's eyes, because she realized that neither of them really believed his promise to return. A door had closed and neither of them had the key to open it again.

The morning dawned cold and blustery as Lt. Colonel John Graves Simcoe led the Queen's Rangers out of Oyster Bay. Sally watched from the front yard as the regiment marched west on Main Road, and she stood rooted to the spot until the last of the rangers disappeared from view.

Simcoe and the Queen's Rangers joined General Benedict Arnold, now of the British army, in operations in Virginia. Some accounts indicate that General Clinton did not fully trust the turncoat general, and Lt. Colonel Simcoe and Lt. Colonel Thomas Dundas (1750–1794) were sent to keep an eye on him. Dunlap's history of New York states, "A gentleman of the most unblemished character, far advanced in years, assured me, that when Arnold departed from New York in command of the army with which he committed depredations in the Chesapeake, a 'dormant commission' was given to the Colonels Dundas and Simcoe, jointly by Sir Henry Clinton, authorizing them, if they suspected Arnold of a sinister intent, to supercede him and place him in arrest. This proves that Clinton did not trust him, and we may reasonably suppose that a watch was set upon his conduct on other occasions.... The gentleman who communicated it to me, was in his youth a confidential clerk in Sir Henry Clinton's office, and copied and delivered the dormant commission as directed. This explains a passage in Clinton's letter to his government, in which he says, 'this detachment is under the command of General Arnold with whom I have thought it right to send Colonels Dundas and Simcoe, as being officers of experience, and much in my confidence."'[1] The "dormant commissions" that Simcoe and Dundas were given apparently went further than specifying that one of them would take charge of Benedict Arnold's brigade in case of Arnold's capture, death or incapacitation. Apparently General Clinton, not fully trusting a turncoat general, also gave Simcoe and Dundas the authority to arrest Arnold if he should prove untrustworthy in any way. The dormant commission was never acted upon.

Simcoe and the Queen's Rangers later left Arnold's command and joined Cornwallis at Yorktown. It proved to be the end of Simcoe and his rangers' military service in the Revolutionary War. Despite his apparent robust physique, Simcoe was plagued by a series of health problems. At Yorktown, Simcoe's health deteriorated to the point where Colonel Banastre Tarleton took over most of the operational command duties of the Queen's Rangers.[2] As the Franco-American siege closed in on Cornwallis's army at Yorktown, it soon became evident that a British surrender was inevitable. Simcoe approached Cornwallis and requested that prior to the capitulation, Simcoe and his rangers would attempt to escape by light boats across the Chesapeake Bay and make their way back to New York. Simcoe argued that since his corps was composed mainly of Loyalists and deserters from the American army, those members would be subjected to a particularly vengeful persecution by the Americans. Simcoe's journal states that Cornwallis, "was pleased to express himself favourably in regard to the scheme, but said he could not permit it to be undertaken, for that the whole of the army must share one fate."[3]

Cornwallis surrendered his army at Yorktown on Thursday, October 19, 1780, and according to the terms of the capitulation, the British were permitted to retain the temporary use of the 14-gun sloop HMS *Bonetta* as a cartel ship. A cartel ship was used for humanitarian purposes, usually to evacuate wounded troops or to convey prisoners who were being exchanged. The *Bonetta* was allowed to make one voyage to New York, after which it was required to be returned to the French as a prize of war.[4] Because of Simcoe's frail health at that time, he was sent to New York on the *Bonetta*, and also primarily because of Simcoe's urging, the *Bonetta* was crammed with as many Loyalists and American deserters from Simcoe's corps as the ship could hold. They were to be exchanged for Americans that were in British ships.

When Simcoe reached New York, he was invalided back to England. In 1782, he married the wealthy Elizabeth Posthuma Gwillim, and they purchased an estate at Wolford near Honiton in Devon. The two eventually had eleven children. In 1790 he was elected to Parliament, and the next year he was appointed lieutenant governor of the new province of Upper Canada.[5] Simcoe was commended for his administration, but he was never able to moderate his obvious prejudice toward the United States. In 1797 he took the position of civil governor of Santo Domingo with the rank of major general, and in 1798 he was appointed lieutenant general of the County of Devon. In 1801, Simcoe commanded at Plymouth in anticipation of Napoleon's invasion, and in 1806 he was named commander-in-chief in India. However, Simcoe's health continued to deteriorate, and he fell ill on the journey to India. He returned home and died in Exeter on Sunday, October 26, 1806. He never returned to Oyster Bay, nor did he ever see Sally Townsend again.

After the war ended, Robert gradually ended his business connections in the city and moved back to Oyster Bay. Like his sister Sally, he never married, and he continued to live in the Townsend family home, sharing it with Sally until his death on Wednesday, March 7, 1838, at the age of eighty-four. Also, like Sally, Robert took the secret of his wartime espionage and his role in the Culper Ring to his grave.

Sally Townsend continued to live in the Townsend home after the war ended, and according to family lore, her two most cherished possessions were the Valentine poem given to her by John Graves Simcoe and her silhouette that was cut by John André. Sally remained unmarried all her life, because as legend has it, she never again met the likes or equal of John Graves Simcoe. She died on Monday, December 19, 1842, at the age of eighty-two, and she is buried near her brother Robert in the Fort Hill Cemetery, in Oyster Bay.[6]

Thoughts Regarding
Agent 355

Because of a growing pervasiveness of the legend of the mysterious and enigmatic female spy known as "355," any story of the Townsends of Oyster Bay or the Culper Ring would be incomplete without some reference to her. She was first mentioned in a 1948 book by Long Island historian Frank Knox Morton Pennypacker, who alluded to a courageous and daring female spy who became the lover of Samuel Culper Junior (Robert Townsend) and who bore his child before being captured by the British and sent to die on one of the Wallabout Bay prison hulks. The legend was first mentioned in Pennypacker's Volume II of *General Washington's Spies on Long Island and in New York*, and was based on a very tenuous thread of evidence that even Pennypacker referred to as circumstantial. Pennypacker of course, deserves considerable credit for not only documenting most of the activities of the Culper Ring, but also for identifying Robert Townsend as Samuel Culper Junior through handwriting analysis. However, an examination of Pennypacker's evidence regarding "355," whether circumstantial or otherwise, does not stand up very well to scrutiny.

Pennypacker's books about the Culpers and Robert Townsend certainly laid the groundwork for the legend of 355, and with a historian of Pennypacker's stature inferring her existence, other authors were certain to follow. In 1965, former OSS officer Corey Ford wrote *A Peculiar Service*, which expanded considerably on the legend of 355. His excellent and exciting book, which detailed the wartime adventures of the Culper Ring, brought them to life as only a historical fiction could. In the process, Ford enhanced the romantic story of the beautiful, daring, resourceful, and ill-fated spy that became associated with the number 355, which in Tallmadge's "numerical dictionary" was merely the code designation for "lady." Ford based her existence on a relatively ambiguous sentence in an August 15, 1779, coded message from Samuel Culper, Sr. (Abraham Woodhull) to John Bolton (Benjamin

Tallmadge). That sentence read, "I intend to visit 727 [New York], before long and think by the assistance of a 355 [lady] of my acquaintance shall be able to outwit them all."[1] From Corey Ford's book, the story of 355 has grown in many circles from mere conjecture to what many consider accepted fact. The legend of Robert Townsend and 355 as intrepid spies and star-crossed lovers has become so popular that a refutation of 355's existence as depicted by Morton Pennypacker and Corey Ford engenders a backlash from many who refuse to consider otherwise. An examination of what we know versus extant documentation with regard to Robert Townsend and 355 will provide a new perspective and perhaps assist in developing different conclusions regarding her existence or quite possibly who she may have been.

There are no other references in Culper Ring messages that refer to a female agent. In fact, one might question whether Woodhull's sentence refers to a female member of the Culper Ring at all. In Tallmadge's numerical code, "355" represented the word "lady" while "371" stood for "man." Other members of the Culper Ring or even people they were in some way associated with had their own designation. For example, John Bolton (Benjamin Tallmadge) was number "721," Samuel Culper (Abraham Woodhull) "722," Culper Junior (Robert Townsend) "723," Austin Roe "724," Caleb Brewster "725," and James Rivington was "726."[2] Not all people who worked with the Culper's had their own designation, but their names were often spelled out by using Tallmadge's monoalphabetic substitution code as in the case of Jonas Hawkins, which was spelled out in coded messages as "Dqpeu Beyocpu."[3] However, other than the one reference to a nonspecific or generic "lady" no other documentation supports the conclusion that "355" referred to a specific operative within the ranks of the Culper Ring.

Yet from that one sentence, coupled with some vague facts and assumptions, Ford has fleshed out and breathed life into the story of the mysterious woman spy known as "355," and with dogmatic statements based on those suppositions, he created a persona that became accepted in many circles as absolute fact. For example, in *A Peculiar Service*, Ford wrote, "We know that sometime in 1780—perhaps at the same moment that Townsend resigned—she became his common-law wife, and their son was christened Robert Townsend Jr. We know that shortly after Arnold defected to the British she was arrested as a spy, on or about October 20th. Woodhull's letter of that date mentions the imprisonment of 'one that hath been ever serviceable to this correspondence.'"[4]

In the above selection, Ford alleges that in 1780, the agent 355 became the lover of Robert Townsend and apparently became pregnant with his child sometime prior to October 20, 1780, around the time she was accused by the

British as a spy and taken into custody. Ford later states that she was imprisoned on the infamous prison hulk *Jersey*, where she subsequently died, perhaps in childbirth, or shortly after giving birth to their son. Ford further speculates that the baby boy was ultimately smuggled ashore by one Mrs. Deborah Franklin of Brooklyn where he was raised by either Mrs. Franklin herself or possibly another unknown woman. According to Ford, the baby was named Robert Townsend Junior (1784–1862), and Robert Townsend paid for the boy's subsequent upbringing. Ford further states that after Robert Townsend's death, he left a larger inheritance to Robert Junior, who was at the time a member of the New York State legislature. Actually, that part of that story is factual. Robert Townsend left four relatives one hundred dollars each but left Robert Junior five hundred dollars.[5] However, as we shall learn, that inheritance does not prove that 355 was the boy's mother. Ford also cited Robert Junior's involvement in the construction of the memorial and monument to the "Wallabout Bay Martyrs" as further proof of his devotion to his mother, who supposedly perished on board the *Jersey*. We'll try to put each of these issues into a truer perspective.

While it is true that a baby was named Robert Townsend Junior, and that Robert provided for the boy's upbringing, it can't be fully ascertained that Robert was the boy's father. However, we can be certain that the mother was not the mysterious 355. To make the math work, 355 would have had to have been pregnant prior to Saturday, October 20, 1780, the approximate date mentioned as the time of her capture. Even assuming that she had become pregnant shortly before her capture, the latest date that her baby could possibly be born would have been toward the end of July or at the latest, the beginning of August 1781. Genealogical records definitively show that Robert Townsend Junior was not born until February 1, 1784,[6] more than three years and four months after 355's supposed capture. That would certainly rule out the possibility of 355 being the mother, even if the British authorities would have been so incredibly cruel as to keep a pregnant woman on board the hellish prison hulks and require her to give birth under those conditions. So who was the mother? The same records that list Robert Townsend's birth date indicate that he was born in New York City to one Mary Margaret Banvard (1759–1841). Mary was from Lunenburg, Nova Scotia, Canada, and according to the St. John's Anglican Church records in Lunenburg, she was the daughter of David and Elizabeth Carlin Banvard. Mary was baptized in St. John's church in Lunenburg on Saturday, October 21, 1759. It's not known when Mary Banvard came to New York, but she took a job in the city as housekeeper for Robert Townsend, who shared his residence with his older brother William and a yet unidentified cousin. William was reputedly a handsome fellow and was referred to by many of the young women of Oyster Bay as the "Flower of the Family."[7] In addition, William had the reputation of being somewhat of a womanizer. While the 31-year-old Robert assumed responsibility for the boy's upbringing, it's been alleged that either 32-year-old William or the unidentified cousin may have impregnated their 24-year-old housekeeper, Mary Banvard. Robert's nephews Solomon and Peter maintained that Robert Junior, with his "large head, broad face, large prominent blue eyes & solemn features,"[8] bore absolutely no resemblance to Robert, his supposed father. As a matter of fact, Solomon kept a scrapbook, which is presently in the possession of the Raynham Hall Museum, in which he wrote that Robert Junior's mother was the housekeeper in the New York City apartment and that William, not Robert, was likely the boy's father. Did Robert choose to provide for Robert Junior out of a sense of family honor, or did Mary possibly have assignations with more than one of the Townsend bachelors and perhaps named Robert, the more serious and responsible of the three, as the father? If she did, Robert accepted the responsibility, giving the boy his name and paying for his upbringing. However, who actually raised the boy remains unknown. Even the inheritance that Robert left Robert Junior does not appear to settle the paternity question. Certainly Robert left Robert Junior five hundred dollars, which was more than the other cash bequests, but the bulk of Robert's estate was placed in trust for the benefit of his niece Phebe Townsend Thorne, and further, he specified that after her death it should be divided equally between whatever of her children should survive her.

After the birth of Robert Junior, Mary Banvard moved on. She left the employ of the Townsends, and the following year, in 1785, she married one Marmaduke Van Buskirk (?—c. 1794), a veteran of the Revolutionary War. They had one child, a baby girl, Hannah Elizabeth Van Buskirk, who died very young in 1788.

Young Robert Townsend Junior's alleged devotion to his supposed martyred mother, agent 355, does not stand up to scrutiny either. Certainly Robert Junior was involved in the proposed memorial to the American prisoners who died on the prison hulks in Wallabout Bay, but it was to a much lesser extent than one would expect from a person honoring his heroic dead mother. The Oyster Bay town historian Harry Macy researched the question of 355 being Robert Junior's mother and of her having died on one of the prison hulks, but in spite of thorough research, Macy was unable find evidence to support the allegations.

Robert Townsend Junior entered politics, which he found more to his liking after first working as a carpenter. He joined the Tammany Society in 1807 and was elected to the New York State Assembly in 1836. Later he was appointed to the seven-member "Wallabout Committee" that was charged with creating a memorial to the victims who died aboard the prison hulks in Wallabout Bay. The memorial is presently located in Fort Greene Park in Brooklyn and is called the Prison Ship Martyrs Monument. As a member of the committee, Robert's name was included on the cornerstone, but there is really nothing to suggest that Robert Junior's involvement was anything more than doing his civic duty as a politician. After passing a measure for the creation of a memorial, the only progress for several years was the collection of what bones of the victims could readily be found. The bones were haphazardly placed in a poorly constructed crypt near Wallabout Bay that quickly deteriorated. By 1864, the vault had fallen apart, exposing the bones. To make matters worse, the site was also used as a refuse dumping area, which caused several citizens to write complaints about the outrageous condition of the martyrs' final resting place. It wasn't until 1873, eleven years after Robert Junior's death, that some "twenty hogsheads of bones" were moved to a more appropriate vault in Washington Park, or present Fort Greene Park, just south of the Brooklyn Navy Yard. Even so, the monument itself was not erected until 1908. An examination of all of the documents and inscriptions associated with the memorial does not reveal any indication of 355 or even that Robert Townsend Junior's mother may have been one of the prison ship victims.

Robert Townsend Junior died in 1862 and was buried in the Sleepy Hollow Cemetery near Tarrytown, New York, and again there is no reference on his grave or grave markers regarding his supposed martyred mother. In addition, despite a thorough search of British General Clinton's papers at the William L. Clements Library at the University of Michigan and other relevant documentation, I have been unable to find any mention or reference to a woman who bears a remote resemblance to the story or circumstances of a female who was accused as a spy and arrested by the British.

What of Woodhull's message dated November 12, 1780, that informed Benjamin Tallmadge of the aftermath of Arnold's defection the previous month? "I then informed you of the severity on watchfulness of the Enemy. Several of our dear friends were imprisoned, in particular one that hath been ever serviceable to this correspondence. This step so dejected the spirits of C. Junr. That he resolved to leave New York for a time. I earnestly endeavored to prevent it but could not, so that I have no person there that I can send the Express to that can rely upon."[9] Does it infer that the "one who hath been ever serviceable to this correspondence" is in fact 355? Of course not. In the aftermath of Arnold's defection and the execution of the popular Major John André, a great hue and cry for revenge arose among the British military. Anyone who came under any suspicion of working for the American patriotic cause was rounded up and locked up in Bridewell or the Provost Prison. Benedict Arnold himself denounced over fifty individuals who were arrested as American sympathizers or probable spies. One of the most productive American spies arrested during this period was the affable and gregarious clothier Hercules Mulligan (1740–1825), who had previously been incarcerated for running afoul of the British authorities. Fortunately, each time he had been able to talk his way out of jail, only to resume his espionage activities.[10] Although he was not a member of the Culper Ring per se, he had worked closely with them since about 1778, primarily through Robert Townsend. On Saturday, October 31, 1778, Woodhull sent Tallmadge a coded message regarding the Culpers' association with Mulligan, which stated they were cooperating with a "faithful friend and one of the first characters in the City," who was "making it his business to keep his eyes open upon every movement and assist me in all respects, and meet and consult weekly in or near the city."[11]

Robert Townsend regularly met with Mulligan and even purchased several articles of clothing from Mulligan, who was considered the most fashionable clothier in New York, if not the American colonies. Records indicate that on Thursday, July 29, 1779, Robert Townsend visited Mulligan's shop and purchased a "plum coloured sateen coat and embroidered waistcoat."[12] Given the Culpers' secretive nature, it is somewhat surprising that Townsend publicly associated with the flamboyant clothier spy, but even more remarkable was Townsend's selection of colorful clothing, since he was a practicing Quaker, a sect known for dressing very plainly. Townsend was playing his role to the fullest as a bon vivant New York businessman, coffeehouse owner, and writer for Rivington's newspaper. It was most likely the arrest of Mulligan that precipitated Townsend's decision to lay low during the flurry of arrests following André's death and Arnold's defection, which Woodhull referred to in his November 12, 1780, coded message.

Does this mean that there was no 355, a daring and resourceful woman who worked with the Culpers and provided them with meaningful and significant intelligence about the British war machine? Was 355 the spy who never was? I believe that the answer is both yes and no. There is absolutely no documentary evidence to support the fanciful legend of the beautiful and mysterious 355 as first described by Morton Pennypacker and Corey Ford. In the context that 355 simply was a generic name for "lady" we can unequivocally state that there were in fact 355s or ladies who assisted the Culpers. Three immediately come to mind: Mary Underhill, Anna "Nancy" Smith Strong, and Culper Junior's sister Sally Townsend. At the time, Woodhull may have been referring to one of them, or quite possibly all three.

Mary was the wife of Amos Underhill, and she was also the sister of Samuel Culper Senior, Abraham Woodhull. Mary and Amos operated Underhill's boardinghouse in New York City and were certainly aware of and involved to some extent in Culper Ring activities. We know that Mary inadvertently caused Woodhull to spill his precious supply of sympathetic stain when she came into his room and startled him. It required a special dispatch across the Devil's Belt via Caleb Brewster's whaleboat commandos to replace Woodhull's invisible ink. Quite possibly, in his August 15th message "by the assistance of a 355 of my acquaintance shall be able to outwit them all,"[13] Woodhull may have been referring to his sister Mary, and that her lodging house was the New York terminus for the Culper Ring.

As described in several books about the Culpers, Anna "Nancy" Strong has perhaps the most evidence to support her assistance to the Culper Ring. First of all, Anna Strong was a neighbor of Abraham Woodhull, and the two lived within sight of each other's residence. According to Strong family lore, Anna's husband, Selah Strong, was imprisoned on board the *Jersey* because of "surreptitious correspondence with the enemy," and their home, St. George's Manor on Strong's Neck near Setauket was taken over by British troops. Anna made frequent visits to her husband on the *Jersey*, bringing him food and other necessities. In the process, she likely saved his life. There is some thought among historians that Anna Strong's visits were the basis for the stories of the woman spy on the *Jersey* that morphed into the legend of 355. Living alone on Strong's Neck with her five children, Anna continued to fight the British by assisting her neighbor Abraham Woodhull and the Culper Ring. With British troops occupying her manor house, Anna was forced to live in a small servant's cottage at the edge of her property. That inconvenience proved beneficial to Culper Ring activities, particularly in facilitating the exchange of messages to and from Washington's headquarters. The little cottage was sited near the shore of Little Bay and was plainly visible from Abraham Woodhull's home. By means of a clandestine signaling system, Anna was able to communicate to Woodhull the presence and location of Caleb Brewster's whaleboat men when they arrived from Connecticut. When Brewster arrived in Conscience Bay, he surreptitiously contacted Anna and told her in which of the hidden coves around the bay his whaleboat was located. Anna then signaled Brewster's hidden location to Woodhull by hanging a combination of a black petticoat and white handkerchiefs on her clothesline, which was visible to Woodhull across the bay. Some argue that Anna Strong could not be the person to whom Woodhull was referring, since he inferred that the lady was in New York City. Actually, Woodhull only mentioned that he was going to visit New York City, but he did not state that the lady resided in the city, only that with her assistance they would be able to outwit the British. Anna was certainly an integral part of the Culper Ring's complex message delivery system that conveyed messages back and forth from Washington's couriers in Connecticut, across the Devil's Belt, on Long Island, and to and from New York City.

In his August 15th message, Woodhull may have been referring to none other than Robert's sister Sally Townsend, the Oyster Bay teenager. There is documentary, anecdotal, and a wealth of circumstantial evidence that supports the probability that Sally gathered intelligence, which she passed along to her brother. Knowing Robert's secretive nature, Sally was most likely not even aware of Robert's involvement with the Culper Ring. She may not have heard of the Culpers, or at best only heard mention of a Long Island espionage ring from Simcoe. Robert quite naturally was concerned that any slipup on Sally's part would undoubtedly lead to him. His concerns magnified when Loyalist officers began living in the Townsend home, but his apprehensions really escalated in November 1778, when Simcoe began living there. He knew by reputation that Simcoe was no fool, and worse yet, he could be ruthlessly brutal. Even more worrisome to Townsend was the knowledge that Simcoe's mission included ferreting out enemy espionage activities on Long Island. In short, the spy hunter was living in the home of the spy he was pursuing. Townsend was worried that any misstep by himself or Sally would place all of the Townsends in peril. Long Island historians like Frances Irwin maintain that Sally had been passing information to Robert for some time, and she continued to do so with intelligence that she gleaned from her association with Simcoe and other Loyalists in the Oyster Bay area. But no one was more aware than her brother Robert of the disastrous consequences her discovery would have on the Townsend family and indeed on the Culper Ring.

Robert realized that Sally's messages regarding André and Simcoe's secretive conversations about West Point and André's use of the alias "James Anderson" put Sally in a very precarious position. If the British somehow learned the details of that message, it would quickly be traced back to Sally, and worse, it would implicate her as a spy. Benjamin Tallmadge was also aware that the details of the message were specific enough to be catastrophic to the person who gathered the information. Whether he deduced that the information came from Robert's sister Sally will never be known, because Tallmadge refused to divulge any details of the message even after the war ended. In his memoirs, Tallmadge circumspectly wrote: "I might enlarge greatly in anecdotes relating to this momentous event in our revolutionary war, and especially those which relate to this most accomplished young man [André]. Some things relating to the detention of André, after he had been sent to General Arnold, are purposely omitted, and some confidential communications which took place of a more private nature, serve rather to mark the ingenuous character of the man, than to require being noticed at this time.... There were only four Officers of our Army who knew all the Circumstances relating to the Capture & detention of Major Andre, with the other Incidents above hinted at, & of this Number I am the only survivor. The Question presented to my mind then is simply this; what benefits can result from a full statem^t of this interesting event? I have deliberately concluded never to disclose the circumstances which relate to that interesting event."[14]

Even with assurances from Tallmadge that the details of Sally's information would never be made public, Robert was undoubtedly filled with consternation regarding the precariousness of his and Sally's situation, and it only got worse with the collapse of the Arnold treason plot. Any euphoria among the British and Loyalists that may have resulted from the defection of Arnold was offset by the deep rage and fury that resulted from the death of the popular Major André. Cries of vengeance and retribution against Americans quickly spread, and scores of people were rounded up and imprisoned for suspicion of carrying on "a treasonable correspondence with the rebels for many years, had acted as spies within the British lines and given rebellion every information in their power."[15] In an attempt to impress his British masters, Arnold began to name names of suspected American spies, but fortunately, he did not have much if any concrete information about Washington's spies. Most of his accusations were without proof of any kind, and the majority of those he had implicated were eventually released. Arnold had tried to learn the identities of Washington's spies before his defection and had queried Washington, Lafayette, and Tallmadge about operatives in New York and on Long Island. Fortunately, the three had been very circumspect about sharing that information even with someone of Arnold's stature.

Robert Townsend decided that it was best to prepare for the worst. He closed his store in New York, left the city, and demanded a meeting with Tallmadge to formulate a plan if the British spy hunt should implicate him or any of his family. Tallmadge tried to reassure Townsend that his identity was safe, and that he should continue his intelligence-gathering efforts. However, Culper Junior feared that his and Sally's safety was never more precarious, and he refused to do anything that might arouse suspicion. Tallmadge and Washington became somewhat frustrated at Culper Junior's reticence to continue operations. On Wednesday, October 11, 1780,[16] Tallmadge wrote to Washington describing his communications with Robert Townsend.

The conduct of Arnold, since his arrival at N.Y. has been such, that though he knows not a single link in the chain of my correspondence, still those who have assisted us in this way, are at present too apprehensive of Danger to give their immediate usual intelligence. I hope as the tumult subsides matters will go on in their old channels.

Culper, Junr. Has requested an interview with me on Long Island on the 13th inst.,[17] but in the present situation of affairs I believe it would be rather imprudent. What makes it particularly so at this time is the swarm of Refugee Boats, which cruise along the shore of Long Island. I have wrote Culper, Junr. Assuring him that his name or character are not even known by any other officer but myself in the army, tho should your Excellency wish to have me meet Culper, Junr. I will appoint an interview at any time. with great Regard Regard [sic]

Sir, Your Excellency's most obedient sert.
Benj. Tallmadge[18]

On Thursday October 26, 1780, Washington wrote back to Tallmadge, endorsing his refusal to meet with Culper Junior. "Dear Sir, I recd. your favr. of the 11th, with C. Junior's enclosed. I think you were right in declining an interview at this time, as the enemy would act with more than common rigor just now."

That same day, October 26th, Woodhull wrote a message to Tallmadge, informing him that Culper Junior had decided to cease his espionage activities and leave the city until the frenzied British hunt for American spies abated somewhat. Woodhull's coded letter read:

Dear Sir, ... I have this day returned from New York, and am sorry to inform you that the present commotions and watchfulness of the Enemy at New York hath resolved C. Jur. for the present to quit writing and retire into the country for a time.—Most certainly the enemy are very severe, and the spirits of our friends very low. I did not think myself safe there a moment, and as nothing is like to be done about New York, perhaps it may not much disadvantage to drop it for a time, and if need requires C. Junr. will undertake again.[19]

When Mulligan and the others were arrested as probable spies in October 1780, it must have hit very close to home for Robert Townsend. He undoubtedly felt that if Mulligan or perhaps one of the others who were arrested would inadvertently or through intense interrogation let slip details of Culper Ring activities, it could cause the collapse of their espionage operations, and worse yet, it would unleash the vengeful wrath of the British military upon the Townsend family and friends. Recalling the arrest of his father four years earlier and the severe treatment meted out by Loyalist troops on Long Island, Townsend was certainly aware that if he were implicated and taken by the British, not only would he likely be executed, but also his entire family, including his sister Sally, would pay a terrible price. As a result, Robert decided to lay low until the dust settled from the flurry of accusations and arrests. It was as simple as that. It wasn't that Robert Townsend dropped out of the picture for a while, because he was heartbroken that the British had captured 355, the love of his life, but rather it was his concerns for the well-being of his friends and family, and particularly the safety of his sister Sally, a 355 who assisted the Culper Ring to "outwit them all."

Afterword

On Tuesday, November 25, 1783, the last of the British army finally marched onto their ships, ending the long occupation of New York and Long Island. With their departure, the wartime espionage activities of Sally Townsend and her brother Robert ended, as did the activities of the Culper Ring and the other agents who operated in and around New York. However, the stories of the major characters encountered in the preceding pages did not end there. As the American radio broadcaster Paul Harvey (1918–2009) used to say, "Here is the rest of the story."

John André (1750–1780)

After Arnold's defection, overtures were made by the Americans to exchange André for Arnold, but however much General Clinton and indeed the British officer corps would have wanted to do so, they knew that if Arnold were returned to the Americans for certain execution, it would deter other Americans from switching sides and coming over to the British. As a result, André was sentenced to die on Monday, October 2, 1780.

André was stoical with regard to his sentence, and only made two requests. He asked that his servant be allowed to bring him a fresh British uniform, and also that he be allowed to choose the manner of his death, a firing squad rather than a death on the gallows. Washington acquiesced on the first request, but demurred on the second. A spy deserved and was expected to die on the gallows, and Washington was concerned that to soften the manner of André's execution would cast doubts on the correctness of his being considered a spy, and indeed on the legitimacy of his execution. To further complicate matters, the personable André had quickly endeared himself to his captors, and eyewitnesses reported that Washington's hand shook as he sadly signed the order for execution.

After breakfast, on the day he was to die, André shaved, dressed himself and cheerfully announced to the officers present, "I am ready at any moment, gentlemen."[1] André still hoped that he would die a soldier's death by firing squad, but when he came in sight of the gallows, he involuntarily stopped and took a step backwards. An officer at his side asked him, "Why this emotion, sir?" and André answered as he regained his composure, "I am reconciled to my death, but I detest the mode."[2]

Eyewitness Dr. James Thatcher[3] wrote: "While waiting and standing near the gallows, I observed some degree of trepidation, placing his foot on a stone and rolling it over and choking in his throat, as if attempting to swallow. As soon, however as he perceived that things were in readiness, he stepped quickly into the wagon and, at this moment, he appeared to shrink, but instantly elevating his head with firmness, he said, 'it will be but a momentary pang.'"[4] André removed his hat and neck stock, then slipped the noose over his own head and adjusted it around his neck. Next he removed two white handkerchiefs from his pocket, and after he blindfolded himself he handed the other to the provost, who tied André's arms. Asked if he had any last words, André said, "I pray you to bear witness that I meet my fate like a brave man."[5] The wagon was pulled out from under him, and eyewitnesses said that the first great swing of the rope killed him almost instantly. It is reported that most of the witnesses wept at the death of the personable and popular young officer. Even Washington later wrote that André was more unfortunate than criminal.

Another of the witnesses to André's execution was John Paulding, one of the men who had captured André. He wrote, "I took Andre the 23 of September 1780 and I seen him hung October 2, 1780 for my children."[6] Paulding and the other two men, Isaac Van Wart and David Williams, who had captured André, were hailed as heroes among the populace, but that was not the case among the military establishment. During his trial, André denounced the three as mere brigands who were more interested in robbing him than doing their duty as militia soldiers. In fact, in 1817, when the three requested an increase in their pension, then Congressman Benjamin Tallmadge strongly urged the government to deny them any additional compensation. Tallmadge, who was intimately involved in the event, accepted André's account of the three men's behavior at the time of his capture. As a result, and despite their semi-heroic status among the populace, Tallmadge publically assailed the men's motives, credibility, and actions, and urged Congress to deny their petition, which he succeeded in doing. Congress decided that the three did not merit an increased pension.

After he was executed, André's body was lowered to the ground and buried at the foot of the gallows on what is now André Hill Road in Tappan,

New York. There is a memorial stone within a circular fenced area to commemorate the spot. However, in 1821, some 41 years after his execution and burial, the remains of Major John André were disinterred at the request of Prince Frederick the Duke of York (1784–1827)[7] and reinterred in the "Poet's Corner" of Westminster Abbey in London.

André was just thirty years old when he died.

Benedict Arnold (1741–1801)

After the surrender of Cornwallis's force at Yorktown, Benedict and Peggy Arnold sailed for England, where they arrived on January 22, 1782. Once in England, Arnold hoped to convince the authorities to send him back to America in command of a sufficient force with which he believed he could defeat Washington, reverse the tide of the war and restore the wayward colonies to the crown. It never happened. It was very evident that Arnold's aggressively bloody campaigns against his former countrymen were in fact causing greater resistance to the British. In addition, the Crown, the military, and the British people had for the most part lost interest in pursuing what appeared to be a lost cause. In desperation, Arnold proposed that at the very least, he be given command of a 40-gun frigate to sail against the American Navy, but even that notion was rejected.

Even after the unpopular war finally ended, the Arnolds found themselves increasingly shunned by much of London society. They were hissed when they attended theater, and frequently attacked in the press. The Arnolds found that even old friends like Silas Deane, who fled to England as a result of a congressional investigation, publically shunned the Arnolds. However, it was rumored that the Arnolds often dined with Deane in private. The most notable rejection came when Lord Cornwallis intervened against Arnold when Arnold applied for a position with the East India Company. The Arnolds made claims for recompense for their lost property in America and also for expenses occurred on behalf of the British during the war, but in 1785 they dropped their claim due to the time and expense it would take to prosecute it.

In 1785, Arnold had a brig, the *Lord Middlebrook*, built, and in October of that year he sailed it to Canada. He arrived in Halifax, where he was not welcomed with open arms, so he continued on to St. John, New Brunswick. Approaching St. John, Arnold happened to be sick in bed with the gout, and the ship was in the hands of a pilot. Unfortunately the pilot ran the *Lord Middlebrook* hard aground, wrecking the ship. To make matters worse, the ship was looted of its cargo of flour, beef, butter, and pork.

Over the winter Arnold had a new ship built, the 300-ton *Sheffield*. In addition, he staked out a thousand forested acres near Maugerville, New Brunswick, where he planned to create a town and build a lumberyard. Arnold bought up other choice properties in the area, including lots in the provincial capital of Fredericton. By 1789, Arnold's fleet had grown to four ships, and in July of that year, he sailed from England to New Brunswick on his newest ship, the *Peggy*, bringing his wife, children, and some close friends.

The Arnolds lived fairly opulently compared to the other settlers in a land where all essentials, including cash, were scarce. Arnold imported most of what was needed by the inhabitants, who often purchased necessary commodities from him on credit. Unfortunately there was very little money to be had, and Arnold was faced with the prospect of taking action against debtors. Eventually Arnold was forced to sue in attempts to collect what he was owed. In many cases his debtors were needy families whose husbands and fathers were liable to be jailed. A few were in fact jailed, but Arnold ultimately could not bring himself to dispossess unfortunate families. Even so and in spite of his generosity, many resented the Arnold family's stature and relative comfort.

In 1788, while Arnold was aboard his ship, a fire destroyed his New Brunswick warehouse, lumberyard, and store. Though the properties were insured, the insurance company tried to evade the liability by saying that Arnold may have deliberately arranged for his sons to set the fires to collect the insurance. To make matters worse, Arnold's business partner, Munson Hayt, publically insinuated that Arnold had torched his own properties. Arnold demanded a public apology from Hayt for blackening his reputation. Hayt replied, "It is not in my power to blacken your character, for it is as black as it can be."[8] Arnold filed suit for slander and won the case against Hayt, but the judges insultingly awarded Arnold only twenty shillings for damage to his reputation. After the trial, a mob ransacked Arnold's house, then burnt an effigy of him with the sign "Traitor" attached.

In September 1791, Arnold advertised his house and property for auction, and later that year, he and Peggy sailed for London. Unfortunately for the Arnolds, they were not well received in England either. Many rumors and whispering campaigns constantly assailed Arnold's character and reputation, and he devoted a great deal of energy and time fighting back.

The French Revolution broke out in 1793, and its resultant reign of terror convinced Arnold that he was correct in having sided with England. He believed that the carnage could easily spill beyond the borders of France, possibly even to America and Canada. In 1794 and 1795, he served as a volunteer with British General Sir Charles "No Flint" Grey. Based on Arnold's

British rank after his defection, he petitioned Grey to make him a senior brigadier, but Grey refused. Instead, Arnold organized the British planters of the area into a militia unit and led them in helping to put down a slave revolt on Martinique. Arnold became so popular with the planters and merchants in the Caribbean that when the British withdrew, the inhabitants petitioned the ministry to send Arnold back in command of a relief expedition.

During the early years of the Napoleonic Wars, Arnold was anxious to once again take command of forces in battle. Though he lobbied hard, the ministry was reluctant to assign him a command over the heads of so many other officers. Instead they awarded him five thousand acres in Upper Canada. In addition his wife, his sister, and each of his five children were awarded twelve hundred acres each. Regardless, Arnold's fortunes soon declined in the face of a series of unfortunate events. In 1796, his oldest son, Benedict Arnold VI, died of wounds received fighting in the Caribbean. Then both his and Peggy's health began to decline. In addition, some of his investments did not pay off as hoped. Arnold owned a fleet of privateers, but his monetary return from them was fairly paltry compared to what he expected. He suspected that his captains were cheating him by keeping most of the prize money from captured French ships. Peggy estimated that the privateer captains had cheated Arnold out of more than £50,000. His poor health and deteriorating financial condition took its toll. In 1801, Peggy wrote of Arnold, "He is at present, in the most harassed wretched shape I have ever seen him in."[9] The indomitable Arnold apparently lost the will to continue the fight. He died in the morning of Sunday, June 14, 1801, and was buried without military honors in the little Church of St. Mary's in Battersea, a rather unfashionable suburb of London. The London Post reported, "Poor General Arnold has departed this world without notice, a sorry reflection this for the Pitts and ... other turncoats."[10] He was sixty years old when he died. Peggy died three years later on August 24, 1804, at the age of forty-four, from cancer of the uterus. Among her personal possessions, her children found a locket that contained a snippet of John André's hair. It was said that her husband Benedict Arnold did not know of its existence.

Caleb Brewster (1747–1827)

After the war, in 1784, Caleb Brewster married Anna Lewis (1760–1834), who was the daughter of the wharf owner in Fairfield, Connecticut. Caleb and Anna moved to a farm at Black Rock, Connecticut, between Fairfield and Bridgeport, and they had several children: Sarah (1785–1875), Jonathon

Lewis (1786–1837), Sturges (1789–?), Anna (1790–?), Elizabeth Burr (1792–1796), Racilia (1794–?), Benjamin (1796–?), and Daniel (1802–?). Brewster worked as a farmer and blacksmith, and in 1786, he was appointed captain of a government ship to patrol the coast and interdict smuggling operations. He remained in that position until 1816, when he retired to his farm at Black Rock. Caleb Brewster died on February 13, 1827, and was buried in the Old Burying Ground on present Beach Road, in Fairfield, Connecticut. His headstone reads, "In memory of Captain Caleb Brewster, who died February 13th 1827; aged 79 years. He was a brave and active officer in the Revolution."

Austin Roe (1749–1830)

Austin Roe attained the rank of captain during his early days in the militia, and he proudly carried the title for the rest of his life. In 1773, Austin married the former Catherine Jones (1752–1820), and the couple eventually had eight children: Justus (1773–1847), Hannah (1775–?), Joanna (1777–1779), Stephen (1779–1851), Ebenezer (1781–?), Joanna (1786–?), Sarah (1791–1863), Mary (1793–?), Lewis (1795–?), and Elizabeth (1788–1868). In 1790, then President Washington visited Setauket and spent the night of Thursday, April 22 in Roe's Tavern. Unfortunately, the intrepid Culper Ring courier Austin Roe fell from his horse and broke his leg while rushing home to greet the president. Austin Roe's Tavern has been moved about a quarter mile away from its original location where it once stood on the corner of present Main Street and Bayview Avenue. It's now a private home. In 1798, the Roe family moved to Patchogue and opened Roe's Eagle Hotel on the north side of Main Street. Today, only a stone marker indicates where Roe's hotel stood. In addition to his Eagle Hotel, Roe bought a large farm at Pine Neck on the south side of Long Island, about a mile or so east of Patchogue. Unlike the other members of the Culper Ring, who were reticent to relate the stories of their espionage activities, Austin was not averse at all about sharing the stories of his Revolutionary War adventures. However, he never revealed the identity of the other members of the Culper Ring. Austin Roe died on November 29, 1830, at the age of eighty-one and is buried in the Cedar Grove Cemetery in Patchogue.

Benjamin Tallmadge (1754–1835)

Prior to the War, Tallmadge was a student at Yale with his good friend and classmate Nathan Hale. After graduating as a teacher in 1773, Tallmadge became superintendent of the school in Wethersfield, Connecticut, but when the Revolutionary War began, he enlisted as an officer in the elite 2nd Connecticut Light Dragoons. Tallmadge remained with his unit, even though he took on extra duties as Washington's spymaster, coordinating the activities of the Culper Ring network in New York and on Long Island.

After the Revolutionary War, Tallmadge retired from the army with the rank of colonel, and in 1784, he married his childhood sweetheart Mary Floyd (1764–1805), the daughter of Major William Floyd of Mastic, Long Island, one of the signers of the Declaration of Independence. The couple moved to Litchfield, Connecticut, and eventually had seven children: William Smith (1785–1822), Henry Floyd (1787–1854), Maria Jones (1790–1878), Benjamin (1792–1831), Frederick Augustus (1794–1869), Harriet Wadsworth (1797–1856), and George Washington (1803–1835).

Tallmadge became wealthy through his investments and was the first president of the Phoenix Branch Bank. In 1792, Tallmadge was appointed postmaster of Litchfield and was also the first treasurer, then secretary and later president of the Society of the Cincinnati. He was elected to the U.S. House of Representatives, where he served as a member of the minority Federalist Party for the entire sixteen years he was in Congress, 1801 to 1817. In 1805, his wife, Mary, died, and in 1808, Tallmadge married Maria Hallett (1776–1838), the daughter of his old friend, Joseph Hallett of New York. In 1817, as one of his last initiatives in Congress, he successfully campaigned against increasing the pensions of John Paulding, Isaac Van Wart, and David Williams, the three men who captured Major André. Tallmadge's objection was based on André's account of the capture, which Tallmadge believed. He argued that despite their militia status, the three men were mere brigands who skulked between the lines preying on any targets of opportunity. Tallmadge argued that when they captured André, they were merely after plunder, and if André could have given the men enough to satisfy them, André never would have been taken prisoner. In 1817, he retired from Congress and then established a training school for Native American and Asian missionaries. In addition, Tallmadge was esteemed for his social qualities and his numerous and generous gifts to public and private charities. When John Trumbull painted Washington's portrait, pressing political matters precluded Washington from sitting until the portrait was completed. As a result, Benjamin Tallmadge posed for Washington's legs after Trumbull pronounced Tallmadge's legs an exact pattern of Washington's. According to legend, "Colonel Benjamin Tallmadge had the reputation of being the handsomest man in the Revolutionary Army."[11] Tallmadge died on Saturday, March 7, 1835, at the age of eighty-one and is buried in East Cemetery at Litchfield, Connecticut.

John Graves Simcoe (1752–1806)

After Simcoe was invalided home in 1781, he convalesced at the estate of his godfather, Admiral Samuel Graves, near Honiton in Devon. While there, Simcoe met Elizabeth Posthuma Gwillim (1762–1850), the ward of Admiral Graves, and heiress to a considerable fortune. They fell in love and were married on Monday, December 30, 1782. Simcoe was fairly wealthy in his own right, but his fortune was trivial in comparison to his wife's. Elizabeth purchased a 5,000-acre estate at Honiton, Devon, and the two constructed "Wolford Lodge," a grand home that would be the Simcoe family seat until 1923. The couple had eleven children: Charlotte (1783–1842), Eliza (1784–1865), Henrietta Maria (1787–1845), Sophia Jemima (1789–1864), Francis Gwillim (1791–1812), Katherine (1793–1794), John Cornwall (1798–1799), Henry Addington (1800–1868), Katherine (1801–1861), Caroline (1788–1858), and Anne (1804–1877).

In 1787, Simcoe wrote and published a book on his experiences in the Revolutionary War titled *A Journal of Operations of the Queen's Rangers: From the End of the Year 1777 to the Conclusion of the Late American War*. The death of John André deeply affected Simcoe, and as a result of the capture and execution of his dear friend, Simcoe carried a profound animosity toward the United States for the remainder of his life. In 1790 he was elected to the House of Commons to represent the Cornish borough of St. Mawes and in 1791 was appointed lieutenant-governor of the new Loyalist province of Upper Canada, where he served under Governor-General of Canada Guy Carleton, the 1st Baron of Dorchester.

John, Elizabeth, and their growing family arrived in Canada in November 1791. They spent the first winter in Quebec City, then the following summer, they took residence at Fort Niagara, where Simcoe initially established the capital of Upper Canada. However, in 1793, he moved the capital to York, which is present Toronto.

Simcoe's agenda was to make Upper Canada so strong that the Americans would never consider invading, and he also hoped to make the province so grand and prosperous that the Americans would come to their senses and be so envious that they would petition the British government to take them back into the fold. Simcoe was an authoritarian lieutenant-governor, and few dared to challenge him. However, he passed laws that were popular with the general populace, such as guaranteeing a trial by jury and establishing town councils as a third-tier government. He even tried to abolish slavery, but the backlash was so great that the best he could accomplish was to prohibit the importation of any new slaves into Upper Canada. Simcoe passed measures that were democratic, but he was not in favor of the type of democracy that caused the Americans to rebel. He wrote passionately of defeating the spirit of democratic subversion that immigrants from the United States might bring to Canada. Although he passed laws granting rights to the populace, he also worked to maintain and strengthen the aristocracy. In general his administration was regarded as commendable despite his occasional displays of prejudice toward the United States. However, some regarded his sometimes controlling method of governance as having "military and aristocratic conceptions quite unsuited to the pioneer conditions,"[12] and thought that his tenure as lieutenant-governor was "rendered ineffective by the impracticable aspects of his projects and the friction which developed between himself and Lord Dorchester, the governor-general."[13]

To promote settlements, particularly along the border with the United States, Simcoe formed the 2nd Queen's Rangers, a military unit patterned after his Queen's Rangers of the Revolutionary War. He used the rangers according to the model of the Roman military colony, where Roman legions on the march established well laid-out camps that eventually became cities. The rangers improved roads, cleared areas, and laid out rudimentary town sites for their winter quarters, and when they moved on, settlers and merchants attracted by the clearing and road building quickly moved into those areas. Disbanded or retired rangers were also expected to form the nucleus of those communities and be the mainstays of the militia in case of a military emergency.

Simcoe continued to worry about an American invasion of Canada, especially with the increase of American border forts during the Ohio Indian wars. Simcoe argued for a real naval force on Lake Ontario and the establishment of military garrisons in Upper Canada that were large and strong enough to meet any threat from the United States. However, the governor-general rejected most of his arguments. In July of 1796, a severe bout of neuralgia and gout forced Simcoe to take a leave of absence in England to recover from his ailments. He never returned to Canada.

While still convalescing in England, he was offered and accepted the post of governor of Santo Domingo (Haiti) and was promoted to lieutenant-general. In July 1797, after only five months of vigorous service on the island, during which time he restored order to the civil administration, checked corruption in the military supply system, reorganized the medical service, and restored an adequate defense of the royalist plantations, Simcoe's health broke and he was forced to return to England to recuperate. In spite of his successes in Santo Domingo, the government was not pleased with the fact that Simcoe greatly exceeded his strict budget, even though the budget was grossly inadequate. Nevertheless, as long as William Pitt was the prime minister and Henry Dundas was secretary of state for war, Simcoe was not considered for another active command.

In July 1806, after Pitt's death, Simcoe was appointed commander-in-chief in India. However, on the way to India, he diverted to render assistance to the Earl of St. Vincent for the relief of England's oldest ally, Portugal. It was to be a joint command, but instead, Simcoe fell grievously ill and was forced again to return to England. He never made it home. John Graves Simcoe died at the age of fifty-four on Sunday, October 26, 1806, at Torbay on the south coast of Devon. He is buried in the little Wolford Chapel on the grounds of his estate in Honiton.

Anna Smith Strong (1740–1812)

After the war, Anna and her husband, Selah (1737–1815), were reunited and resumed their lives at St. George's Manor on Strong's Neck near Setauket. Different sources list different numbers of children for the couple, but a record taken from the Strong family Bible seems to be the most reliable. Prior to Selah's imprisonment, the couple had seven children, six of whom survived infancy. They were: Keturah (1761–1790), Thomas Shepherd (1765–1840), Margaret (1768–?), Benjamin (1770–1851), Mary (1773–1773), William Smith (1775–1794), and Joseph (1777–1794). After the war, they had another child, whom they named George Washington Strong (1783–1855).[14]

The story of Anna and Selah's life during and after the war is somewhat sketchy. Other than the accounts of Anna's assistance to the Culper Ring, not much else is known about her. Some sources indicate that while Selah was imprisoned on the *Jersey*, Anna likely saved his life by visiting and bringing him food, medicine and other necessities, and that Selah remained in captivity until the end of the war. Some accounts indicate that Anna used her influence with Loyalist friends to secure Selah's release, after which he moved to the safety of Connecticut for the duration of the war, leaving Anna in Setauket to look after the estate on Strong's Neck. It is not known whether Selah was aware of Anna's involvement with the Culper Ring spy network at the time, but it seems unlikely that he would leave his wife to continue her potentially fatal espionage activities, especially since he was the reason the family was under scrutiny by the British in the first place.

After the war, like the majority of American spies, Anna chose to keep her wartime exploits private and let them fade into the mists of time. She simply resumed her prewar roles of mother, housewife, and lady of St.

George's Manor, while Selah resumed an active political career. Anna Smith Strong died in 1812 at the age of seventy-two, and Selah died three years later in 1815. They are buried side-by-side in the Strong family cemetery on Strong's Neck, not far from where Anna hung her wash to signal Caleb Brewster's hiding place in Conscience Bay.

Robert Townsend (1753–1838)

Benjamin Tallmadge visited New York prior to the British evacuation in 1783 to establish contact with American agents who might be in jeopardy after the British departed. A good number of the spies had taken on a Tory character as their cover during the war, and Tallmadge was worried that they were in danger of misguided retribution from American patriots. Tallmadge knew some of his agents personally, having met them at one time or another before or during the war, but Samuel Culper Junior, the New York head of the Culper Ring, was still only a code name to Tallmadge. Tallmadge had been given the address of Underhill's boardinghouse, and when he arrived, he finally met Robert Townsend.[15] Tallmadge commended Townsend for his service during the war and told him that Washington wanted to personally thank and reward him when the general arrived in the city in November. Townsend demurred and told the astonished Tallmadge that he would not stay in the city to meet Washington, and he further insisted that Tallmadge never reveal his identity to anyone, not even to Washington. Townsend added that all he wanted was to be forgotten.[16] As a result, Washington never learned that Robert Townsend was Culper Junior. In fact, Tallmadge and all of the members of the Culper network who knew the true identity of Culper Junior respected Townsend's wishes and carried the secret of Culper Junior's identity to the grave.

Townsend continued to operate his New York business after the war, living in an apartment that he shared for a time with his older brother William and an unidentified cousin. Robert Townsend never married, although he may have fathered a child in 1784 with his New York housekeeper, Mary Banvard. Though Robert assumed responsibility for the child, even giving him his name, there is speculation that the child was actually fathered by either William or the unidentified cousin.[17]

Sometime later, Robert sold his New York business interests and retired to Oyster Bay, taking up residence in the Townsend family home. He reoccupied the same room that Simcoe had used during the time the commander of the Queen's Rangers stayed with the Townsends in Oyster Bay. Robert was content to live in obscurity and was reluctant to discuss what he had done during the war, much less allude to any espionage undertakings in which he may have been involved. When relatives periodically learned of a rumor, or uncovered some articles or artifacts of Robert's that seemed to pertain to his activities during the war, Robert seemed embarrassed by their discovery. Even in those circumstances and regardless of repeated coaxing, Townsend would offer little or no explanation.

While serving as Culper Junior, Robert Townsend had a pervasive fear that his handwriting style might betray his identity. Ironically, that is precisely what happened, although not for well over 150 years. In 1930, the Long Island historian Frank Knox Morton Pennypacker came into possession of documents that had been written by Robert Townsend. Pennypacker also had copies of messages that had been signed with the alias "Samuel Culper Junior." He noticed a similarity between the two writing styles, and as Samuel Culper Junior once feared, handwriting experts confirmed Pennypacker's suspicions that the same person wrote the documents.

Robert shared the Townsend family home with his sister Sally, who also never married. Sally died in Oyster Bay in 1842 at the age of eighty-two, four years after her brother Robert died in 1838. Robert was eighty-four at the time of his death. Both Sally and Robert are buried along with their father, mother, and sister Phebe near their home in the Fort Hill Burying Ground, which is atop the hill where John Graves Simcoe had constructed his Oyster Bay fort.

Abraham Woodhull (1750–1826)

After Cornwallis surrendered at Yorktown, major hostilities gradually wound down. It was apparent that the British had lost the will and the desire to continue the war. In an attempt to disassociate themselves with what they believed was a lost cause, many of the British officers including the commander-in-chief General Clinton, requested transfer back to England. General Guy Carleton assumed command of the British forces, and the very humane Carleton made it plain in his unprecedented meetings with Washington that he was most interested in restoring order out of the bedlam of war. Even so, it took Washington some time to become convinced that the British were sincere, and wind down intelligence-gathering operations in New York and on Long Island. By the summer of 1783, the activities of the Culper Ring had ceased altogether.

Abraham Woodhull's last message as Samuel Culper Senior was sent to

Tallmadge on Saturday, July 5, 1783, and it pertained to expenses that Woodhull had accrued in conjunction with his espionage activities. "I am unable to particularize dates … for I kept only the most simple account that I possibly could, for fear it should betray me, but I trust it is a just one—and do assure you I have been as frugal as possibly could. I desire you would explain to the Genl. the circumstances that attended this lengthy correspondence that he may be satisfied we have not been extravagant. And in the Interim wishing you health and prosperity I remain your ever mindful and Humble Servant, Samuel Culper."[18]

Woodhull married his cousin, Mary Anna Smith (1759–1806), in 1781, and the couple eventually had three children, two girls and a boy. They were Elizabeth (1785–1856), Mary (1794–1853), and Jesse Smith (1796–1844). After the war, Woodhull spent the remainder of his life in Setauket, where in addition to his farming operation, he held civic positions including that of Suffolk County magistrate from 1799–1810.

Woodhull's wife, Mary, died in 1806 at the age of forty-seven, and Abraham remained on his farm where he raised his children alone. In 1824 at the age of seventy-four he married thirty-three-year-old Lydia Terry (1791–1864) of Aquebogue, Long Island. The two did not have any children, and Abraham only lived two years longer.

On Monday, January 23, 1826, Abraham Woodhull, the former leader of Washington's Long Island and New York spy network, the Culper Ring, died at the age of seventy-six. He was buried in the graveyard of the Setauket Presbyterian Church. Woodhull's home burned down in 1931, and bricks from the home surround his headstone. There is a brass memorial on top of his tomb, which reads in part: "Friend and confidant of George Washington. Head of the Long Island Secret Service. During the American Revolution he operated under the alias Samuel Culper Sr. To him and his associates have been credited a large share of the success of the Army of the Revolution."

Although Washington knew the identity of Samuel Culper Senior, Washington and Woodhull never met. Like Robert Townsend, Benjamin Tallmadge, and the rest of the Culper Ring, Woodhull shunned public recognition, and he never publicly discussed his wartime espionage activities. Interestingly, his second wife, Lydia married, one Gilbert Floyd (1771–1864) in 1826, and in 1827, they had a son that they named "Abraham Woodhull Floyd."

Epilogue

Sally Townsend, her brother Robert, Caleb Brewster, Anna Smith Strong, Austin Roe, and Benjamin Tallmadge are all gone now, as are the rest of Washington's espionage network in New York and on Long Island. The New York City they knew is gone too, buried beneath concrete, steel, and asphalt. Even the shape of Manhattan or York Island, as it was known, has been altered. However, on Long Island, vestiges of the world they knew still exists. In Oyster Bay and Setauket one can walk the paths and fields and enter some of the buildings where Sally and the other Long Island spies lived, worked, played, loved, and where they secretly carried on their deadly game of espionage.

In Setauket, you can stand near the intersection of Bob's Lane and Dyke Road, where Abraham Woodhull's farmhouse stood until it was destroyed by fire in 1931, and look due east across Little Bay to where Anna Smith Strong hung her black petticoat and however many white handkerchiefs to signal the rendezvous location with Caleb Brewster and his whaleboat commandos. The little sand spit over which Brewster and his men dragged their whaleboat in and out of Conscience Bay is unchanged, and Brewster's home off Main Street in Setauket is much the way he left it when he went to become part of Tallmadge's clandestine group. It's possible to see Austin Roe's Tavern, although it's not in its original location on the corner of present Main Street and Bayview Avenue. It was moved about a quarter mile away, and it is now a private home. The Loyalist Caroline Church, with its curiously warped steeple and musket ball holes, still dominates one corner of the triangular green in Setauket opposite the rebuilt Whiggish Presbyterian Church on the adjacent corner of the green. The Presbyterian Church is where Benjamin Tallmadge's father served as pastor during the Revolution. Abraham Woodhull is buried behind the Presbyterian Church, and Anna Strong is buried near her home in the family cemetery on Strong's Neck.

In Oyster Bay the Townsend family home still stands, although it was enlarged around 1851 and renamed Raynham Hall. However, the original part

Left: The grave of Sally Townsend—Fort Hill Burying Ground, Oyster Bay. *Right:* The grave of Robert Townsend—Fort Hill Burying Ground, Oyster Bay (author's photographs).

Fort Hill Burying Ground sign—Oyster Bay (author's photograph).

of the house that faces Main Street has been restored to the way Sally and Robert would likely remember it. The windows in Sally's upstairs bedroom face south toward Main Street onto the area where Oberleutnant Wintzingerode and the rest of von Wurmb's Jägers assembled in January of 1777. There is also a window in Sally's room that faces west, through which she often watched for Simcoe and his Queen's Rangers to proudly march back into Oyster Bay.

Graves of Daniel and Susannah Youngs—Youngs Memorial Cemetery, Oyster Bay (author's photograph).

When one examines the artifacts, the environment, the tools and techniques that were used by Sally and the members of the Culper Ring, they appear simplistic, naïve, and amateurish. They were indeed amateurish, because Sally and the other Long Island spies were in fact amateurs, who in spite of the potentially fearsome consequences, did not hesitate to fight the only way they knew against the most powerful, sophisticated, and technologically superior military force on the face of the earth. Armed with nothing more than their wits, some invisible ink, and Major Tallmadge's rudimentary code, they unhesitatingly went off to war in the dangerous and shadowy world of espionage. They had no experience or training as spies, but had to learn on their own and develop their techniques as they went. The odds against them were great, and the price of failure was unthinkable. If they were captured, the best they could hope for was a quick death on the gallows rather than the rotting hell of the prison hulks. There were no second chances. That they survived at all is remarkable, and that they prevailed is almost

Grave of John Graves Simcoe—Wolford Chapel on the Simcoe Estate in Honiton, Devon, England (author's photograph).

beyond belief. Their success was due to their innate talents, incredible adaptability, resourcefulness, bravery, and their patriotism. They did not serve for accolades, fame, glory, renown or other tangible rewards, and they were content if not adamant about keeping their clandestine activities private after the war, and indeed throughout their lives.

They all gave more than was expected of them, and they all paid a price to varying degrees. However, none paid a heavier price for their wartime experiences than Sally Townsend. Though she was a remarkably beautiful, vivacious and extremely popular young woman, Sally never married and lived the remainder of her life in the Townsend home. It is surmised that the reason she remained single was because she never again met the likes or equal of the dashing and gallant enemy officer, Lieutenant Colonel John Graves Simcoe, who was perhaps the one real love of her life. Simcoe, in turn, loved Sally, but tragically could not reconcile his personal feelings that on some level all Americans were responsible for the death of his dear friend André, and that Sally was an American. At the same time, Sally's most heart-rending secret was that she was more complicit in André's death than Simcoe ever realized. Even today, visitors to the Townsend home report experiencing a feeling of profound sadness in the vicinity of Sally's bedroom. Sally never talked about her wartime experiences, but chose to let that segment of her life drift into the misty and forgotten past. However, she never forgot John André, John Graves Simcoe or the times and experiences they shared together. In the privacy of her room, she often looked at André's sketches and the silhouettes he cut of her, and she also smiled at the other mementos of those happy and heady times. She read and reread the Valentine that Simcoe gave her so frequently that over the years the pages separated along the folded creases.

Regrettably, there are no known portraits or other likenesses of the remarkable Sally Townsend, but we do have documents, articles and artifacts that help us get a sense of who she was and what she did: the etched windowpanes that read "The Adorable Miss Sally Townsend," Mrs. Elizabeth Titus's recollection that Sally was beloved by every one of the officers who occupied Oyster Bay, Sarah Thorne's remembrance that Sally was the favorite of the Jäger Captain Ernst Wintzergerode. Of course Simcoe's Valentine and André's silhouette attest to her beauty and popularity, but it is important to remember that she was much more than a lively, vivacious, and popular teenage girl. She was also a very brave and resourceful young woman, who, when caught up in the whirlwind of a war that engulfed her community, fought back as courageously as any soldier on a conventional battlefield.

Chapter Notes

Preface

1. Morton Pennypacker, *General Washington's Spies on Long Island and in New York,* Vol. II (East Hampton: Pennypacker, 1948).
2. Corey Ford, *A Peculiar Service* (Boston, Toronto: Little, Brown, 1965).
3. George Washington, George Washington Papers at the Library of Congress, 1741–1799: Series 4, General Correspondence, 1697, Image 1020–1021.

Prologue

1. Benson J. Lossing, ed., *The American Historical Record, and Repertory of Notes and Queries* (Philadelphia: Chase and Town, 1872), p. 68.
2. A sect founded in England in 1650 by George Fox that was noted for its unwavering pacifism.
3. Wilson Armistead, *Journal of George Fox; Being an Historical Account,* Vol. I (London: W. and F.G. Cash, 1852), pp. 381–383.
4. Ben Johnson, *The Works of Ben Johnson* (Boston: Philips, Samson, 1853), p. 789.
5. Corey Ford, *Donovan of OSS* (New York: Little, Brown, 1970), p. 4.
6. Frances Irwin, *Oyster Bay, A Sketch* (New York: Oyster Bay Historical Society, 1987), pp. 147–148.
7. Frances Irwin, *Oyster Bay, In History* (Oyster Bay: Oyster Bay Historical Society, 19??), p. 109.

Chapter 1

1. Daughter of William and Mary (Hicks) Stoddard.
2. Irwin, *Oyster Bay, A Sketch,* p. 47.

3. Irwin, *Oyster Bay, In History,* p. 7.
4. Margaret Townsend Tagliapietra, *Townsend—Townshend, 1066-1909* (New York: Press of the Broadway, 1909), p. 72.
5. Irwin, *Oyster Bay, A Sketch,* p. 51.
6. *Ibid.,* p. 51.
7. Presently West Main Street.
8. John Cox Jr., ed., *Oyster Bay Town Records* (New York: Tobias Wright, 1930), 5:611–613.
9. Irwin, *Oyster Bay, A Sketch,* p. 50.
10. Samuel's wife Sarah had been baptized in the Episcopal Church, but she preferred the Friends or Quakers.
11. Tagliapietra, *Townsend—Townshend, 1066-1909,* p. 72.
12. Tunis Garret Bergen, *Genealogies of the State of New York: Long Island Edition,* Vol. III (New York: Lewis Historical Publishing Co., 1915), p. 1,116.
13. Irwin, *Oyster Bay, A Sketch,* p. 51.
14. *Ibid.,* p. 51.
15. As was their brother Robert, Sally and Phebe were taught by Sarah Wright Townsend (1719–1780) who was married to John Townsend (1703–1786) on July 24, 1738.
16. Irwin, *Oyster Bay, A Sketch,* p. 51.

Chapter 2

1. Irwin, *Oyster Bay, In History,* p. 96.
2. The Province of New York (1664–1783), which was named for James, Duke of York and brother to Charles II in 1664, when the colony was won from the Dutch.
3. A "freeholder" is a landowner or someone who owns land *fee simple.* In essence, it is absolute ownership only limited by certain government powers, such as taxation, eminent domain, and police power.

4. Henry Onderdonk Jr., *Documents and Letters Intended to Illustrate the Revolutionary Incidents of Queens County* (New York: Leavitt, Trow and Company, 1846), pp. 25–26.

5. *Ibid.*, p. 26.

6. Franklin B. Hough, *The New-York Civil List, From 1777 to 1860* (Albany, NY: Weed Parsons & Co., 1860), p. 59.

Chapter 3

1. Most historians believe the group to have numbered 60 to 70 men arrayed in two lines. The 1826 deposition of Sylvanus Wood indicates a lesser number. Wood said that Parker formed a single line and walked from one end to the other counting exactly 38 men.

2. Robert Debs Heinl Jr., *Dictionary of Military and Naval Quotations* (Annapolis, MD: United States Naval Institute, 1966), p. 82.

3. Paul David Nelson, *William Tryon and the Course of Empire: A Life in British Imperial Service* (Chapel Hill: University of North Carolina Press, 1990), p. 129.

4. Turtle Bay was a small inlet located on the east side of Manhattan Island between present 42nd and 53rd Streets opposite Roosevelt Island. The bay itself was filled in and is now the site of the United Nations Headquarters.

5. He remained living on board until the British Army arrived in New York in August 1776.

6. Irwin, *Oyster Bay, A Sketch*, p. 53.

7. Abraham Whipple (1733–1819), arguably America's most experienced naval officer. During the French & Indian War, as a privateer captain in command of the *Game Cock*, he captured 23 French vessels. Whipple also led the 50-man party in the "Gaspée affair" in 1772.

8. The Raynham Hall Museum lists the year of his death as 1773, and the Townsend Society of America lists the year of his death as 1775. I have used the date cited by the Townsend Society, since it has comprehensive data pertaining to Townsend family history.

9. Other members of the committee were Colonel John Broome, Colonel Charles De Witt, William Duer, John Sloss Hobart, John Jay, Robert R. Livingston, Governeur Morris, General John Morin Scott, William Smith, Henry Wisner, Abraham Yates, and Robert Yates.

Chapter 4

1. Irwin, *Oyster Bay, In History*, p. 96.

2. The present site of the Verrazano Narrows Bridge.

3. Silas Wood, *A Sketch of the First Settlement of the Several Towns on Long Island; with their Political Condition, to the end of the American Revolution* (Brooklyn: Alden Spooner, 1828), pp. 132–133.

4. *Ibid.*, p. 133.

5. During the French and Indian War, Alexander served as an aide to Governor William Shirley. In 1756, he accompanied Shirley to England and learned of the vacant seat of Stirling in Scotland, after which he pursued a claim to the title. The British House of Lords refused to accept his title as "Earl of Stirling," but instead granted him the lesser title "Lord Stirling." He built a grand estate at Basking Ridge, New Jersey, filled with the furnishings and trappings appropriate for a Scottish Lord.

6. David McCullough, *1776* (New York: Simon & Schuster, 2006), p. 145.

7. Increase Carpenter (1743–1807). In addition to operating an inn, he was a church elder and served as a 1st lieutenant quartermaster during the Revolutionary War. In 1774 a meeting to protest British taxation policies was held at his house.

8. Oliver DeLancey Jr. (1749–1822) was the son of Brigadier General Oliver DeLancey Sr. He was educated at Eton and later purchased a position as coronet in the 14th Dragoons in 1766 and later a lieutenancy in 1773. In 1773 he purchased a captaincy in the 17th Light Dragoons, and a majority in 1778. He became head of British Intelligence, and in 1781, he was appointed Adjutant General of the Forces in North America, replacing John André.

9. Kip's Bay originally stretched from about present E. 38th St. south to E. 32nd St. and inland to about 2nd Ave. Landfill over the years has widened Manhattan Island considerably. The present F.D.R. Dr. lies approximately over the line where Admiral Howe's ships were anchored at the time of the assault on Manhattan.

10. Presently Park Avenue and 37th Street.

11. Charles Monaghan, *The Murrays of Murray Hill* (New York: Urban History Press, 1998), p. 66.

Chapter 5

1. Irwin, *Oyster Bay, In History*, p. 97.
2. Morton Pennypacker, *The Two Spies* (Boston & New York: Houghton Mifflin Company, 1930), p. 55.
3. According to Native American legend, the local tribes used warriors and medicine magic to chase the devil out of their land. The devil picked up huge boulders and threw them into the water and used them as his stepping-stones to make his escape across Long Island Sound.
4. Irwin, *Oyster Bay, In History*, p. 99.
5. Pennypacker, *The Two Spies*, p. 57.
6. *Ibid.*
7. A method of binding several cornstalks together for strength.
8. A smoothbore long gun used primarily for hunting fowl; an 18th century relative of the shotgun.
9. Morton Pennypacker, *General Washington's Spies on Long Island and in New York* (Brooklyn: Long Island Historical Society, 1939), p. 106.
10. *Ibid.*, p. 106.
11. *Ibid.*, p. 106.
12. William Cunningham, b. Dublin 1738; died in London 10 August 1791. Arrived in New York in 1774. He went to Boston in 1775, where Thomas Gage appointed him provost marshal to the Royal Army. In 1778 he had charge of the prisons in Philadelphia and later in New York. In both places his cruelties to the American prisoners became notorious. Of the prisoners under his care, more than 2,000 were starved to death, and more than 250 were hanged without trial. He is most well known for conducting the execution of the American spy Nathan Hale. After the war Cunningham went to England. An unsubstantiated, but popular, legend has it that in London, he mortgaged his half-pay, and subsequently forged a draft. For this offense he was tried, convicted and executed by hanging.
13. Whitehead Hicks was born in Bayside, Long Island, in 1728 and was admitted to the bar in 1750. From 1766 to 1776, he was the mayor of New York. In 1776, he was appointed a judge of the Supreme Court of Judicature, and subsequently retired to Jamaica, Long Island. Upon the death of his father, he took possession of the family home in Bayside and died there in 1780.
14. Pennypacker, *The Two Spies*, pp. 13–14.
15. Later Columbia University.
16. Timothy Guilfoyle, *City of Eros* (New York: W. W. Norton, 1992), pp. 23–24.
17. *Ibid.*, p. 24.
18. Alexander Rose, *Washington's Spies* (New York: Random House, 2006), p. 154.

Chapter 6

1. Oliver DeLancey Sr. (1718–1785), merchant, Loyalist politician and soldier during the American Revolution. Born in New York City, he served as city alderman and was a member of the New York assembly from 1756 to 1761. In 1768, he allied himself with Isaac Sears and the Sons of Liberty in speaking out against the Boston Port Bill, but he did not support non-importation and he remained a Loyalist. In 1773, he was appointed colonel-in-chief of the Southern Military District. On Sept. 21, 1776, he was commissioned a brigadier general of the Royal Provincial Forces, and drawing on his considerable personal wealth, he raised and equipped at his own expense three battalions of troops, consisting of Loyalist volunteers from New York City, Long Island, and Westchester and Fairfield Counties to form DeLancey's Brigade.
2. Some sources use the spelling *Greene*.
3. The site is presently north of the intersection of Cove Road and Cove Neck Road, across the road from the Youngs Cemetery, in which Theodore Roosevelt is buried.
4. St. George's Episcopal Church, Hempstead, NY, Registry of Marriages.
5. Pennypacker, *General Washington's Spies on Long Island and in New York*, p. 106.
6. *Ibid.*, p. 106.
7. Early in the war, DeLancey's Regiments, like many of the Loyalist units, wore a green uniform. Later they changed to a red regimental coat with dark blue facings, white breeches and waistcoat, black cocked hat and dark leggings.
8. After the war, Joseph Green and Hannah moved to Ireland. Hannah died in 1797.

Chapter 7

1. Fort Washington was located where the present George Washington Bridge reaches

Manhattan Island. Fort Washington Park presently occupies the site.

2. Ravelin: a projecting, V-shaped outwork that protects the main fortification from direct assault.

3. Redoubt: a small fort or outwork of varying shape usually without flanking defenses.

4. Near Alpine, NJ, in what is now Palisades Interstate Park.

5. The straight-line distance was approximately six miles, but by the roads of the time, the distance was about ten miles.

6. Henry Cabot Lodge, *George Washington*, Vol. 1 (Boston and New York: Houghton, Mifflin, 1899), p. 178.

7. *Ibid.*, p. 178.

Chapter 8

1. Joseph. J. Ellis, *Revolutionary Summer: The Birth of American Independence* (New York: Alfred A. Knopf, 2013), p. 118.

2. In 1777, von Wurmb was given command of the entire Jäger Corps, which included all Jäger troops of Hesse-Cassel, Hesse-Hanau, and Anspach serving in America.

3. Steven Mintz, *Huck's Raft: A History of American Childhood* (Cambridge, MA: Belknap Press of Harvard University Press, 2004), p. 64.

4. Charles Bracelen Flood, *Rise and Fight Again: Perilous Times Along the Road to Independence* (New York: Dodd, Mead, 1976), p. 100.

5. *Ibid.*, p. 100–101.

6. Pennypacker, *The Two Spies*, p. 65.

7. There were two "T." Townsends in the Oyster Bay area during the winter of 1776–1777: Timothy and Thomas. At this time it cannot be determined which, if either, provided quarters to Lt. Wintzingerode.

8. I could not find a record of a D. Mudge in the Oyster Bay area during the winter of 1776–1777. The farm of Moses Mudge passed to his son Jarvis, but both died prior to 1776. Quite possibly, Lt. Ochse was quartered with their descendent Jane Mudge, who had never married and retained the family name.

Chapter 10

1. Edwin P. Adkins, *Setauket: The First Three Hundred Years, 1655–1955* (New York: Three Villages Historical Society), pp. 20–21.

2. Additional Continental Regiments were regiments that were formed without any administrative connection to an individual state. Webb's regiment was raised in Danbury, CT, on Jan. 11, 1777, and was composed mostly of Connecticut men. In 1780, Webb's Additional Regiment became the 9th Connecticut Regiment of the Continental Army.

3. Swivel guns were small cannon mounted on a swiveling stand or fork that allowed a wide range of movement. They were antipersonnel weapons, typically measuring less than a yard in length that, depending on the size of the bore, could fire up to a one-pound ball or one pound of shot.

4. The family of Francis Chadsey was one of the early landowners in the vicinity of this fording place on Brandywine Creek early in the 18th century. Sometime around 1725, Francis's son John Chadsey dropped the *ey* and began spelling his name Chads. The fording place became known as Chads' Ford. Spelling in the 18th century was mostly done phonetically and occasionally the name was spelled with two *d*'s. Sometime during the 19th century it became more common to see the name spelled *Chadds* with two *d*'s and the town that grew up there is now officially known as *Chadds Ford*. Even so, the house built in 1725 that was the residence of John and Elizabeth Chads is still referred to as the Chads' Home.

5. Edmund Fanning (1739–1818). Born Southold, Long Island, graduated from Yale in 1757, studied law in New York. Moved to Hillsboro, North Carolina, in 1761 where he became a protégé of William Tryon. Fanning followed Tryon to New York in 1771, and in 1777 he raised a corps of 460 Loyalists and was commissioned a colonel in command of the unit, which he named the "associated refugees" or "King's American Regiment." During the war he was twice wounded, and near the end of the war he moved to Nova Scotia, where in 1783, he was named Lieutenant Governor. Later he became governor of Prince Edward Island. He retired to London and died there in 1818.

6. Ray Raphael, *A People's History of the American Revolution* (New York: The New Press, 2011), p. 1778.

7. David Hackett Fischer, *Washington's Crossing* (New York: Oxford University Press, 2004), p. 376.

8. Onderdonk Jr., *Documents and Letters Intended to Illustrate the Revolutionary Incidents of Queens County,* p. 192.

9. Dorothy Horton McGee, *Sally Townsend, Patriot* (New York: Dodd, Mead, 1952), p. 188.

10. Crudely or irregularly fashioned verse, often of a humorous or burlesque nature.

11. Fischer, *Washington's Crossing,* p. 73.

12. Tuesday, January 6, 1778, David Bushnell, inventor of the submarine "turtle" set a number of incendiary mines or "infernals," afloat in the Delaware River above Philadelphia. The mines were constructed of kegs, and were cast adrift to float down among the British fleet. A mine exploded against a barge, killing four sailors and injuring several others, after which the ships and troops ashore were ordered to fire at anything they could see floating. The ships were able to avoid all other mines without damage or injuries.

13. Samuel B. Griffith II, *The War for American Independence* (Garden City, NY: Doubleday, 1976), p. 463.

14. Catherine S. Crary, "The Tory and the Spy: The Double Life of James Rivington," *William and Mary Quarterly* (January, 1959): pp. 70–71.

15. Steuben (1730–1794). Former Prussian officer in the army of Frederick the Great. He was discharged for obscure reasons in 1763 at the age of 33. He became chamberlain (Hofmarschall) in the court of Hohenzollern-Hechingen, where he was made a Baron (Freiherr). His prince became bankrupt, and Steuben had to seek other employment. After several unsuccessful attempts to join foreign armies, he was endorsed by Benjamin Franklin in France, who wrote a letter to Congress introducing Steuben as a lieutenant general in the King of Prussia's service. With these bogus credentials, he was accepted into the American army as an unpaid volunteer. Steuben was so effective training troops that Washington recommended his appointment to major general on May 5, 1778, which Congress approved.

16. Near present Freehold, New Jersey.

17. Paul David Nelson, *The Life of William Alexander, Lord Stirling: George Washington's Noble General* (Tuscaloosa: University of Alabama Press, 1987), p. 126.

18. Mark M. Boatner III, *Encyclopedia of the American Revolution* (Mechanicsburg. PA: Stackpole Books, 1966), p. 722.

19. Scott most likely was not present when Washington confronted Lee, so it is not known what is the basis of Scott's recollection of the event.

20. Boatner III, *Encyclopedia of the American Revolution,* p. 722.

Chapter 11

1. The Queen's Rangers was a Loyalist regiment that was founded and organized by the French and Indian War hero, Major Robert Rogers. In 1776, Rogers was replaced by Colonel French, who in turn was replaced by Captain James Wemyss, who led the regiment during the Battle of Brandywine. In October 1777, Wemyss was in turn replaced as commander by then Major John Graves Simcoe.

2. Presently near the intersection of Prospect Street and Simcoe Street in Oyster Bay.

3. Long bundles of sticks tied together used as a framework in constructing fortifications or also during an assault to throw into moats and ditches to create a crossing point.

4. A wicker basket of cylindrical form, usually open at both ends and filled with dirt. It was used for field fortifications and other works of military engineering.

5. A small vee-shaped earthwork pointed out from a fortification to create additional strong points. The fleche was open at the rear, so if captured it could not be used by besieging forces against a fortification.

6. Obstacles of felled trees facing toward the enemy, sometimes with the tips of the branches sharpened and used to impede an enemy advance. Used much like barbed wire in later wars.

7. John Graves Simcoe, *A History of the Operations of a Partisan Corps, Called the Queen's Rangers, Commanded by Lieut. Col. J. G. Simcoe* (New York: Bartlett & Welford, 1844), pp. 93–94.

8. John Graves Simcoe, *Simcoe's Military Journal* (New York: Bartlett & Welford, 1844), p. 95.

9. "Early Canada Historical Narratives—John Graves Simcoe," accessed Nov. 4, 2013, www.uppercanadahistory.ca/simcoe/simcoe1.html.

10. *Ibid.*

11. Irwin, *Oyster Bay, In History*, p. 101.

12. E. Littell, *Littell's Living Age*, Vol. II, *From 10 August to 26 October, 1844* (Boston: Littell, Son & Co., 1844), p. 177.

13. Irwin, *Oyster Bay, In History*, p. 101.

14. Benson J. Lossing, *The Pictorial Field Book of the Revolution*, Vol. II, p. 137.

15. Simcoe, *Simcoe's Military Journal*, pp. 98–99.

16. *Ibid.*, p. 99.

17. Located on what is now a private estate off Fort Hill Dr. on the western shore of Lloyd's Neck.

18. William Franklin (1731–1813), the illegitimate son of Benjamin Franklin. His mother's identity is unknown, and he was raised by his father and his father's common-law wife, Deborah Read. He accompanied his father on several diplomatic missions, and when he was twenty-one, in 1752, he assisted his father in his famous kite experiment. William studied law in London and there married Elizabeth Downes. They had one son, William Temple Franklin, who by mutual decision was raised by Benjamin Franklin. In 1763 he was appointed Royal Governor of New Jersey, and as Governor, he signed the charter for Queen's College, which became Rutgers University. Though Benjamin took up the patriot cause, William remained steadfastly loyal to the Crown. As Royal Governor, he was arrested by the rebels in 1776 and imprisoned for two years. He was released in 1778 and went to New York, where he remained active among the Loyalist community. In 1782, he went to England, never to return. William reconciled with his father through a letter 1n 1784. He saw his father one last time in 1785, when Benjamin visited in England. In spite of Benjamin Franklin's wealth, he left his son virtually none of it. Benjamin said that if England had won the war, he would not have had any wealth to leave his son anyway. Franklin Township in Bergen County, New Jersey, was named in his honor, rather than for his father Benjamin Franklin.

Chapter 12

1. Irwin, *Oyster Bay, A Sketch,* pp. 142–143.

2. Rose, *Washington's Spies*, p. 110.

3. Irwin, *Oyster Bay, In History,* p. 103.

4. In colonial America, an "ordinary" was synonymous with "tavern," in which food, drink, and spirits were served, but accommodations were not available. An "inn" provided accommodations.

5. Pennypacker, *General Washington's Spies on Long Island and in New York*, p. 55.

6. Ralph E. Weber, *United States Diplomatic Codes and Ciphers: 1775–1938* (Chicago: Precedent Publishing, 1979), p. 277.

7. Some accounts claim that she preferred to be called "Nancy" by her friends, others that "Nancy" was a nom de guerre.

8. Anna (Nancy) Smith (1740–1812), the affluent daughter of William and Margaret Smith of Brookhaven, Long Island. Granddaughter of William "Tangier" Smith, who built St. George's Manor on Strong's Neck. Most of Anna's relatives were sympathetic to the Loyalist cause. In 1760 she married Judge Selah Strong (1737–1815), who favored the Whig cause, and they moved to Anna's family home, St. George's Manor. Nine children are recorded in the family Bible. Anna and Selah are buried side-by-side in the family cemetery on Strong's Neck.

9. Lisa Tendrich Frank, ed., *An Encyclopedia of Women at War* (Santa Barbara, CA: ABC-CLIO, 2013), p. 522.

10. Anna eventually appealed to her Tory relatives, who used their influence to secure Judge Strong's release.

11. Presently near the southwestern end of Bridge Road on Strong's Neck. The servant's house is plainly visible in the left center portion of the painting *Eel Spearing at Setauket* by William Sidney Mount, 1845.

Chapter 13

1. Onderdonk Jr., *Documents and Letters Intended to Illustrate the Revolutionary Incidents of Queens County*, p. 212.

Chapter 14

1. Pennypacker, *General Washington's Spies on Long Island and in New York*, p. 7.

2. McGill was born in Scotland in 1752 and emigrated to Virginia in 1773. At the beginning of the Revolutionary War he joined the Loyal Virginians, and in 1777 he trans-

ferred to the Queen's Rangers. He surrendered with his regiment at Yorktown in 1781 and after the war settled in New Brunswick, Canada. He died at Toronto in 1834.

3. "Relics at Oyster Bay," *New York Times*, July 20, 1902, accessed November 3, 2013, http://query.nytimes.com/mem/archive-free/pdf?res=F10816F93A5F12738DDDA90A94D F405B828CF1D3.

4. Lossing, *The American Historical Record*, p. 68.

5. *Ibid.*, p. 68.

Chapter 15

1. John André (1751–1780), British officer and spy. Son of a Swiss merchant from Geneva. He was educated in Geneva.

2. James Thomas Flexner, *The Traitor and the Spy: Benedict Arnold and John André* (New York: Harcourt, Brace, 1953), p. 269.

3. In Greek mythology, Sisyphus was a king who was punished by the gods for tricking them. Sisyphus was compelled to roll a huge boulder to the top of a hill only to have it roll down before reaching the top. He was forced to begin again and again, repeating this effort throughout eternity. Sisyphean is used to describe activities that are unending, repetitive and sometimes pointless and unrewarding.

4. I have not found any sources that confirm the duration of André's stay in Oyster Bay, or even the specific time period. Based on André's letter and Simcoe's journal, my best guess would be the last two weeks of April through the first week of May 1779.

5. Robert McConnell Hatch, *Major John André, A Gallant in Spy's Clothing* (Boston: Houghton Mifflin, 1986), p. 139.

6. The Raynham Hall Museum has two silhouettes on display. The male silhouette was once thought to be of Robert Townsend, but is now believed to be of Captain Solomon Townsend, Sally's oldest brother. The female silhouette is of an unidentified female, possibly Sally, or one of her two sisters, Audrey or Phebe. While André likely was acquainted with Robert in New York, it is unlikely that he encountered him in Oyster Bay. In any event, André never met Solomon Townsend, and it's doubtful that André had cut the silhouettes that are presently on display in the Townsend Home.

7. Flexner, *The Traitor and the Spy*, p. 269.

8. *Ibid.*, p. 269.

Chapter 16

1. David Breackenridge Read, *The Life and Times of Gen. John Graves Simcoe* (Toronto: George Virtue, Publisher, 1890), pp. 37–38.

2. Silliman (1732–1790) graduated from Yale in 1752, was colonel of the Connecticut Regiment and subsequently was promoted to brigadier general of the Connecticut militia. He had commanded a regiment at Long Island and White Plains. In 1777 he saw action in Tryon's Danbury raid.

3. Silliman and his son were fortunate in that they were paroled on Long Island and were exchanged a year later in April 1780. Silliman's friend and Yale classmate Thomas Jones, who was a prestigious noncombatant, Loyalist historian, and author of the only history of the Revolution from the standpoint of a Loyalist, was arrested by the Americans on Saturday, November 6, 1779, specifically to be exchanged for General Gold Selleck Silliman and his son.

4. Judge Richard Woodhull (1712–1788).

5. Both men were descended from Richard Woodhull (1620–1690).

6. George Washington, George Washington Papers at the Library of Congress, 1741–1799: Series 4. General Correspondence, 1697–1799, Samuel Culper to John Bolton, June 5, 1779, Images 562–564.

Chapter 17

1. The Amboys are two municipalities in Middlesex County, New Jersey, "Perth Amboy," and "South Amboy." They are located across from each other on Raritan Bay.

2. This most likely should have been dated Oct. 26, 1779.

3. Henry Lee III, called "Light Horse Harry," (January 29, 1756–March 25, 1818) was a cavalry officer in the Continental Army during the American Revolution. He was the Governor of Virginia and a U.S. Congressman, as well as the father of American Civil War general Robert E. Lee.

4. Littell, *Littell's Living Age*, Vol. II, p. 180.

5. A mittimus is a writ issued by a court

or magistrate, directing the sheriff or other executive officer to convey the person named in the writ to a prison or jail and directing the jailor to receive and imprison the person.

6. Simcoe, *Simcoe's Military Journal,* pp. 283–285.

Chapter 18

1. William Alexander, born 1726 in New York, died Jan. 15, 1783, in Albany, was an American major general during the Revolutionary war. In 1756, Alexander attempted to claim the vacant title of Earl of Stirling. A Scottish jury accepted his claim, but the English House of Lords refused to do so. However, Alexander was satisfied with the partial acceptance of his claim, and when he returned to America in 1761, he began to use the title Lord Stirling.

2. Simcoe, *Simcoe's Military Journal,* pp. 129–130.

Chapter 19

1. Clare Brandt, *The Man in the Mirror: A Life of Benedict Arnold* (New York: Random House, 1994), p. 177.

2. *Ibid.,* p. 178.

3. *Ibid.,* pp. 178–179.

4. *Ibid.,* p. 182.

5. McGee, *Sally Townsend, Patriot,* p. 274.

6. The date of the gathering is listed differently in several different sources. I selected Saturday, September 2, 1780, because it most fits within the timeline of André and Simcoe's activities during the month of September 1780.

7. Pennypacker, *General Washington's Spies on Long Island and in New York,* p. 114.

8. McGee, *Sally Townsend, Patriot,* p. 261.

9. Harry Thayer Mahoney and Marjorie Locke Mahoney, *Gallantry in Action: A Biographic Dictionary of Espionage in the American Revolutionary War* (Lanham: University Press of America, 1999), p. 56.

10. This date was derived by extant documents regarding a timeline of André's movements.

11. A round, gathered or pleated cloth bonnet, usually linen, consisting of a caul to cover the hair, a frilled or ruffled brim, and often a ribbon band, worn by women during the Colonial Era.

12. Pennypacker, *General Washington's Spies on Long Island and in New York,* p. 114.

13. *Ibid.,* p. 114.

14. Some sources indicate the letter was addressed to *John Anderson.*

Chapter 20

1. Mahoney and Mahoney, *Gallantry in Action,* p. 56.

2. Irwin, *Oyster Bay, In History,* p. 30.

3. Daniel (1748–1809) and Susannah Kelsey Youngs (1752–1847) are buried in Youngs Cemetery in Oyster Bay across Cove Road from their home. It is the same cemetery where President Theodore "Teddy" Roosevelt is interred. According to the Youngs Family Society, Daniel and Susannah hosted President George Washington. A marker at the site of their home states, "George Washington rested here on April 23/24, 1790."

4. A quire is usually 25 sheets.

5. A traveling case or bag to carry clothing; usually a leather trunk or suitcase that opens into two halves.

6. McGee, *Sally Townsend, Patriot,* p. 272. "Dr." most likely meant "daughter" (of Samuel Townsend).

7. Sinclair Hamilton Collection of American Illustrated Books, *Library of American History; Containing Biographical Sketches* (Cincinnati: U. P. James, 1855), pp. 99–101.

8. Tagliapietra, *Townsend—Townshend, 1066–1909,* p. 72.

9. Pennypacker, *General Washington's Spies on Long Island and in New York,* p. 116.

10. The minister at the time was Reverend Benjamin Tallmadge, father of Major Benjamin Tallmadge, chief of Washington's espionage network.

11. Referred to both as *Robinson House* or *Beverly House.* It was the home of Col. Beverly Robinson, a staunch Loyalist, who was serving with the British and had been taken over by the American commander of West Point.

12. Pennypacker, *General Washington's Spies on Long Island and in New York,* pp. 136–137.

Chapter 21

1. Now Lewisboro, NY, which is about 3 miles southeast of Ridgefield, Connecticut.

2. Benjamin Tallmadge, "To George Washington from Benjamin Tallmadge, 19 September 1780," Founders Online, National Archives, accessed Dec. 29, 2013, http://founders.archives.gov/documents/Washington/99-01-02-03344.

3. Pennypacker, *General Washington's Spies on Long Island and in New York*, p. 117.

4. "Inst." is the shortened form of the Latin, "instant" or "instant mense," which refers to the current month. "Ult." is the shortened form of "ultimo" or "ultimo mense," which refers to the previous month. "Prox." is the shortened form of "proximo" or "proximo mense," which refers to the following month.

5. Pennypacker, *General Washington's Spies on Long Island and in New York*, pp. 117–118.

6. Winthrop Sargent, *The Life and Career of Major John André: Adjutant-General of the British Army in America* (Boston: Ticknor and Fields, 1861), p. 298.

7. Originals in Washington Papers, Library of Congress, No. 20155.

8. Referred to both as *Robinson House* or *Beverly House*. It was the home of Col. Beverly Robinson, a staunch Loyalist who was serving with the British.

9. Pennypacker, *The Two Spies,* photo adjacent to p. 68.

10. Some sources spell his name as Van Wert.

11. Allen C. Beach, *The Centennial Celebrations of the State of New York* (Albany, NY: Weed, Parsons & Co., 1879), p. 204.

12. William Abbatt, *The Crisis of the Revolution: Being the Story of Arnold and André* (New York: William Abbatt, 1899), p. 29.

13. Benton Rain Patterson, *Washington and Cornwallis: The Battle for America, 1775–1783* (Lanham, MD: Taylor Trade Publishing, 2004), p. 208.

14. Abbatt, *The Crisis of the Revolution,* p. 30.

15. *Ibid.*, p. 31.

16. Boatner III, *Encyclopedia of the American Revolution,* p. 39.

17. Hamilton Collection of American Illustrated Books, p. 101.

18. George Washington,, *The Writings of George Washington,* Vol. VII, ed. Jared Sparks (Boston: Ferdinand Andrews, Publisher, 1838), p. 530.

19. Traveling under a flag of truce to conduct a parley.

20. James Thomas Flexner, *The Traitor and the Spy: Benedict Arnold and John André* (New York: Harcourt, Brace, 1953), p. 369.

21. William Heath, *Memoirs of Major General William Heath* (New York: William Abbatt, 1901), pp. 235–236.

22. Read, *The Life and Times of General John Graves Simcoe,* p. 86.

23. Abbatt, *The Crisis of the Revolution,* p. 63.

24. The location or the content of the letter from Peggy Arnold to her husband is not known at this time.

25. Alexander Hamilton, *The Papers of Alexander Hamilton,* Vol. II, *1799–1781* (New York: Columbia University Press, 1961), pp. 445–446.

26. Isaac Newton Arnold, *The Life of Benedict Arnold: His Patriotism and His Treason* (Chicago: Jansen, McClurg & Company, 1880), p. 308.

27. Hatch, *Major John André, A Gallant in Spy's Clothing,* p. 264.

28. Sargent, *The Life and Career of Major John André,* p. 384.

29. *Ibid.*, p. 378.

30. Janet Uhlar, *Freedom's Cost: The Story of General Nathaniel Greene* (Indianapolis: Dog Ear Publishing, 2011), p. 285.

Chapter 22

1. Richard Brookhiser, *Alexander Hamilton, American* (New York: Touchstone, 1999), p. 38.

2. Benson John Lossing, *Reflections of Rebellion: Hours with the Living Men and Women of the Revolution* (Charleston: History Press, 2005), p. 212.

3. Simcoe, *Simcoe's Military Journal,* p. 152.

4. Samuel Johnson (1709–1784), who is regularly referred to simply as Dr. Johnson, is among England's best known literary figures. Dr. Johnson was an essayist, poet, biographer, lexicographer and a critic of English literature. Considered to be a great wit and prose stylist, he was well known for his aphorisms. The single most-quoted English writer after Shakespeare, Dr. Johnson has been de-

scribed as being among the most outstanding figures of 18th-century England.

5. James Boswell, *The Life of Samuel Johnson,* Vol. III (Oxford: Talboys and Wheeler, 1826), p. 259.

6. Read, *The Life and Times of Gen. John Graves Simcoe,* p. 90.

7. Pennypacker, *General Washington's Spies on Long Island and in New York,* p. 186.

8. *Ibid.,* p. 188.

9. Paul R. Misencik, *The Original American Spies: Seven Covert Agents of the Revolutionary War* (Jefferson: McFarland, 2014), pp. 92–124.

Chapter 23

1. William Dunlap, *A History of New York, for Schools,* Vol. II (New York: Collins, Keese, & Co., 1837), p. 242.

2. Simcoe, *Simcoe's Military Journal,* p. 252.

3. *Ibid.,* pp. 253–254.

4. The *Bonetta* was employed by the French, but was recaptured by the British on January 3, 1782.

5. The Province of Upper Canada was a British colony located in what is now the southern portion of the Province of Ontario in Canada. Upper Canada officially existed from 1791 to 1841 and generally comprised present-day southern Ontario; until 1797 it included the Upper Peninsula of the State of Michigan. Its name reflected its position closer to the headwaters of the St. Lawrence River.

6. The Fort Hill Cemetery is located adjacent to the site of Simcoe's hill fort, presently immediately east of the end of Simcoe Street in Oyster Bay.

Chapter 24

1. George Washington, George Washington papers at the Library of Congress, 1741–1799: Series 4, General Correspondence, 1697, Image 1020–1021.

2. Thomas B. Allen, *George Washington, Spymaster* (Washington: National Geographic Society, 2004), p. 164.

3. Rose, *Washington's Spies,* 172.

4. Ford, *A Peculiar Service,* p. 206.

5. Pennypacker, *General Washington's*

Spies on Long Island and in New York, Vol. II, p. 4.

6. Natalie Naylor, "Surviving the Ordeal: Long Island Women During the Revolutionary War," *Long Island Historical Journal* 20, nos. 1–2 (Fall 2007/Spring 2008).

7. Rose, *Washington's Spies,* p. 276.

8. *Ibid.,* p. 276.

9. Pennypacker, *The Two Spies,* p. 75.

10. Misencik, *The Original American Spies,* pp. 92–124.

11. *Ibid.,* p. 115.

12. Ford, *A Peculiar Service,* p. 194.

13. George Washington, George Washington papers at the Library of Congress, 1741–1799: Series 4, General Correspondence, 1697, Image 1020–1021.

14. Benjamin Tallmadge, *Memoir of Colonel Benjamin Tallmadge,* ed. Henry Phelps Johnston (New York: Gillis Press, 1904), pp. 136–137.

15. Thomas Jones, *History of New York During the Revolutionary War,* Vol. I (New York: New-York Historical Society, 1879), p. 382.

16. Tallmadge erroneously dated the message October 11, 1778.

17. The present month.

18. Pennypacker, *The Two Spies,* p. 70.

19. *Ibid.,* p. 73.

Afterword

1. William Sterne Randall, *Benedict Arnold: Traitor and Patriot* (New York: Quill/William Morrow, 1990), pp. 568–569.

2. *Ibid.,* p. 569.

3. James Thatcher (1754–1844), American physician and writer.

4. Randall, *Benedict Arnold: Traitor and Patriot,* p. 569.

5. *Ibid.,* p. 569.

6. *Ibid.,* p. 568.

7. Son of King George III.

8. Randall, *Benedict Arnold: Traitor and Patriot,* p. 602.

9. *Ibid.,* p. 611.

10. *Ibid.,* pp. 612–613.

11. Arthur White Tallmadge, *The Talmadge, Tallmadge, and Talmage Genealogy* (New York: Grafton Press, 1909), p. 88.

12. Boatner III, *Encyclopedia of the American Revolution,* p. 1010.

13. Hugh Chisholm, ed., *The Encyclopædia*

Britannica, Eleventh Edition, Vol. XXV (New York: Encyclopædia Britannica Co., 1911), p. 121.

14. Jeannie F. J. Robinson and Henrietta C. Bartlett, eds., *Genealogical Records: Manuscript Entries of Births, Deaths and Marriages Taken from Family Bibles, 1581–1917* (New York: Colonial Dames of the State of New York, 1917), p. 203.

15. Ford, *A Peculiar Service,* p. 310.

16. *Ibid.,* p. 311.

17. See Chapter 24: Thoughts Regarding Agent 355.

18. Ford, *A Peculiar Service,* p. 308.

Bibliography

Abbatt, William. *The Crisis of the Revolution: Being the Story of Arnold and André.* New York: William Abbatt, 1899.

Adkins, Edwin P. *Setauket: The First Three Hundred Years, 1655–1955.* New York: Three Villages Historical Society.

Allen, Thomas B. *George Washington, Spymaster.* Washington: National Geographic Society, 2004.

AmericanRevolution.org—Your Gateway to the American Revolution. www.americanrevolution.org.

André, John. Letter of André to Simcoe, dated April 6, 1779. Huntington Library.

Armistead, Wilson. *Journal of George Fox; Being an Historical Account.* Vol. I. London: W. and F.G. Cash, 1852.

Arnold, Isaac Newton. *The Life of Benedict Arnold: His Patriotism and His Treason.* Chicago: Jansen, McClurg & Company, 1880.

Bakeless, J. *Turncoats, Traitors & Heroes—Espionage in the American Revolution.* New York: J.B. Lippincott, 1959.

Beach, Allen C. *The Centennial Celebrations of the State of New York.* Albany, NY: Weed, Parsons & Co., 1879.

Bergen, Tunis Garret. *Genealogies of the State of New York: Long Island Edition.* Vol. III. New York: Lewis Historical Publishing Co., 1915.

Boatner, Mark M., III. *Encyclopedia of the American Revolution.* Mechanicsburg, PA: Stackpole Books, 1966.

Boswell, James. *The Life of Samuel Johnson.* Vol. III. Oxford: Talboys and Wheeler, 1826.

Brandt, Clare. *The Man in the Mirror: A Life of Benedict Arnold.* New York: Random House, 1994.

Brookhiser, Richard. *Alexander Hamilton, American.* New York: Touchstone, 1999.

Chisholm, Hugh, ed. *The Encyclopædia Britannica.* Eleventh Edition, Vol. XXV. New York: Encyclopædia Britannica Co., 1911.

Collin, John David. *Fortunes of War—Benedict Arnold.* Monograph, 1999.

Cooper, M. "Out of the Spy's Stocking and into the Wash." *New York Times,* September 8, 2005.

Cox, John, Jr., ed. *Oyster Bay Town Records.* New York: Tobias Wright, 1930.

Crary, Catherine S. "The Tory and the Spy: The Double Life of James Rivington." *William and Mary Quarterly* (January 1959).

Currie, C. *Anna Smith Strong and the Setauket Spy Ring.* East Hampton Taproot Workshops, 1990.

DeWan, G. "The Culper Ring Foils the British by Delivering Critical Information to Washington." Newsday.com (2008). Accessed November 3, 2012.

Dunlap, William. *A History of New York, for Schools.* Vol. II. New York: Collins, Keese, & Co., 1837.

"Early Canada Historical Narratives—John Graves Simcoe." www.uppercanadahistory.ca/simcoe/simcoe1.html. Accessed November 4, 2013.

Ellis, Joseph J. *Revolutionary Summer: The Birth of American Independence.* New York: Alfred A. Knopf, 2013.

Fischer, David Hackett. *Washington's Crossing.* New York: Oxford University Press, 2004.

Flexner, James Thomas. *The Traitor and the Spy: Benedict Arnold and John André.* New York: Harcourt, Brace, 1953.

Flood, Charles Bracelen. *Rise and Fight Again: Perilous Times along the Road to Independence.* New York: Dodd, Mead, 1976.

Ford, Corey. *Donovan of OSS.* New York: Little, Brown, 1970.

_____. *A Peculiar Service.* Boston, Toronto: Little, Brown, 1965.

Frank, Lisa Tendrich, ed. *An Encyclopedia of Women at War.* Santa Barbara, CA: ABC-CLIO, 2013.

Griffith, Samuel B., II. *The War for American Independence.* Garden City, NY: Doubleday, 1976.

Guilfoyle, Timothy. *City of Eros.* New York: W.W. Norton, 1992.

Hamilton, Alexander. *The Papers of Alexander Hamilton.* Vol. II, *1799–1781.* New York: Columbia University Press, 1961.

Hamilton, Sinclair. *Sinclair Hamilton Collection of American Illustrated Books. Library of American History; Containing Biographical Sketches.* Cincinnati: U.P. James, 1855.

Hatch, Robert McConnell. *Major John André, A Gallant in Spy's Clothing.* Boston: Houghton Mifflin, 1986.

Heath, William. *Memoirs of Major General William Heath.* New York: William Abbatt, 1901.

Heinl, Robert Debs, Jr. *Dictionary of Military and Naval Quotations.* Annapolis, MD: United States Naval Institute, 1966.

Hough, Franklin B. *The New-York Civil List, From 1777 to 1860.* Albany: Weed Parsons & Co., 1860.

Irwin, Frances. *Oyster Bay, A Sketch.* New York: Oyster Bay Historical Society, 1987.

_____. *Oyster Bay, In History.* Oyster Bay: Oyster Bay Historical Society, 19??.

Johnson, Ben. *The Works of Ben Johnson.* Boston: Philips, Samson, and Co., 1853.

Jones, Thomas. *History of New York During the Revolutionary War.* Vol. I. New York: New-York Historical Society, 1879.

Lefferts, Charles M. *Uniforms of the Armies in the War of the American Revolution, 1775–1793.* New York: New-York Historical Society, 1926.

Littell, E. *Littell's Living Age.* Vol. II, *From 10 August to 26 October, 1844.* Boston: Littell, Son & Co., 1844.

Lodge, Henry Cabot. *George Washington.* Vol. 1. Boston and New York: Houghton, Mifflin, 1899.

Lossing, Benson J., ed. *The American Historical Record, and Repertory of Notes and Queries.* Philadelphia: Chase and Town, 1872.

_____. *The Pictorial Field Book of the Revolution or Illustrations, by Pen and Pencil, of the History, Scenery, Relics and Traditions of the War for Independence.* Vol. II. New York: Harper Brothers, 1860.

Lossing, Benson John. *Reflections of Rebellion: Hours with the Living Men and Women of the Revolution.* Charleston, SC: History Press, 2005.

Mahoney, Harry Thayer, and Marjorie Locke Mahoney. *Gallantry in Action: A Biographic Dictionary of Espionage in the American Revolutionary War.* Lanham, MD: University Press of America, 1999.

McCullough, David. *1776.* New York: Simon & Schuster, 2006.

McGee, Dorothy Horton. *Sally Townsend, Patriot.* New York: Dodd, Mead, 1952.

Mintz, Steven. *Huck's Raft: A History of American Childhood.* Cambridge, MA: Belknap Press of Harvard University Press, 2004.

Misencik, Paul R. *George Washington and the Half-King Chief Tanacharison: An Alliance That Began the French and Indian War.* Jefferson, NC: McFarland, 2014.

_____. *The Original American Spies: Seven Covert Agents of the Revolutionary War.* Jefferson, NC: McFarland, 2014.

Monaghan, Charles. *The Murrays of Murray Hill.* New York: Urban History Press, 1998.

Nagy, John A. *Invisible Ink: Spycraft of the American Revolution.* Yardley, PA: Westholme, 2010.

Naylor, Natalie. "Surviving the Ordeal: Long Island Women during the Revolutionary War." *Long Island Historical*

Journal 20, nos. 1–2 (Fall 2007/Spring 2008).

Nelson, Paul David. *The Life of William Alexander, Lord Stirling: George Washington's Noble General.* Tuscaloosa: University of Alabama Press, 1987.

_____. *William Tryon and the Course of Empire: A Life in British Imperial Service.* Chapel Hill: University of North Carolina Press, 1990.

O'Brien, M.J. *Hercules Mulligan, Confidential Correspondent of General Washington.* New York: P.J. Kennedy & Sons, 1937.

Onderdonk, Henry, Jr. *Documents and Letters Intended to Illustrate the Revolutionary Incidents of Queens County.* New York: Leavitt, Trow and Company, 1846.

Patterson, Benton Rain. *Washington and Cornwallis: The Battle for America, 1775–1783.* Lanham, MD: Taylor Trade Publishing, 2004.

Pennypacker, Morton. *General Washington's Spies on Long Island and in New York.* Brooklyn, NY: Long Island Historical Society, 1939.

_____. *General Washington's Spies on Long Island and In New York.* Vol. II. East Hampton, NY: Pennypacker, 1948.

_____. "Old Roe Tavern, Setauket, L.I." http://aphdigital.org/projects/culperspyring/items/show/495. Accessed January 1, 2015.

_____. *The Two Spies.* Boston & New York: Houghton Mifflin, 1930.

Randall, William Sterne. *Benedict Arnold: Traitor and Patriot.* New York: Quill/ William Morrow, 1990.

Raphael, Ray. *A People's History of the American Revolution.* New York: New Press, 2011.

Read, David Breackenridge. *The Life and Times of Gen. John Graves Simcoe.* Toronto: George Virtue, Publisher, 1890.

"Relics at Oyster Bay." *New York Times,* July 20, 1902. http://query.nytimes.com/mem/archivefree/pdf?res=F10816F93A5F12738DDDA90A94DF405B828CF1D3. Accessed November 3, 2013.

Robinson, Jeannie F.J., and Henrietta C. Bartlett, eds. *Genealogical Records: Manuscript Entries of Births, Deaths and Marriages Taken from Family Bibles, 1581–1917.* New York: Colonial Dames of the State of New York, 1917.

Robson, Lucia St. Clair. *Shadow Patriots.* New York: Forge Books, 2005.

Rose, Alexander. *Washington's Spies.* New York: Random House, 2006.

St. George's Episcopal Church, Hempstead, NY. Registry of Marriages.

Sargent, Winthrop. *The Life and Career of Major John André: Adjutant-General of the British Army in America.* Boston: Ticknor and Fields, 1861.

Seymour, George Dudley. Papers, Manuscripts and Archives. Sterling Memorial Library, Yale University. Online. Accessed December 14, 2014.

Simcoe, John Graves. *A History of the Operations of a Partisan Corps, Called the Queen's Rangers, Commanded by Lieut. Col. J. G. Simcoe.* New York: Bartlett & Welford, 1844.

_____. *Simcoe's Military Journal.* New York: Bartlett & Welford, 1844.

Tagliapietra, Margaret Townsend. *Townsend—Townshend, 1066–1909.* New York: Press of the Broadway, 1909.

Tallmadge, Arthur White. *The Talmadge, Tallmadge, and Talmage Genealogy.* New York: Grafton Press, 1909.

Tallmadge, Benjamin. *Memoir of Colonel Benjamin Tallmadge.* Edited by Henry Phelps Johnston. New York: Gillis Press, 1904.

_____. "To George Washington from Benjamin Tallmadge, 19 September 1780." Founders Online, National Archives. http://founders.archives.gov/documents/Washington/99-01-02-03344. Accessed December 29, 2013.

Tillotson, H. S. *The Beloved Spy.* Caldwell, ID: Caxton,1948.

Uhlar, Janet. *Freedom's Cost: The Story of General Nathaniel Greene.* Indianapolis: Dog Ear Publishing, 2011.

Washington, George. George Washington Papers at the Library of Congress, 1741–1799: Series 4. General Correspondence, 1697. Image 1020–1021.

_____. George Washington Papers at the Library of Congress, 1741–1799: Series 4. General Correspondence, 1697–1799.

Samuel Culper to John Bolton, June 5, 1779. Images 562–564.

_____. Washington Papers, Library of Congress, No. 20155.

_____. *The Writings of George Washington.* Vol. VII. Edited by Jared Sparks. Boston: Ferdinand Andrews, Publisher, 1838.

Weber, Ralph E. *United States Diplomatic Codes and Ciphers: 1775–1938.* Chicago: Precedent Publishing, 1979.

Whitehead, W. A. *Contributions to the Early History of Perth Amboy and Adjoining Country, with Sketches of Men and Events in New Jersey during the Provincial Era.* New York: D Appleton & Co., 1856.

Wood, Silas. *A Sketch of the First Settlement of the Several Towns on Long Island; with their Political Condition, to the end of the American Revolution.* Brooklyn, NY: Alden Spooner, 1828.

Woodhull, Abraham. *Washington Papers, Letters,* XXXIII, 203. Letter of June 5, 1779, from Woodhull to Washington.

Wrixon, Fred B. *Codes, Ciphers & Other Cryptic & Clandestine Communications.* New York: Black Dog & Leventhal, 1998.

Index

Numbers in **bold italics** indicate pages with photographs.